Containment
Concept and Policy

Containment
Concept and Policy

Based on a Symposium Cosponsored by
the National Defense University
and
the Foreign Service Institute

Edited by

Terry L. Deibel
John Lewis Gaddis

IN TWO VOLUMES

VOLUME ONE

1986

National Defense University Press
Washington, DC

National Defense University Press Publications

To increase general knowledge and inform discussion, NDU Press publishes books on subjects relating to US national security.

Each year, the National Defense University, through the Institute for National Strategic Studies, hosts about two dozen Senior Fellows who engage in original research on national security issues. NDU Press publishes the best of this research.

In addition, the Press publishes other especially timely or distinguished writing on national security, as well as new editions of out-of-print defense classics, and books based on University-sponsored conferences concerning national security affairs.

Page proofs of this book were proofread by Editorial Experts, Inc., Alexandria, VA, under contract DAHC32-86-A-0009. The index was prepared by SSR, Inc., Washington, DC, under contract DAHC32-86-A-0009.

NDU Press publications are sold by the US Government Printing Office. For ordering information, call (202) 783–3238 or write to the Superintendent of Documents, US Government Printing Office, Washington, DC 20402.

Library of Congress Cataloging in Publication Data

Containment: concept and policy.

Includes bibliographies and index.
1. United States—Foreign relations—1945– . 2. World politics—1945– . 3. United States—Foreign relations—Soviet Union. 4. Soviet Union—Foreign relations—United States. I. Deibel, Terry L. II. Gaddis, John Lewis. III. National Defense University. IV. Foreign Service Institute (U.S.)
E744.C7615 1986 327.73   86–23582

First printing, November 1986

Contents

VOLUME ONE

VOLUME TWO

Part Three: Applications

Part Four: Containment's Future

Foreword

The concept of containment, originated by George F. Kennan, has influenced US policy toward the Soviet Union since 1947. To reexamine the concept, and to recognize Kennan's contribution, the National Defense University and the Center for the Study of Foreign Affairs of the Foreign Service Institute cosponsored a symposium called *Containment and the Future*. Symposium participants from universities, foreign affairs institutes, and the US government—scholars and practitioners, historians and current policy analysts—considered containment as it originated, as it has developed over forty years, and as it is likely to affect future US national security policy.

Containment: Concept and Policy represents the work and wisdom of those participants, whose views span four decades and a broad political spectrum. Professor John Lewis Gaddis, a leading historian and Symposium chairman, frames the book with an opening historical essay and an epilogue. Part I, "Origins of Containment," presents the views of individuals who gave the concept of containment life: Walt and Eugene Rostow, Dean Rusk, Clark Clifford, Alexis Johnson, and of course George Kennan. Part II contains essays on "Determinants and Instruments of Containment," including public opinion, economics, and military means. Part III examines the past and future of containment in various regions of the world. Part IV provides observations and opinions for policymakers contemplating the future of containment.

The principal ideas of containment have been applied by eight different administrations, in ways George Kennan could not have anticipated. The concept, though, which shall always be identified with George F. Kennan, continues to be a factor in formulating US policy. The National Defense University is pleased to publish this work as both a tribute to and consequence of the work he began.

Richard D. Lawrence
Lieutenant General, US Army
President, National Defense
University

Containment
Concept and Policy

1

Introduction:
The Evolution of Containment

John Lewis Gaddis

B IOGRAPHERS, AS A RULE, need to be very careful in
speculating about what was in the minds of their subjects
at any given point. Nevertheless, I think it safe enough to say
that when George Kennan, almost forty years ago, sat down to
draft his call for a "long-term, patient but firm and vigilant containment of Russian expansive tendencies,"[1] he had no idea of
what he was letting himself in for. He himself has compared the
experience to that of inadvertantly loosening "a large boulder
from the top of a cliff and now helplessly witness[ing] its path
of destruction in the valley below, shuddering and wincing at
each successive glimpse of disaster."[2] As this book indicates,
the geopolitical landscape has yet wholly to stabilize itself, even
after all these years. The boulder still bounces back and forth
from time to time.

John Lewis Gaddis is Distinguished Professor of History at Ohio University.
Winner of the Bancroft Prize for *The United States and the Origins of the
Cold War*, he is also the author of *Strategies of Containment* and is currently
working on a biography of George Kennan.

But biographers must also guard against exaggerating the influence of their subjects, and I suspect George Kennan would be the first to acknowledge that something like a strategy of containment would have evolved, in any event, even if he had chosen to devote his life to what he has admitted he would really like to have been doing all this time—writing a long, leisurely biography of Anton Chekhov. After all, the breakdown of Soviet-American cooperation after World War II resulted not from the actions of any one man, or even any one nation, but from the workings of a political principle so ancient that Thucydides would have found it familiar: that great powers, separated only by power vacuums, tend not to get along. Nor would the old Greek have found it surprising that nations would seek, in such a situation, to "contain" one another. For "containment" was just another way of talking about restoring a balance of power in the world, and that idea would surely have developed in any event after World War II, even if Chekhov had had his biography.

George Kennan's importance lies not so much in the fact that he coined the term *containment,* but rather that he called for implementing it in a particular way. As he himself has reminded us, that approach has not always found favor in official Washington or in the country at large; indeed, Kennan has spent more of the past four decades as a critic rather than as a defender of strategies that have nonetheless proceeded under the rubric of the term he originated. That brings me to the central point I want to make: that the idea of "containment" has taken on not just a life of its own, but several lives; that different people—indeed, different administrations—have understood it to stand for very different things over the years; and that even today, use of the term is more apt to start than to settle arguments.

What I would like to do here is to set out—very briefly and in an admittedly oversimplified way—what seem, in retrospect, to have been the principal points at issue in this long debate over the meaning of *containment*. My intent is by no means to try to resolve these arguments—an improbable task, in any event—but rather to introduce several of the issues that figure prominently in the more detailed discussions of containment that follow.

The Question of Interests

Let us begin, as all good strategists should, with interests: just what is it that a strategy of "containment" is supposed to defend? The very term *containment* suggests defense rather than offense, and that in turn implies some conception of what is at stake in the first place. But not everyone has always agreed about that.

Kennan's own views were clear enough: the fundamental American interest throughout the twentieth century, he used to tell students at the National War College, had been to keep key centers of military-industrial capability from falling under hostile control. It had been for that reason that the United States had twice gone to war to prevent the German domination of Europe; after 1945 the same interest required ensuring the defense of Western Europe and Japan against an ambitious but nervously insecure Soviet Union. Other parts of the world, most conspicuously China, did not fall within Kennan's list of interests to be defended for the simple reason that, lacking the requisite sources of industrial and military strength, their control by unfriendly regimes could pose no threat.

But Kennan's conception of interests proved easier to articulate than to implement. He himself acknowledged the need to defend Greece in 1947 and South Korea in 1950—neither of them centers of industrial-military capability at the time—because the *psychological consequences* of their loss could be devastating to areas that *were* critical, like Western Europe and Japan. But this is where things get tricky, because once you introduce psychology into the equation, it becomes very hard to draw the line: if the loss of South Korea would be psychologically devastating, why not South Vietnam? Why not Quemoy and Matsu?

It was not all that difficult to slide from Kennan's insistence on distinguishing vital from peripheral interests to a very different approach, which in effect admitted no such distinction. The authors of NSC–68 expressed the second view very clearly in 1950 when they wrote that "in the context of the present polarization of power a defeat of free institutions anywhere is a defeat everywhere."[3]

It followed from this that the fundamental American interest was not so much territory, or industrial-military capacity, but credibility: if the United States allowed itself to be successfully challenged in any part of the world, then its determination to resist aggression would be called into question everywhere else. "If we are driven from the field in Viet-Nam," Lyndon Johnson proclaimed in 1965, "then no nations can ever again have the same confidence in . . . American protection."[4] And it was left to an appalled Kennan to point out, the following year, that "there is more respect to be won in the opinion of this world by a resolute and courageous liquidation of unsound positions than by the most stubborn pursuit of extravagant and unpromising objectives."[5]

What was the problem here? How could containment evolve, in slightly over a quarter of a century, from a conception of interests so narrowly focused as to appear to require little more than the defense of Western Europe and Japan to one that seemed incapable of excluding any territory not already under communist control? Part of the answer, I suspect, has to do with the difficulty of defining security in the first place. It is, after all, a state of mind, and once you acknowledge that, you have rendered it subject to considerations that go beyond cool logic; you must take into account, whether within your own thinking or—more often—within that of allies, the illogical effect of anxieties, apprehensions, panics, phobias, and the fear of "things that go bump in the night." Psychology, in short, provides the mechanism by which precise conceptions of interest become imprecise, creating a real problem for the strategist who is attempting to be clear on just what interests containment is supposed to be defending in the first place.

But this imprecision about interests is not altogether a matter of illogic: there is a very rational reason for it as well, and that has to do with what we might call the "Hobson's choice" of containment. If you differentiate between vital and peripheral interests, you retain the advantage of selecting how and where you will deploy your forces, but you also run the risk of inviting attacks on what may appear to be exposed and undefended flanks. Dean Acheson discovered this in the most painful way when he attempted to delineate a "defensive perimeter" in the Western Pacific, only to wind up inadvertently signaling the Russians that we would not defend South Korea. But if you treat all interests as vital, you run into another problem, which is relinquishing the initiative altogether: you then have to be prepared to commit resources in places and at times chosen by your adversary, not yourself. It was probably "no accident," as the Russians like to say, that Moscow did so little to help us extricate ourselves from Vietnam; the Soviets even at one point—although in an unguarded moment—advised the Johnson administration to *escalate* the American commitment there.[6]

What this suggests, then, is that one should be sufficiently vague about interests as to reassure allies and deter adversaries, but at the same time sufficiently precise as to retain control over how, when, and where one might act to defend those interests. And that, I would be the first to admit, is easier to say than to do.

What is to be Contained?

A second area of disagreement over containment has involved the question of who, or what, is to be contained. Once again, Kennan was very precise about this: to pose a significant threat to American interests, he argued, potential adversaries had to combine both hostility and capability. It was not enough just to be unfriendly; one also had to be able to do something about it. In the immediate postwar years, only the Soviet Union met this test; where communists were not under Moscow's control, as was clearly the case in Tito's Yugoslavia, and as seemed likely to be the case in Mao Tse-tung's China as well, Kennan's strategy looked to the possibility of working with rather than against them to contain the Soviet Union.

That tradition of identifying adversaries in terms of capability rather than ideology began to erode in 1949 and 1950, primarily as a result of the victory of communism in China and the political repercussions set off in the United States by that event. The Korean War—with which the People's Republic had had little to do until overzealous American military action provoked its intervention—only reinforced the public trend toward seeing all communists everywhere as equally dangerous. We now know from the documents that official perceptions were a good deal more sophisticated than that: no less an ideologue than John Foster Dulles himself assumed an eventual split between Moscow and Peking and sought, through his own policies, to bring that about.[7] Similar strategies existed within the Kennedy and Johnson administrations as well. But what came across in public was the rhetoric of ideological non-differentiation: containment came to be understood as aimed at all communists, not just the Russians.

It is an indication of the strength of this sentiment that not until the coming to power of Richard Nixon and Henry Kissinger did an administration feel secure enough publicly to exploit Sino-Soviet differences that had been there for all to see for more than a decade: it did so by refocusing containment back toward its original target, the Soviet Union. But even then it confused the issue by continuing to regard indigenous Marxism outside of China and Yugoslavia—even, as in Chile, constitutionally legitimate Marxism—as a threat. Nor have our more recent policies in Central America provided any clearer answer to the question of just what it is we are seeking to contain.

One of the fundamental principles of strategy is to define enemies parsimoniously: never take on more than you need to at any given time.[8] And yet, the issue of what it is that containment is supposed to contain—whether it is a specific country, or an ideology, or simply patterns of behavior we don't much like—is one about which there has been, and still is, a surprising amount of disagreement.

The Issue of Means

A third area of disagreement about containment relates to means: having identified interests to be defended and threats to be contained, what methods does one choose with which to implement containment? To say that the means chosen must be appropriate to the ends one has in view is axiomatic, but that does not make the task of selecting them any easier. Indeed, the strategy of containment confronts us with the perpetual dilemma of how, in seeking to contain our adversaries, we can avoid coming to resemble them.

George Kennan viewed the problem with uncharacteristic optimism in 1947: "to avoid destruction," he wrote in the 'X' article, "the United States need only measure up to its own best traditions and prove itself worthy of preservation as a great nation."[9] We could, he seemed to be saying, contain the Russians and still be true to ourselves. Certainly, the first chosen instrument of containment—economic assistance to Western Europe through the Marshall Plan—provided a remarkably effective way to reconcile American geopolitical interests with American ideals.

But that coincidence of interests and ideals did not last very long. The Truman administration found it necessary to exaggerate the Soviet threat in order to win necessary appropriations from an economy-minded Congress. "We made our points clearer than truth," Dean Acheson later acknowledged, adding the barb that this was a tactic in which "we did not differ from most other educators."[10] Kennan himself reluctantly supported development of a covert action capability for the Central Intelligence Agency on the grounds that the Russians already had and were using such a capability. And, of course, a strategy originally designed to contain a non-military threat by non-military means quickly became heavily militarized, not because Washington actually expected the Russians to invade Western Europe, but because the Europeans themselves demanded insurance, even against unlikely threats; it was a similar desire for insurance against uncertainty—not any identifiable military requirements at the time—that led to the decision to build the hydrogen bomb.

Reinhold Niebuhr liked to point out that it is sometimes necessary to do evil in order to accomplish good, and I suspect few practitioners of containment over the years would quarrel with that rather bleak proposition. The more difficult question is the one of degree: how many departures from the way one would like the world to be can one justify without bringing about the very conditions one hopes to avoid? Paul Nitze and his co-authors of NSC–68, drawing on Alexander Hamilton and the *Federalist Papers,* provided one answer: "the means employed must be proportioned to the extent of the mischief."[11] But this left unclear what the proper proportion was, or how such matters were to be decided. Dwight Eisenhower, in one of those remarkably candid letters one finds in his papers, went a bit further in 1955: "Truth, honor, justice, consideration for others, liberty for all—the problem is how to preserve them, nurture them and keep the peace—if this last is possible—when we are opposed by people who scorn to give any validity whatsoever to these values. I believe we can do it, but *we must not confuse these values with mere procedures, even though these last may have at one time held almost the status of moral concepts.*"[12]

The procedural latitude that Eisenhower assumed with regard to means—and that was indeed granted strategists of containment throughout much of the history of the Cold War—has in recent years been called into question. Kennan himself has seen it as leading to disproportionate excess, both in Vietnam and in the nuclear arms race: we can, he has been telling us, no longer afford to employ means that risk destroying the very ends we seek to secure. During the 1970s, spokesmen for human rights—from both liberal and conservative ends of the domestic political spectrum—made a point of assailing Nixon and Kissinger for compromising ideals in their search for geopolitical stability. New congressional restraints on executive authority, together with print and electronic media not easily put off by appeals for discretion, have forced recent administrations to think more than their predecessors did about finding means that can be convincingly justified in terms of ends sought. The fact that we have spent several years now *overtly* debating the merits of *covert* aid to the contras in Nicaragua is only the most obvious example of how much more sensitive we have become to the way in which we implement containment—but, as that very example illustrates, this certainly has not made the task of implementing that strategy any easier.

The Issue of Costs

Yet another area of disagreement about containment—closely related to the one about means—has had to do with what it should cost: does one allow the requirements of containment to determine what one spends, or does one first consider what one can spend and then let that determine who, or what, one should contain? It makes a difference, and yet there has been little consistency on this point. Indeed the whole history of containment can be written in terms of oscillations between the belief on the one hand that means should be expanded to bring them into line with perceived interests, and the conviction on the other that interests should be restricted to keep them in line with perceived means.

It is often forgotten that the original strategy of containment proceeded from an assumption of severely limited resources: the atomic bomb was of little use short of an all-out war; American military forces had evaporated in the postwar rush to demobilize; President Truman was adamant in maintaining a $15 billion ceiling on military spending; and Kennan himself had profound doubts about the competence of

Americans to manage any kind of global strategy in the first place. As a consequence, his view of containment was selective as to means—the emphasis would be almost entirely on economic assistance—and as to the places in which it would be implemented—Western Europe, the Mediterranean and Japan, but not China, not Southeast Asia, and definitively not what we would today refer to as the Third World. That skepticism about American capacity and competency has never really left him.

It was Paul Nitze and his colleagues who suggested the alternative approach in NSC–68: that when confronted by what appeared to be an all-out threat, it made no sense to restrict oneself to limited means, especially when the nation had unused productive capabilities. NSC–68 proposed a tripling of the defense budget; it also showed how this could be done—through the use of deficit spending to stimulate the economy—without setting off damaging inflation or unacceptable taxation. Whether in the absence of the Korean War President Truman would have accepted that argument is an interesting but academic question: as has happened time and time again, the Russians themselves provided the most convincing justification for a more expansive approach to containment, this time by authorizing the North Korean attack on South Korea.

President Eisenhower faced a dilemma with respect to this question of means: he agreed with Nitze's perception of a worldwide Soviet threat, but he emphatically did not accept the assumption that the nation could spend whatever was necessary to contain it. Convinced that deficit spending was just as dangerous as the communists, Eisenhower and Dulles sought ways to make containment work more effectively at less cost: the result was the first real integration of nuclear weapons into the strategy of containment. Deterrence would provide the mechanism by which global interests could be defended and, at the same time, budgets balanced.

There was, of course, a shift back to the doctrine of expandable means during the Kennedy and Johnson administrations—not least because of their desire to get away from

Eisenhower's heavy dependence on nuclear weapons. But with Nixon, Ford, and Kissinger, the pendulum swung back the other way again: the Nixon Doctrine, the opening to China, and indeed detente itself, together can be seen as yet another attempt to make containment work more effectively at less cost—albeit this time without increased reliance on a nuclear superiority we no longer possessed. Carter, too, for all his differences with preceding administrations on moral issues, came into office determined to keep the lid on defense spending, at least until the Russians persuaded him otherwise by invading Afghanistan. And with the Reagan administration, we have come back to the opposite idea that the requirements of containment should determine what is spent on containment, even if that means spending a good deal less on everything else.

Why are these disagreements over costs important? They have an obvious bearing on how one allocates resources within a society, of course, but there is another less obvious consideration as well: there is reason to think that a linkage may exist between the perception of means available, on the one hand, and the perception of interests and threats, on the other. The history of containment suggests that when means have been perceived as expandable, conceptions of interests have tended to broaden; as conceptions of interests broaden, perceptions of threat tend to also. Conversely, perceptions of means as limited have forced differentiations between vital and peripheral interests, and, as a result, a somewhat less apocalyptic perception of threat.

All of which is to suggest a curious thing about containment: that it is as often a reflection of our internal state of mind at any given moment as it is a response to external reality. If this is true, then it would behoove us not to exclude from our considerations the internal roots as well as the external determinants of that doctrine.

The Impact of Domestic Politics

That brings me to the relationship between domestic politics and containment. George Kennan has never been noted for the enthusiasm with which he greets the intrusion of political considerations into the making of foreign policy. But there is a real problem here, and it has to do with the extent to which American foreign policy is capable of consistency. No competent strategist would allow his calendar to dictate when to switch from one strategy to another, and yet the domestic political process in the United States has imposed procedures very much like that upon the strategy of containment. Each new administration's approach to foreign policy tends to be determined, not by a calm and rational assessment of interests and threats, but rather by a desperate determination to do something—anything—new, something above all that will avoid association with the discredited policies of the preceding administration.

Thus, the Eisenhower administration's "New Look" was first worked out during the 1952 campaign, as a reaction to the Democrats' perceived vulnerability resulting from the "no-win" war in Korea. The "flexible response" strategy of Kennedy and Johnson grew out of the Democrats' campaign critiques of Eisenhower's excessive reliance on nuclear weapons. The Nixon Doctrine reflected the belief that the Johnson administration had overcommitted itself in Vietnam. The Carter "human rights" campaign was an obvious reaction to the perceived "amorality" of Henry Kissinger. And, of course, the Reagan administration's military buildup had been promised during the 1980 campaign as a means of closing the so-called "window of vulnerability" left open by Carter.

Now, no one would question the benefits of learning from the mistakes of one's predecessors. To the extent that the American system provides mechanisms for detecting and correcting failures in strategy in relatively short order, it has some advantages over, say, the Soviet system, where incompetence can be institutionalized for years without anyone being able to do anything about it. Our problem is that, because we depend upon our interminable and at times somewhat irrational presidential selection process to provide the occasion for evaluating past policies and suggesting new ones, we tend to distort reality by magnifying the errors of incumbents and by over-simplifying the necessary solutions. The effect is that each new administration faces a lengthy process—and it seems to get lengthier all the time—of adjusting its own rhetorical commitments to the circumstances of the real world.

This is one area in which the Russians have a legitimate complaint: how can they deal with us, they ask, when we keep shifting our priorities in response to mysterious and unpredictable internal forces whose effects we ourselves seem unable to anticipate or to comprehend? In this sense, there is much to be said for what Kennan has been calling for all along: a greater insulation of the national security decisionmaking process from the whims and caprices of domestic politics. But how do we do this without violating the constitutional requirement of checks and balances? How do we secure the public support foreign policy needs to be effective without misleading the public as to what it can expect? How do we make new administrations see that it is really not necessary to throw out the baby with bathwater every time?

The Goals of Containment

The last point that I wish to raise is, in many ways, the most fundamental: it is the question of what result, in the end, containment is supposed to produce. It is, after all, a strategy, and having a strategy implies having an objective. It is supposed to lead to something; otherwise, as Clausewitz reminded us a century and a half ago, it is meaningless. George Kennan read Clausewitz while he was at the National War College, and partly as a result of that experience—but partly also because it is just common sense—he has always insisted that containment be viewed as a means toward a larger end, not as an end in itself.

Stated in this way, the point seems unexceptionable enough. But how often do you actually hear a discussion of what containment is supposed to lead to? The process of "containing," during these past four decades, has received far more attention than the question of where containment is supposed to take us, or of what might replace it once we get there.

One point is clear: containment has never implied the complete elimination of Soviet power, in the same way that we sought the unconditional surrender of Germany and Japan during World War II. Even if you could defeat the Soviet Union, Kennan used to ask his War College students, how would you occupy it? What kind of a regime would you replace it with? How could you be sure that such a regime would be any easier to live with than the old one? Containment, instead, sought a modification of Soviet behavior through a combination of deterrents and rewards—sticks and carrots, if you will. The disagreements have focused largely on what the proper mix of these should be, and on precisely what kind of behavior they are supposed to produce.

Kennan's own criticism of the way containment has been implemented over the years has focused on what he considers to have been its neglect of the carrots: we have failed, he argues, to reward the Russians for the restraint they have shown, and hence have been unable to move toward the next logical step beyond containment, which should be a negotiated resolution of differences looking toward stabilization of—and mutual respect for—our respective positions in the world. But others have been critical of containment for neglecting the sticks: we have failed, they assert, to deter the Russians from expanding their military power at home and their influence in the world at large, and hence have had to witness a corresponding and dangerous decline of our own.

Neither side has really made it clear just what kind of behavior we expect from the Russians in the first place. Do we require an abandonment of world revolutionary ambitions? The relaxation of controls over Soviet satellites? A dismantling of the Soviet military machine? Liberalization of the Soviet internal system? Respect for our security interests and those of our allies? Participation in the international system by generally accepted rules of the game? Acknowledgment of what a war between our two countries would mean? Some of these objectives might be easier to achieve than others. And yet, because we so rarely talk about objectives in the first place, we provide ourselves few opportunities to think about which of them are feasible and which are not.

Strategy is largely a matter of getting from where you are to where you want to go. But if you don't know—or can't agree on—the intended destination, getting there is indeed likely to be a problem.

George Kennan: A Personal Note

I cannot end this essay without including a word, in a more personal sense, about George Kennan. I first interviewed him eleven years ago when he was setting up the Kennan Institute and was keeping an office in the old Smithsonian castle, the same building in which his namesake, the first George Kennan, had both lived and worked. I was intrigued to note that as the interview progressed, first his jacket came off, then he loosened his tie, then he rolled up his sleeves, then his shoes came off, and he finally wound up absolutely horizontal on the couch, his feet propped up, his hands behind his head, as wave after wave of eloquent Kennanesque prose came rolling forth. Indeed, the more horizontal he got, the more eloquent he became. I have since learned—from Dorothy Hessman, his long-time secretary—that this is the standard Kennan dictating posture: that in fact the "long telegram" and several of the other great Kennan literary efforts were composed in precisely this manner.

I have not yet decided, as a biographer, just what to make of this. But I think it does illustrate at least one important point: that there is a personal side to great men, and that it may not always accord with their public image. It has been my privilege to learn that the Kennan who so often comes across as a man preoccupied with visions of decline, decay, and catastrophe is in fact a man of generally optimistic temperament who takes great and vigorous delight in work, family, friends, and of course his farm, his sailing, his guitar, and even an occasional lighthearted or irreverent poem now and then.

He is also a man who understands—as few others would—the necessarily ambivalent relationship that must exist between a biographer and his subject. It is one that involves, on the part of the biographer, both sympathy and the ability to stand apart: the capacity to understand as well as the capacity to evaluate. On the part of the subject of the biography, it involves, above all else, great tolerance, and great trust. George Kennan has more than kept his part of that bargain; it is now up to me to keep mine.

Notes

1. George F. Kennan (writing as 'X'), "The Sources of Soviet Conduct," *Foreign Affairs* 25 (July 1947), p. 575.

2. Kennan, *Memoirs: 1925–1950* (Boston: Little, Brown, 1967), p. 356.

3. NSC–68, "United States Objectives and Programs for National Security," 14 April 1950, US Department of State, *Foreign Relations of the United States: 1950,* Vol. I, p. 240.

4. Johnson press conference, 28 July 1965, *Public Papers of the Presidents: Lyndon B. Johnson, 1965* (Washington: 1966), p. 794.

5. US Congress, Senate, Committee on Foreign Relations, *Supplemental Foreign Assistance Fiscal Year 1966—Vietnam* (Washington: 1966), pp. 335–336.

6. See, on this point, John Lewis Gaddis, *Strategies of Containment: A Critical Appraisal of United States National Security Policy* (New York: 1982), p. 269.

7. Ibid., pp. 142–143.

8. See Frederick H. Hartmann, *The Relations of Nations,* 4th Edition (New York: 1973), p. 83.

9. Kennan, "The Sources of Soviet Conduct," p. 582.

10. Dean Acheson, *Present at the Creation: My Years in the State Department* (New York: 1969), p. 375.

11. NSC–68, 14 April 1950, *Foreign Relations: 1950,* Vol. I, p. 244.

12. Eisenhower to Lewis Douglas, 29 March 1955, Dwight D. Eisenhower Papers, Ann Whitman File, "DDE Diary," Box 6, "Mar. 55(1)." Emphases in original.

Part One

Origins

2

The Origins of Containment

George F. Kennan

B EFORE I TURN TO THE SUBJECT OF THIS PAPER, I would like to say a word or two about the National War College.

I had the position of Deputy for Foreign Affairs at the National War College in the first year of its existence—in the academic year, that is, of 1946–47. I look back on that year as one of the happiest and most exciting of my life. My colleagues on the command staff of the College were Admiral Harry Hill, General Alfred Gruenther, and General Ted Landon of the Air Force. I don't think I've ever been associated with three finer people. It was a joy to work with them. There was also a marvelous student body (if you can call it that): mostly men of senior rank in the armed services who had performed distinguished service in the Second World War—mature men, keen, enthusiastic, interested in all that I had to offer but never hesitant to give it the critical scrutiny and the questioning it deserved.

George F. Kennan is Professor Emeritus at the Institute for Advanced Study in Princeton, New Jersey. A former career diplomat in the Foreign Service, he was the first chairman of the State Department's Policy Planning Staff and served as ambassador to the Soviet Union and Yugoslavia.

And the work itself was exciting. The war had brought great changes in the strategic and political environment of this country as well as in all forms of weaponry. We were aware that our country would now have to develop an entirely new set of strategic-political concepts, to take account of these tremendous changes; and we all had the feeling that it was here, at this newly created National War College, that the thinking out of which these concepts would evolve had to take its beginning; because that was what a war college was all about. So it was a marvelously exhilarating and richly profitable experience, for which I shall always be grateful.

When the first class at the National War College came together in 1946, I believe it was really the first time in our history that people representing the armed services and the other departments of government—particularly, the Department of State—had ever come together in an organized way in what was a mixture of teaching and research to examine something greater and deeper than foreign policy, which we had always had. That was national policy, taking into account the civilian and the military and the security needs of this country. That was an innovation which was probably overdue, but it was a profound innovation; it was destined to have the greatest of consequences for our lives every since, and will continue to have them into the future.

It is a source of great gratification and reassurance to me to see that we are going to have a comprehensive national policy of that sort, and that men in uniform are going to work with others in evolving that policy—to see the development of that concept in the form of the National Defense University since I was here. And I can only express my deepest conviction of the importance of what is now going on at the University, and what is going to go on there in the coming years.

And now, one or two reflections about "containment."

The word itself, of course, was not new in the year 1946. What was new, perhaps, was its use with relation to the Soviet

Union and Soviet-American relations. And what brought it to public attention in this connection was indeed its use in an article that appeared in 1947, in the magazine *Foreign Affairs*, under the title of "The Sources of Soviet Conduct," and was signed with what was supposed to have been an anonymous *X*. This piece was not originally written for publication; it was written privately for our first Secretary of Defense, James Forrestal, who had sent me a paper on communism and asked me to comment on it. And it was written, as I recall it, in the month of December 1946, in the northwest corner room on the ground floor of the National War College building. So I suppose it is fitting that I, for my sins, should try to explain something about how the word *containment* came to be used in that document, and what it was meant to signify.

I would ask you to try to picture, if you can, the situation that existed in that month of December 1946. The Second World War was only a year and some months in the past. Our armed forces were still in the process of demobilization; so, too, though to a smaller extent (because the Russians proposed to retain a much larger peacetime establishment than we did), were those of the Soviet Union.

In no way did the Soviet Union appear to me, at that moment, as a military threat to this country. Russia was at that time utterly exhausted by the exertions and sacrifices of the recent war. Something like 25 million of its people had been killed. The physical destruction had been appalling. In a large portion of the territory of European Russia, the devastation had to be seen to be believed. Reconstruction alone was obviously going to take several years. The need for peace, and the thirst for peace, among the Russian people was overwhelming. To have remobilized the Soviet armed forces at that time for another war effort, and particularly an aggressive one, would have been unthinkable. Russia had then no navy to speak of and virtually no strategic air force. She had never tested a nuclear weapon. It was uncertain when she would test one, and it was even more uncertain when, or whether, she would ever develop the means of long-range delivery of nuclear warheads. We had, ourselves, not yet developed such delivery systems.

In these circumstances, I reiterate, there was no way that Russia could appear to me as a military threat. It is true that even then she was credited—and credited by some of my colleagues at the War College—with the capability of overrunning Western Europe with her remaining forces, if she wanted to do it. But I myself regarded those calculations as exaggerated (I still do); and I was convinced that there was very little danger of anything of that sort. So when I used the word *containment* with respect to that country in 1946, what I had in mind was not at all the averting of the sort of military threat people are talking about today.

What I *did* think I saw—and what explained the use of that term—was what I might call an ideological-political threat; and I will tell you why. Great parts of the Northern Hemisphere— notably Western Europe and Japan—had just then been seriously destabilized, socially, spiritually, and politically, by the experiences of the recent war. Their populations were dazed, shell-shocked, uncertain of themselves, fearful of the future, highly vulnerable to the pressures and enticements of communist minorities in their midst. The world communist movement was at that time a unified, disciplined movement, under the total control of the Stalin regime in Moscow. Not only that, but the Soviet Union had emerged from the war with great prestige for its immense and successful war effort. The Kremlin was, for this and for other reasons, in a position to manipulate these foreign communist parties very effectively in its own interests. And as for the intentions of the Stalin regime toward ourselves, I had no illusions. I had already served three tours of duty in Stalin's Russia—had in fact just come home from the last of these tours when I came to the War College; and I had nothing but suspicion for the attitude of the Stalin regime toward us or toward the other recent Western allies. Stalin and the men around him were far worse—more sinister, more cruel, more devious, more cynically contemptuous of us—than anything we face today. I felt that if Moscow should be successful in taking over any of those major Western countries, or Japan, by ideological-political intrigue and penetration, this would be a defeat for us, and a blow to our national security, fully as serious as would have been a German victory in the war that had just ended.

Now you must also remember that during that war, and to some extent into the post-hostilities period as well, our government had tried to win the confidence and the good disposition of the Soviet government by fairly extensive concessions to Soviet demands with respect to the manner in which the war was fought and to the prospect for the postwar international order. We had raised no serious objection to the extension of the Soviet borders to the west. We had continued to extend military aid to the Soviet Union even when its troops were overrunning most of the rest of Eastern Europe. We had complacently allowed its forces to take Prague and Berlin and surrounding areas even when there was a possibility that we could arrive there just as soon as they did. They were refusing to give us even a look in their zone of occupation in Germany but were demanding a voice in the administration and reconstruction of the Ruhr industrial region in Western Germany. Now there seemed to be a danger that communist parties subservient to Moscow might seize power in some of the major Western Europe countries, notably Italy and France, and possibly in Japan. And what I was trying to say, in the article I am talking about, was simply this: "Don't make any more unnecessary concessions to these people. Make it clear to them that they are not going to be allowed to establish any dominant influence in Western Europe and in Japan if there is anything we can do to prevent it. When we have stabilized the situation in this way, then perhaps we will be able to talk with them about some sort of a general political and military disengagement in Europe and in the Far East—not before." This, to my mind, was what was meant by the thought of "containing communism" in 1946.

Now you may wish to compare that situation with the one we face today, and to take account of the full dimensions of the contrast—between the situation we then confronted and the one we confront today. I must point out that neither of the two main features of the situation we were confronting in 1946 prevails today; on the contrary, the situation is almost exactly the reverse.

I saw at that time, as I say, a political-ideological threat emanating from Moscow. I see no comparable ideological-political threat emanating from Moscow at the present time. The Leninist-Stalinist ideology has almost totally lost appeal everywhere outside the Soviet orbit, and partially within that orbit as well. And the situation in Western Europe and Japan has now been stabilized beyond anything we at that time were even able to foresee. Whatever other dangers may today confront those societies, a takeover, politically, by their respective communist parties is simply not in the cards.

You may say, yes, but look at Soviet positions in such places as Ethiopia and Angola. Fair enough. Let us look at them, but not exaggerate them. Aside from the fact that these places are mostly remote from our own defensive interests, what are the Russians doing there? With the exception of Afghanistan, where their involvement goes much further, they are selling arms and sending military advisers—procedures not too different from many of our own. Do you think they can translate those operations into ideological enthusiasm or political loyalty on the part of the recipient Third World regimes? No more, in my opinion, than we can. These governments will take what they can get from Moscow—take it cynically and without gratitude, as they do from us. And they will do lip service to a political affinity with Moscow precisely as long as it suits their interest to do it and not a moment longer. Where the Russians acquire bases or other substantial military facilities, this has, of course, greater military significance. But it is not an ideological threat.

On the other hand, whereas in 1946 the military aspect of our relationship to the Soviet Union hardly seemed to come into question at all, today that aspect is, of course, of prime importance. But here, lest I leave you with a misunderstanding, I must voice a caveat.

When I say that this military factor is now of prime importance, I do so not because I see the Soviet Union as threatening us or our allies with armed force. It is entirely clear to me that Soviet leaders do not want a war with us and are not planning to initiate one. In particular, I have never believed that they have seen it as in their interests to overrun Western Europe militarily, or that they would have launched an attack on that region generally even if the so-called nuclear deterrent had not existed. But I recognize that the sheer size of their armed force establishment is a disquieting factor for many of our allies. And, more important still, I see the weapons race in which we and they are now involved as a serious threat in its own right, not because of aggressive intentions on either side but because of the compulsions, the suspicions, the anxieties such a competition engenders, and because of the very serious dangers it carries with it of unintended complications—by error, by computer failure, by misread signals, or by mischief deliberately perpetrated by third parties.

For all these reasons, I am free to admit that there is now indeed a military aspect to the problem of containment as there was not in 1946; but what most needs to be contained, as I see it, is not so much the Soviet Union as the weapons race itself. And this danger does not even arise primarily from political causes. One must remember that while there are indeed serious political disagreements between the two countries, there is no political issue outstanding between them which could conceivably be worth a Soviet-American war or which could be solved, for that matter, by any great military conflict of that nature.

And the weapons race is not all there is in this imperfect world that needs to be contained. There are many other sources

of instability and trouble. There are local danger spots scattered
about in the Third World. There is the dreadful situation in
Southern Africa. There is the grim phenomenon of a rise in several parts of the world of a fanatical and wildly destructive religious fundamentalism, and there is the terrorism to which that
sort of fundamentalism so often resorts. There is the worldwide
environmental crisis, the rapid depletion of the world's
nonrenewable energy resources, the steady pollution of its atmosphere and its waters—the general deterioration of its environment as a support system for civilized living.

And finally, there is much in our own life, here in this
country, that needs early containment. It could, in fact, be said
that the first thing we Americans need to learn to contain is, in
some ways, ourselves: our own environmental destructiveness,
our tendency to live beyond our means and to borrow ourselves
into disaster, our apparent inability to reduce a devastating
budgetary deficit, our comparable inability to control the immi-
gration into our midst of great masses of people of wholly different cultural and political tradition.

In short, if we are going to talk about containment in the
context of 1985, then I think we can no longer apply that term
just to the Soviet Union, and particularly not to a view of the
Soviet Union drawn too extensively from the image of the Stalin
era, or, in some instances, from the even more misleading image of our Nazi opponents in the last great war. If we are going
to relate that term to the Soviet Union of today, we are going to
have to learn to take as the basis for our calculations a much
more penetrating and sophisticated view of that particular country than the one that has become imbedded in much of our public rhetoric. But beyond that, we are going to have to recognize
that a large proportion of the sources of our troubles and dangers lies outside the Soviet challenge, such as it is, and some of
it even within ourselves. And for these reasons we are going to
have to develop a wider concept of what containment means—a
concept more closely linked to the totality of the problems of
Western civilization at this juncture in world history—a

concept, in other words, more responsive to the problems of our own time—than the one I so light-heartedly brought to expression, hacking away at my typewriter there in the north-west corner of that War College building in December of 1946.

This—the development of this concept—is the task to which I hope future discussions will be devoted; and I wish only that I were young enough, and still enough of a citizen of this age, to be of greater use in getting on with that undertaking.

3

Reflections on Containment

Remarks by

W. W. Rostow
Eugene V. Rostow
Dean Rusk
Clark Clifford
U. Alexis Johnson
George F. Kennan

W.W. Rostow, *Professor of Economics*
and History, University of Texas

My connection with containment and with George Kennan does
not relate to the time when I held relatively reputable posts in
the bureaucratic structure in the sixties, but to two other occasions. One was when I was nearly as junior as one could be in
the State Department: Assistant Chief of the German-Austrian
Economic Division. But I was also shoulder to shoulder with
George on very much the same array of issues when Stalin died,
and we both were brought in to speak our piece. My perspective
on George's "long telegram" of 22 February 1946 differs a bit
from those of my distinguished colleagues because I was then
still in my twenties and held a distinctly minor post. Above me

were five levels before one reached the Under Secretary, Dean Acheson, let alone the somewhat peripatetic Secretary of State, Mr. James Byrnes, who was out negotiating (in a kind of permanent floating crap game) the peripheral treaties.

My first reaction to the cable was sheer admiration for George's boldness, even panache, in seizing on the occasion of a routine inquiry to European posts when his boss, Averell Harriman, was out of town to unload an eloquent, five-part essay on his unsuspecting colleagues back home.

My second reaction was more substantive. I agreed almost totally with George's analysis of Soviet attitudes and intentions and their deep historical roots. I agreed with the challenge they represented to the United States, with the extent to which he believed Soviet thought and action were affected—as they are today—by US performance at home as well as abroad, and with the urgent need for the United States to generate a policy to frustrate Stalin's ample but rather elastic ambitions.

But what policy? The long cable, you may recall, was mighty short on specific proposals. I took its main thrust to be that the US government and public must be promptly galvanized into action to throw their weight behind a Western bloc.[1]

Here, I had reservations. It so happened that, along with some of my colleagues, I was engaged at just that time in an even more outrageous bureaucratic initiative than George's long cable. We working-level economists had decided that, before the United States accepted the split of Germany and of Europe toward which the interplay of Soviet and American policy was palpably moving every day, we should mobilize all our bargaining power vis-a-vis the Soviet Union short of going to war and use it to back the following propositions:[2]

- A long-run, regional United Nations Security Council for Europe, in which the Soviet Union and the United States would participate fully.

- A Germany united by secret and free elections, but held by the United States and the USSR via the European Security Council to a low, agreed level of armaments.

- A United Nations Economic Commission for Europe, embracing East as well as West, with special committees for transport, coal, steel, electricity, etc.

- A US offer to provide all of such a Europe with substantial additional resources for reconstruction.

- Settlement of the sensitive, unresolved issues in the peripheral treaty negotiations (for example, the long-run management of the Danube) in terms of this all-European plan. We also argued that the plan should constitute the framework for Byrnes' presentation at the April meeting of the Foreign Ministers in Paris.

As of February 1946, Stalin had not fully consolidated his control over Eastern Europe, and there were significant democratic elements in the governments of Poland, Czechoslovakia, and Hungary. Still, it is often forgotten that not only the Soviet Union, but also France and Britain and others in Europe, assumed from our extraordinary behavior that we were repeating the slide into isolationism that occurred after the First World War. And for those in diplomacy, there was the haunting, open statement at Yalta of Franklin Roosevelt, who said that we could not keep troops in Germany more than two years.

The plan made its way to the top of the State Department bureaucracy in February, just as George's cable arrived. Despite support from Acheson and Clayton, plus Jean Monnet in the wings, an important assist from my brother Gene down the table here, and a splendid leak by Dean Acheson to the Alsop brothers—despite all this, Mr. Byrnes turned down the plan by pocket veto. To the best of my archival knowledge and Clark Clifford's memory, it was never laid before President Truman for decision. By a lateral route, it did lead directly to the creation of the UN Economic Commission for Europe in Geneva, and it is part—not the central part but a serious part—of the setting out of which the Marshall Plan emerged a year later.

I do not recall this minor strand in the history of the period to argue that the division of Germany and Europe could have been avoided if only our plan of early 1946 had been adopted as the US strategy at Paris in April. We can never know if a different outcome would have been possible if President Truman had rallied US political life around a positive, all-European proposal in 1946, rather than one to salvage Greece, Turkey, and Western Europe a year later. I still wish we'd tried. But in reflecting on the story some four decades later, I'm inclined to conclude it's altogether possible that the outcome might have been much the same.[3] And I'm prepared to respect, if not wholly to agree with, A. W. DePorte's brilliantly argued case for the division of Germany and Europe as the best possible outcome, given the multiple, deeply rooted interests and forces in play in those turbulent days.[4]

I recall this mainly failed bureaucratic effort for two quite different reasons. One is long-run in character; the other, rather urgent.

In the long run, I have no faith that the division of Germany and Europe is historically stable. The forces at work in Central and Eastern Europe as the generations succeed each other are almost certain to tip toward increasingly assertive nationalism and an increasingly determined demand for enlarged political freedom. And in the West, as memories of the Second World War fade, succeeding generations are likely to search for increasingly European solutions to their security problems, which would dilute the authority of the United States in their region and of the Soviet Union in the East. We should take seriously Helmut Schmidt's observation in his 1985 Henry Stimson lecture at Yale: "No one should have any illusion—the Germans will be as stubborn as the Poles, who got together again after having been divided for almost 130 years."

In short, the problem of reconciling the abiding and legitimate US and Soviet security interests in Europe with the aspirations of Europeans, East and West—a problem we sought to address in 1946—is likely to rise on the diplomatic agenda with the passage of time. It behooves thoughtful officials in Moscow and Washington, as well as in Europe, to give some thought to a transition which could be dangerous for all if not handled with wisdom and care.

In the short run, the most important lesson to be drawn from this story relates to summitry. Mr. Reagan is the ninth American president in a row to take part in summit meetings with Soviet leaders. Most advice about summitry from those who earned their wound stripes centers on the need for careful preparation. Now, like any good bureaucrat, and as a certified intellectual, I am all for careful preparation. But the fact is that every single summit has been different. Preparation in each case had to be and was different. And in the case of the Open Skies proposal at the Geneva summit in 1955, a quite good immediate result was obtained by a hasty command decision on the spot by President Eisenhower in the face of a hitherto hopelessly divided US delegation.

The one summit I had anything directly to do with, at Glassboro, New Jersey, was hasty and opportunistic in many ways. But I'm inclined to think that the two meetings of President Johnson and Mr. Kosygin, alone for many hours—as Dean Rusk will remember, we sat outside in the modest study of the president of Glassboro State College—did help the serious process of advancing the first major arms control agreement that came about in Mr. Nixon's time.

Now return to 1946 and the division of Germany and Europe, which occurred essentially in that year. That division of Europe in 1946 illustrates the one universal rule about summits I am prepared to commend: namely, that the outcome of a summit depends not so much on the agreements reached, but on the seriousness and stubbornness of the American follow-through.

The agreements at Yalta and Potsdam were clearly equivocal, but they did include hard elements which represented US interests as then formulated and which, if pursued firmly by the United States—by the president, the Congress, and the citizenry—might have yielded a better result than the one with which we have lived for forty years. The fact is that our post-summit efforts to implement those agreements were feeble and cosmetic, and I am inclined to attribute the emergence of the Cold War in Europe more to US confusion and weakness in 1945 and 1946 than to a rigid, implacable plan of Stalin's.

Put another way, I conclude that no agreement reached at a summit is likely to be self-enforcing. We should not seek agreements that we are not prepared to back. If we achieve an agreement, we should be prepared to invest at least as much, if not more, national effort in insisting on its implementation as we put into achieving the agreement in the first place.

Eugene V. Rostow, *Distinguished Visiting Professor*
of Law and Diplomacy, National Defense University

I came into the history of containment as a very junior officer in
the State Department during the latter part of World War II.
One of my assignments was as the Lend-Lease officer of the
State Department. And my first contact with George Kennan
was over a plan I developed to offer a reconstruction loan under
one of the provisions of the Lend-Lease Act to the Soviet
Union.

The Soviets had initiated talks with us about the possibility
of a reconstruction loan. Everybody was conscious of the enor-
mous hostility of Soviet policy, and the risk that the Soviet
Union would refuse to participate in the emerging state system
under the UN Charter as a colleague and a cooperator. So the
effort to meet the Soviet request for reconstruction loans had all
sorts of wider political implications. I was writing telegrams in
the name of the Secretary of State in Washington, and Ambassador Kennan was writing the answering telegrams from
Moscow. So the context of hostility and the emergence of a split
between the Soviet Union and the United States were parts of
the background of the containment policy which I shared
with him.

The questions Mr. Gaddis posed at the end of his
introduction—What was the goal of containment? If containment was the means, what was the end it sought?—are very
good questions, and fundamental ones. I think the answers relate to the fact that the containment policy was not our first
postwar policy toward the Soviet Union. It was our second
postwar policy. The first policy, which I think necessarily and
permanently remains our goal so far as the Soviet Union is concerned, is to persuade, induce, bring the Soviet Union somehow
to see that the only possible future and highest national interest
of the Soviet Union is that it participate with other leading powers in managing the modern state system. We must operate very
much as the great powers managed the European state system,

the Concert of Europe, during the nineteenth century: with strict respect on both sides for its rules.

If I differ with the formulation that George Kennan and Professor Gaddis have made, it is because each one, it seems to me, tried to explain the phenomenon with which we're dealing as a very natural hostility, a rivalry among great powers with whose parameters Thucydides would have been familiar. That is very true, I think, but it's not the whole of the truth, because it neglects the fact that the Soviet Union sought then and is seeking now to expand its area of control in ways which threaten the long-term security interest of the United States, as George Kennan said very well in his opening remarks. It is trying to do so by gaining control of the whole of the Eurasian land mass plus Japan, whereas US policy and interest is in preventing such an accumulation of power and in establishing and helping to manage a state system which operates in accordance with the generally accepted rules of the UN Charter. I think the tendency to equate Soviet behavior and American behavior is something we must examine carefully in the course of this conference, and I wanted to take advantage of this occasion to draw attention to its significance.

Dean Rusk, *Former Secretary of State, Professor of International Law, University of Georgia*

I listened with the greatest of interest and appreciation to the reflections which George Kennan shared with us, and also to the remarks made by others. I would like to comment on just two points, for the moment.

Most of us know, either from direct experience or from our history books, about the sad story of the 1930s, a period during which my generation of students was led into the catastrophe of a World War II which could have been prevented. But most people have forgotten, if they ever knew, what happened just after VJ Day. We demobilized almost completely, and almost overnight. By the summer of 1946, we in the State Department were being told by officers on the Joint Staff that we did not have one division in our Army nor one group in our Air Force that could be considered ready for combat. The ships of our Navy were being put into mothballs about as fast as we could find berths for them. Those that remained afloat were being manned by skeleton crews. Our defense budget for three fiscal years—I think it was 1947, 1948, and 1949—came down to a little over $11 billion, groping for a target of $10 billion.

Now, most of you have heard the story that, in a wartime conference, Churchill spoke to Mr. Stalin about the views of His Holiness, the Pope, on a particular point. And Stalin was reported to have said, "The Pope? How many divisions does he have?" In any event, Stalin looked out across the West and saw the divisions melting away.

And what did he do during this period? He tried to keep his forces in the northwest province of Iran, Azerbaijan—the first case before the UN Security Council. He demanded two eastern provinces of Turkey, Kars and Ardahan, and a share in the control of the straits connecting the Mediterranean with the Black Sea. He supported the guerrillas going after Greece, using bases and sanctuaries in places like Yugoslavia, Bulgaria, and Albania. He established in Eastern Europe a colonial empire

which today remains the only significant empire found anywhere in the world. He had a hand in the communist coup d'etat
in Czechoslovakia. He blockaded Berlin. He gave the green
light to the North Koreans to go after South Korea.

Now, the revisionist historians can write until all their ink
runs out; those were the events which launched the Cold War.
We were disarmed. Indeed, from his own point of view, I suspect that Mr. Stalin made a rather serious mistake. Because if
he had followed World War II with a period of ten or fifteen
years of genuine peaceful coexistence, he would, I suspect,
have produced a disarmed and isolationist America.

But by those events, he alerted the West. Those events
made up the background of the launching of NATO and much
of the background for the famous National Security Council paper, NSC–68. Indeed, those events, unhappily, cracked open
the door to let in an evil phenomenon in the history of this nation that we know as "McCarthyism," producing a period
which, perhaps, reached its lowest point when a Senator from
Indiana accused George Marshall of being a traitor, without an
immediate and stinging rebuke from then President of the
United States Dwight Eisenhower.

But I suspect that we, ourselves, bear some responsibility
for launching the Cold War, because it may well be that we exposed Josef Stalin to intolerable temptations through our own
weakness. And, if so, we must be careful about that. I draw a
distinction between adequate national defense, which we did not
have in those days, and the kind of arms race in which we are
involved today, which is reaching the edges of insanity.

The second comment I wanted to make is that, in this year
of 1985, the human race has put behind it forty years since the
firing of a nuclear weapon in anger, despite a number of very
serious and sometimes dangerous crises we've had since 1945. I
think we have learned during those forty years that the fingers
on the nuclear triggers are not itchy, not just waiting for a pre-
text on which to launch these dreadful weapons. If anyone has

any doubt about that as far as the United States is concerned, bear in mind that we have taken almost 600,000 casualties, dead and wounded, in support of collective security since the end of World War II, without the firing of nuclear weapons. I think we've learned during those forty years that the Soviet leaders have no more interest in destroying Mother Russia than our leaders have in destroying our beloved America.

Now, of course, these forty years are by no means a sure guarantee for the future. So we still have to be careful. We and the Russians should not play games of chicken with each other to see how far one side or the other can go without crossing that lethal line, because down that trail lies the possibility of miscalculation and mistake, which can produce a situation that no one wants. I think we also ought to watch the level of rhetoric between the two capitals, because if that rhetoric becomes too vitriolic over too sustained a period of time, there's always the possibility that one side or the other will begin to believe its own rhetoric, and then we are going to have some problems.

George Kennan mentioned something else that appealed to me. I hope that when we think of superpower summits we'll realize how short a time the two leaders have with each other. For example, if they meet for eight hours, you have to divide that in half for interpretation; divide it in half again for equal time. So in eight hours, each man will have about two hours in which to present his point of view. Given these constraints, leaders should not waste time exchanging ideological sermons with each other. Mr. Reagan has indicated he doesn't expect to make a capitalist out of Mr. Gorbachev, and Mr. Gorbachev is not going to make a communist out of Mr. Reagan. I hope that they will not use their time to launch threats at each other, because a threat becomes too dangerous, as we found after the Vienna summit between Kennedy and Khrushchev in 1961.

I would hope that instead they try to find those elementary, simple, common interests on which we might be able to build. We and the Soviet Union share a fundamental, common interest in preventing nuclear war. No one in his right mind in Moscow or Washington could deny that we and they also share a primordial responsibility to the entire human race, because we are the only two nations whose mortal conflict would raise serious questions about whether this planet could any longer sustain mankind.

But George Kennan mentioned something else. After all, we and the Russians belong to the species *Homo sapiens*. Now, in the coming decades, the entire human race is going to face a series of problems which are different in kind and in scale from any we have faced before. George mentioned the energy problem, with regard to which we are living in a Fool's Paradise at the present time. He mentioned the possibility that man himself might inflict irreparable damage upon this thin biosphere around the earth's surface in which we must live. Down the road is a coming hunger problem, caused by a combination of the population explosion and the shortage of resources. Indeed, one of the oldest causes of war in the history of the human race is being revived in a nuclear world. Difficult as these people are in Moscow—and they are difficult—we should search persistently for points of common interest and points of agreement on large matters or small, in order to try to broaden that base of common interest and reduce the range of issues over which violence might occur.

A nuclear war must never be fought, because such a war would not only eliminate the answers, it would also eliminate the questions. Now, that means that we ought to do something about these fantastic inventories of nuclear weapons in the world. To me, the only rational purpose of nuclear weapons is to guarantee that someone else will not use them against us. And on both sides, we could achieve that purpose with about ten percent of present inventories. I would hope, somehow, that we would get away from these minuets we dance with each other, and get down to the business of cutting back these inventories simply and drastically.

I remain optimistic about the possibilities of avoiding a nuclear war. I regret that our young people are being battered with so much Doomsday talk these days, because a lot of it is nonsense. And I don't wear a hair shirt about the invention of some notions of containment. I happen to believe that the American people have acted with responsibility and restraint and generosity in this postwar period. We've made our mistakes; we've had our frustrations and disappointments. But I wish that all those who exercise so much power would act in the same responsible and thoughtful mood.

Clark Clifford, *Former Secretary of Defense, Law Firm of Clifford & Warnke*

When a man is asked to serve on a panel of this kind, I think it places a special responsibility upon him to provide his own particular experience with the subject that is under discussion. Rather than devote myself to the general subjects and complexities that present themselves, therefore, let me go back some forty years and give a very personal account of President Truman and his reaction to what was taking place in that period long ago.

President Truman came into office upon the death of Franklin Roosevelt in April 1945. Truman went to Potsdam, as the first important event of his administration, in June and July. And he prepared well for it. I think that he was uneasy, because it came so early in his administration. He was awed, somewhat, by the opportunity of being with Winston Churchill and Josef Stalin, and he talked a good deal about that. But at the same time, he looked forward to being an important figure in this historic conference.

When he returned, he returned in an attitude of temporary euphoria. He thought it had gone very well. I heard him on two or three occasions tell about the incident in which Mr. Stalin had come over to pay a courtesy call, intending to stay maybe five minutes. Instead, President Truman began to discuss a number of matters with him, talked about his boyhood on his difficult farm in northern Missouri, and pretty soon he felt a breaking down of the hostility between them. He finally persuaded Mr. Stalin to stay for lunch, and he thought that that was an unusual accomplishment.

Much of his attitude toward the accomplishments of Potsdam, I think, was due to his basic optimism and to a certain ingenuousness that accompanied the early period of his presidency. It was his most fervent and deepest hope that we would be able to arrive at a type of concord with the Soviet Union that could bring about peace in the world. We had worked with them so closely and so effectively as allies. He said, "If we can go through that kind of experience together in war, then I think that we can do it in peace."

He continued to be optimistic for a time; but week by week and month by month, the optimism deteriorated as we began to experience one serious problem after another with the Soviet Union. Ultimately, his optimism disappeared almost entirely, and in its place came a deep questioning on his part as to what the future might hold for the relationship between the two nations.

He called me into his office in the Spring of 1946—I was serving as counsel at the White House at the time—and we had a long talk. He went back over the hopes that he had had for the relationship, and how those hopes had been dissipated by a consistent pattern of activity on the part of the Soviet Union. And he said, "I need now to find out where we have been, where we are now, and where we're going. I would like you please to undertake a study. I want you to go to the top individuals in our country, men who have lived through these past periods, civilian and military, and interview them. Notify them ahead of time of the purpose of the inquiry, so that they might have time to prepare themselves and prepare papers. And then, by Fall, I would like you to submit your report."

Well, I had the great good fortune at the time to have an intelligent, well-prepared, and extraordinarily able assistant named George Elsey. Elsey took over the responsibility of most of the interviews, and the report, to a great extent, was the result of the expertise and experience he brought to it.

So at the end of the day on 24 September 1946, I took in to President Truman a copy of the report. We had sent it over to the printing office of the government which handled top secret items. With the report, I sent a letter. Just to show you the breadth of the report, my letter of 24 September 1946 said,

My dear Mr. President: In the course of complying with
your directive to prepare a summary of American relations
with the Soviet Union, I have consulted the Secretary of
State, the Secretary of War, the Attorney General, the
Secretary of the Navy, Fleet Admiral Leahy, the Joint
Chiefs of Staff, Ambassador Pauley, the Director of Central Intelligence and other persons who have special
knowledge in this field.

Then I described, in effect, what their preparation was. The
concluding sentence of the letter was, "Factual statements, studies and opinions have been assembled and summarized, and
there is submitted herewith a report entitled, 'American Relations with the Soviet Union.'"

About quarter of seven the next morning, my telephone
rang at home; it was the president. I got on the phone and I
thought his tone was quite sharp. He said, "I stayed up late last
night reading that report." (It would have been late; the report
was eighty-two pages long.) "Are there any more copies?"

I said, "There are."

He said, "How many more?"

I said, "Eleven." (I had had twelve copies made.)

He said, "I wish that you would come down at once and
get the other eleven copies and bring them upstairs to me."

And I said, "Well, I really haven't gotten up yet and I
haven't shaved and all."

He said, "You can do that later. I want to be absolutely
certain that no copy of any kind gets out. This would blow the
roof off of the White House."

He thought, in other words, that there were still real hopes
for Soviet-American cooperation. He had them. His was an exceedingly tactical and pragmatic approach.

I took the other eleven copies in to him, he put them away in the safe, and they did not appear for twenty-five years. They went into the Truman Library.

Now, I think you will be interested—I hope even fascinated—to know what the distillation of the attitude of our government was. The report, very definite in tone, was a synthesis of the opinions of others, from the Secretary of State through the entire top hierarchy of our government. My task mainly was an assembly job, an attempt to present it as succinctly as possible. Yesterday I got the report out, went through it, and picked out maybe the thirteen or fourteen principal points that were made. Keep in mind, now, this is almost forty years ago, just at the beginning of our postwar relationship with the Soviet Union. I'll just paraphrase them very quickly:

'The gravest problem facing the United States is its relationship with the Soviet Union. It is becoming apparent that Soviet goals are in direct conflict with US aims and ideals.

'Our major effort first must be to gain accurate knowledge of the motives and methods of the USSR.' (You see, this was an almost complete mystery to us at the time, because we had never really faced it directly before.)

'It is the considered opinion of these men that the Soviets proceed on the assumption that the peaceful coexistence of communist and capitalist nations is impossible.' Again and again, that thread came back from the various men. 'They believe that the conflict between the USSR and capitalist states is inevitable.' But the report also indicated that the Soviets wished to postpone the conflict. And the substance of opinion was that the Kremlin sought delay not because the Soviets thought there might be an answer other than conflict, but because they wanted, first, to have greatly strengthened their military power.

'They will continue to exert control over Eastern Europe, and will brook no opposition to such control.' (Much of this, you may feel as we go along, has a certain clairvoyance to it, but it is because these men had been living through it.)

'The Soviet Union is, clearly, looking toward controlling Greece and Turkey, so as to become an important factor in the eastern Mediterranean. With regret, it must be reported that agreements reached at Tehran and Yalta and Potsdam have been consistently violated, and will very likely continue to be violated in order to suit Soviet policy.

'It now seems apparent that the Soviet Union is attempting to weaken the United States and weaken other countries by conducting subversive activities in those other countries, and especially within the United States.'

Then we turn to the concluding chapter in the report, which may be the last twenty pages. And that deals with the recommended US policy toward the Soviet Union. Again, I remind you that this is the synthesis of the opinions of these top men:

'a. The primary objective of the United States is to convince the Soviets that it is in the Soviet interest to participate in a system of world cooperation.

'b. The United States must establish and maintain sufficient and adequate military strength to restrain the Soviet Union.

'c. We should try to demonstrate to the Soviets that the peaceful coexistence of communism and capitalism is possible.'

And then, clearly, there is the statement just made by Secretary Rusk, 'The Soviets have not been easy to get along with. They are not easy to get along with now. And it is the opinion of the group that they will always be difficult to get along with.

'We must prevent any effort of the Soviet Union to expand into areas which are vital to American security. As far as the Soviet attitude toward us is concerned, the prospect of defeat is the main deterrent, and must continue to be the main deterrent, to the Soviets.'

Then, lastly, 'In addition to maintaining our own strength, the United States should support democratic countries endangered by the Soviet Union. But this support should be in the form of economic support. Military support should be considered only as a last resort.'

Let me read the concluding sentence, which contains the basic philosophy of the entire eighty-two pages:

Even though Soviet leaders profess to believe that the conflict between Capitalism and Communism is irreconcilable and must eventually be resolved by the triumph of the latter, it is our hope that they will change their minds and work out with us a fair and equitable settlement when they realize that we are too strong to be beaten and too determined to be frightened.[5]

U. Alexis Johnson, *Washington Institute of Foreign Affairs*

I have been throughout my life an operator in the foreign affairs field, rather than a "theoretician" or a writer on it. I've had to deal with practical and immediate problems, so I bring a few observations out of my own experience.

First, about the basic nature of the Soviet Union and our relationship with it. I can make no pretense of being a Kremlinologist or an expert on Russia; I've never served in the Soviet Union. My first direct contact with Soviet diplomats was during the Geneva Conference in 1954 and 1955. My next direct contact with them was as head of our SALT delegation, from 1973 to 1977.

My opposite member was Vladimir Semenov, who had also been the principal delegate during the time of Gerry Smith's conversations with the Soviets leading up to the SALT I accords. I used to say to him on occasion, "Isn't it utterly absurd that the two of us are sitting here across this table, talking about these beasts of weapons with which we can wipe each other out in fifteen or twenty minutes? What has led us to this situation, this confrontation between us? We've never had a war. We have no direct territorial disputes. Our economic relations are minimal, so we do not have the frictions of economic strife."

I said, "The problem in my own mind is," and I take this from George Kennan's thesis, "that you people are still living in the Dark Ages. We Christians slaughtered other Christians and slaughtered the heathens in an effort to make them believe as we believed. And, finally, we, as a Christian civilization, came to the conclusion that that was not very profitable, that we had to tolerate diversity and live and let live."

And when we did that, we made the big step of getting along with each other. The Moslems have done somewhat the same thing. You know, there's something about monotheism that leads to intolerance. And when we learned to live with each other, we were able to mitigate most of that.

So I told my Soviet colleague, "The problem, in my view, with the Soviet system is that you have a monotheistic view of the rest of the world, in that you believe that you must make the rest of the world conform to your system. And to a degree, you have a point, because lacking the automatic controls of free enterprise, and a tolerant attitude, you feel you have to control the means of production—land, labor, capital, particularly people—and make them conform to the program and the plan. Inevitably, you're forced into a position of forcing people to react to a plan, rather than letting nature take its course.

"Someday you are going to have to arrive at the point of being willing to live and let live, willing to modify your doctrine to the degree that you do not feel under a compulsion to change the rest of the world to conform to it. And then we will be able to find a pattern of living together.

"We do not have detente or 'coexistence' with the UK or with Japan or with the rest of the noncommunist countries. We live together and tolerate each other's diversity. And someday, if you get to that point—and I hope that you are going to get to that point—then problems with these weapons and other problems between us are going to take their proper proportions and will look entirely different than they now do because of the thrust of your doctrine."

I used to try to get an argument out of him on it—in private conversation, obviously. But I never could get one. His response to me was always, "Well, there are those of us who feel differently about this, and you've got to give us time." I simply pass that on as a past observation.

I want to add two footnotes to what has been said. First, I think it's useful to remind ourselves that our last three wars, including World War II, all started in the Pacific. And the thrust of our population, the thrust of our economy, the whole thrust of our civilization is more and more into the Pacific. Note that when we were isolationist toward the rest of the world we were always very interventionist in the Pacific. Our early ancestors who arrived here on the Virginia coast immediately started thrusting westward, and they kept thrusting westward throughout our history. I often point out to the Japanese that our first settlers at Jamestown arrived at the same time that Ieyasu was closing Japan for its 250 years of hermit existence.

But coming from a Pacific background, I have a feeling that we tend in our relations with the Soviets to focus so thoroughly upon the Atlantic and the problems of Europe that we ignore the problems of the Pacific. And I think we should pay much more attention to them.

My final footnote is to stress George Kennan's point that dangers arise not just from military confrontation, but also from instabilities that develop in our society and the world's society. I am a child of the Depression. I graduated from college in 1931, the year after the Smoot-Hawley tariff had gone into effect, in a period during which the United States' gross national product had dropped fifty percent, catastrophically, in one year. Most of the rest of the world was doing the same: the United Kingdom was moving toward imperial preference, and each country was seeking autarky for itself.

My own view is that Japanese militarism and the Hitlers and Mussolinis in Europe developed out of this thrust toward economic autarky, which led toward political autarky and then military autarky, and to competition for living space and for resources. I am very concerned that we are forgetting the lessons of the past and tending again toward this autarkical approach to the world.

It's not gone too far yet; there are sober heads. My concern is not that history repeats itself exactly, but that some of the historical thrusts that led to World War II are present now in our management of our finances and our economies. And I think that we need to get back to the broader vision that the men around this table had at the end of World War II, and restore some of the elan and some of the thought that we put into the postwar organization of the world.

I, myself, am very uneasy. Aside from the Soviet Union, a collapse in Latin America, for example, would be most catastrophic to the United States. You've got Mexico on the south of our border, its population doubling every sixteen to eighteen years, with resources unable to keep up with it. There is a large Hispanic population in this country. If the Mexican society and government were to collapse into anarchy, it would not be something we could blame on the Soviet Union, but it's something the Soviets would be very quick to take advantage of. And my guess is that in the next generation, if not sooner, we're going to find our relationships with Mexico overriding in importance our relationships with the Soviet Union.

I merely throw out those few ideas for you to chew on, and I would like to see more study of the relationship of economic autarky in the 1930s to the rise of the extremists, both in Europe and in Japan, and to the disaster of World War II. I think you'll find there's a very close connection.

Questions from the floor

Question (Professor James Nathan, University of Delaware): I have a question for Ambassador Kennan. This ongoing dispute about what was really meant by "containment"—when you authored the notion and as it was later implemented—is a great concern to professional historians, as well as contemporary policymakers. One of the things Joseph Alsop quoted you as saying in 1950 was that you were really pleased, in a way, that the Soviets had authorized the advance in Korea, because it showed the Soviet hand. I wonder if you were quoted correctly in this, and if it casts any light on your general vision of Soviet purposes in this period.

Ambassador Kennan: I don't recall that precise reaction on my part. We had had many tests of our patience, I must say, in the years between 1947 and 1949, ones where it was very baffling to know what the reply should be. I do recall a certain sense of relief that at least here we had a very definite offense against our interests, to which a definite reply could be given. But I think I would have preferred that the whole crisis not arise.

Question (Professor Lou Kashevsky, Sam Houston State University): My question is for Ambassador Kennan, also. You mentioned in your paper that you chose the term *containment* in a sort of light-hearted way. I wonder if you have any reflections on the choice of the term, whether it prejudiced the way the policy was subsequently applied. Were there other words, such as *coping* or *resisting,* that would have been better?

Ambassador Kennan: You know, there were people at that time who had been inclined to believe that we were going to have a wonderful collaboration with the Soviet Union after the war was finished, and who then were rather shattered by the realization that this cooperation was not going to take place. These people tended to say—and some of them said it to me—"Ah, we see it now. Collaboration, as Franklin Roosevelt and others defined it, is not going to be possible. Therefore, a war between us and the Russians is inevitable." This is precisely what I could not accept. And it was precisely against this thesis that the 'X' article was actually written.

It was written to say, "Look, just stop making these concessions; do the proper thing; stand fast here, and the day will come when we can talk to these people about our problems." And I must say that one of my greatest disappointments in the years that followed was the feeling that there were successive occasions where we could have talked to the Russians about the split of Europe, and about the other great issues of the time, and that we missed those opportunities. We didn't realize that the time had come to take advantage of them.

There was, in fact, a moment, I believe in 1948, when Chip Bohlen and I, together, came to the conclusion that the Russians had had enough, that we had demonstrated to them, through the Marshall Plan and the foundation of NATO and so forth, that they were really stymied in Europe; that they were not going to get further than they'd gone—that now the time had come to make a conciliatory gesture, to see whether we couldn't discuss some of our problems.

Well, this suggestion commended itself to Dean Acheson and to the president. And the president did say something along the lines that he would always be glad to talk with the Soviet government. The result was quite different than we expected. The press hopped onto it and took it as a bid for a summit meeting, and the president had to retract it immediately. There was even great criticism and ridicule of him in the press for suggesting it. I remember a cartoon, in *The Washington Post* I think, that showed the president up at bat and the ball whizzing past him and the umpire saying, "Strike one!" And I felt very bad about that. But I still think that we were quite right at that time, that the moment had come when, perhaps in a little different way, we should have sought a clarification of these issues by a discussion with the Russians.

Question (Professor Ole R. Holsti, Duke University): This is a follow-up on the question that you just answered. What about at the time of Stalin's death in 1953? You were in your last few months in the State Department. What opportunity did you feel might have been present then?

Ambassador Kennan: Well, personally, I think that the situation in Russia was at that time, under the shock of his death, too unstable for the Soviet government to have formulated any proposals it could have lived with. There were various signs of erraticism at that time.

I think that this is a question on which perhaps some of the others on the panel could also offer something. Dean, I wonder if you could.

Secretary Rusk: George, wasn't it true that during a rather long period of transition following Stalin's death we did achieve the Austrian State Treaty, which was a rather significant step?

Ambassador Kennan: If you take the next two or three years, you're quite right. Not only that, but also the Trieste settlement, as I remember it.

Question: I would like to ask the panel a very sweeping question concerning the future of American containment policy. My speculation is that if we continue our present policy of confrontational relations with the Soviet Union we are courting the danger of alienating both Western Europe and Asia. Essentially, America would be left alone in the world. A second speculation is that continuing the present policy of confrontation also risks a mutual economic suicide of both the Soviet Union and the United States, leading to a greater role in world affairs for both Western Europe and Japan and some of the rising powers in Asia. How would you react to these thoughts?

Secretary Rusk: This suggests one question I would like to put to Clark Clifford. When Harry Truman made his principal statement about support for aid to Greece and Turkey, he used language that seemed to have worldwide application, and that came to be known as the Truman Doctrine. My own impression at the time was that we were in no sense nominating ourselves to be the world's policeman, but that that was a part of the rhetoric needed to get support for Greek and Turkish aid. After all, some of those votes in the Congress were very close at that time.

While I was still in office, the State Department counted more than 400 situations of violence somewhere in the world since 1945. And the United States had been involved in about seven or eight of them. We have not gone around the world looking for places in which to intervene. And the containment idea has not been generalized into the role of a world policeman, in my judgment.

Clark, what do you think about that?

Secretary Clifford: I have the feeling that the Greece-Turkey crisis has more importance than history has given it. The British informed us at the beginning of 1947 that they could no longer continue to extend economic and military aid to Greece and Turkey. They suggested in a note to our government that that burden be taken up by the United States. It was an unattractive prospect to our government. That had never been an area under our aegis; the British had always controlled the Mediterranean, with particular emphasis on the eastern Mediterranean. And now they were pulling out. It was leaving a vacuum.

I think in many respects the decision to aid Greece and Turkey was one of the most courageous that President Truman made, and possibly had greater significance than was then thought. President George Washington, in his farewell address, indicated that the most serious and even fatal decision we could make was to become entangled in "foreign alliances." (He was referring, of course, to Western Europe.) That had been our policy all the way through: don't get involved in these age-old quarrels in Europe. Now, here, the president was being asked really to reverse the policy of generations. And it came hard to him. But the vacuum there would have been an exceedingly ominous one, so he wanted to go to the defense of Greece and Turkey.

Now, interestingly enough, there wasn't that degree of interest on the Hill at the time. I think Arthur Vandenberg had a good deal to do with creating it. He said, "We must make this a greater issue than just Greece and Turkey." So the language we used—and if we had to write it again, I think we might have chosen some different words—said, "It must be the policy of the United States to come to the defense of those nations who are being beset by armed minorities from within or from without." Too inclusive. But at the time it seemed the correct thing to do. We were stating a principle.

I suggest to you that a thrill of hope went around the world that wasn't there before those words went out, because they did not mean just Greece and Turkey. The Truman Doctrine showed other peoples that they could look to us for assistance. I think we felt that the major value was the warning directed at the Soviet Union, that they would have to face us from then on if they expected to use aggressive means beyond what they had already done.

Question (Professor Joseph Nye, Harvard University): I have a question for Mr. Clifford and for Mr. Kennan. It relates to domestic change and how rapidly one thinks it will occur. When one looks at the Clifford Report as you described it, there is nothing in there about expecting change inside the Soviet Union. But if one looks at the 'X' article or the long telegram, there is an expectation that there would be change inside the Soviet Union.

Can you recall the frame of mind that you had in 1946, Mr. Clifford? Did you think that some change would be necessary in the Soviet Union before any realistic accommodation could be reached? And, Mr. Kennan, how rapidly did you think the change would have to occur?

Secretary Clifford: Transpose yourself, if you can, to the thinking of late 1945 and early 1946. President Truman's hope that we could find some agreement with the Soviet Union had been badly used by the Soviets. Their aggressive designs—aggressive designs on all the nations in their western periphery—took different forms. They had violated the agreements—Tehran, Yalta, Potsdam—a long list of violations. They displayed the most extreme cynicism in the handling of these delicate and sensitive problems abroad, so that it would be difficult to find anybody, at that stage, who believed there was going to be much change within the Soviet system. It looked as though Stalin would live forever. Their attitude was so consistent, they constituted an immediate and ever-present threat.

But you may remember, from two or three sentences I read, that it was one of our aims to continue working with the Soviets so that they might ultimately find that they could develop some kind of understanding with us. We continued our effort. It's generally forgotten, I believe, that we offered to include the Soviet Union in the Marshall Plan and attempted to use some influence to get them to accept the offer. They rejected it arbitrarily, out of hand. So I would say to you that, at the time, there was not any real thought that there would be a change in the Soviet system.

But we still had the hope, and we would continue to work on it, that we could ultimately reach some type of agreement. George?

Ambassador Kennan: You will probably recall that the term used in the 'X' article with regard to future possibilities in the Soviet Union was for a "mellowing" of Soviet power. I think—if one takes the situation that we confronted at that time and the personalities of the men then in power, and compares them with what we have today—that mellowing has certainly occurred. It took a long time. I was thinking then in the shorter term, and I thought that if it were demonstrated to them that their hopes for extending their power further in Europe and Asia were not justified, then it would become possible to talk with them.

I am not sure to this day that that wouldn't have been possible. Dean Rusk has already pointed out, and very pertinently, that shortly thereafter we were able to get the Austrian Peace Treaty, one of the great successes of East-West negotiation and a source of stabilization for the whole Balkan and Central European area. I have never been convinced that we could not have talked to them about a German settlement at an earlier date. I did state my position on this on two memorable occasions: first in the submission of the Policy Planning Council's "Program A" proposal for Germany in 1949, and second in my Reith Lectures in 1957. And actually the difficulty that we ran into was not so much the dispositions of our own government—although they came in there, too—but more the anxieties of our Allies in Western Europe, the French and the British, who didn't really want the division of Europe removed at that time. They were still more afraid of Germany than they were of the Soviet Union. So there we are. There's not much more I can say about that.

None of us knew how long Joe Stalin would live. I think that, if anything, I somewhat underestimated the immediate repercussions of his death. On the other hand, this has been a complicated problem ever since, because while the Soviet government has evolved, and Khrushchev was entirely different from Stalin (as is Gorbachev from any of his predecessors), nevertheless, there have been strains of Stalinism in the internal administration of the Soviet Union which I hold to be very unfortunate, and which have endured to this day. Unless the Soviets can succeed in getting rid of those strains, unless they can remove the Secret Police from the inordinate position that they have had—not only in internal policy, but in foreign policy as well—in the Soviet apparatus of power, despite my belief that you could probably reach a sensible arms agreement with them, beyond that I think we have to beware and not hope to go too far and too fast.

Notes

1. In a cable from Moscow on 6 March 1946, Kennan argued explicitly for the division of Germany and "the incorporation of these [British and American] zones into general economic and political patterns of Western Europe. . . ." Kennan had argued in a letter to Charles Bohlen more than a year earlier—just before the Yalta Conference—that the United States should accept the division of Europe into Soviet and Western spheres of influence. For references and other schismatic views of the time, see W.W. Rostow, *The Division of Europe after World War II: 1946* (Austin: University of Texas Press, 1981), pp. 38–50.

2. The story of this plan and its fate is told in ibid., pp. 51–62.

3. Ibid., pp. 83–93.

4. Anton W. DePorte, *Europe Between the Superpowers: the Enduring Balance* (New Haven: Yale University Press, 1979).

5. See Thomas H. Etzold and John Lewis Gaddis, eds., *Containment: Documents on American Foreign Policy and Strategy, 1945–1950* (New York: Columbia University Press, 1978), pp. 64–71.

Part Two

Determinants
and
Instruments

4

Public Opinion and Containment

Ole R. Holsti

> *Since the time when Thomas Jefferson insisted upon a "de-cent respect to the opinions of mankind," public opinion has controlled foreign policy in all democracies.*
>
> Cordell Hull, 5 December 1936

> *To hell with public opinion.... We should lead, and not follow.*
>
> State Department official
> quoted by Bernard Cohen
> in *The Public's Impact on Foreign Policy*

IT IS RELATIVELY EASY to identify the requirements for examining the relationship between public opinion and containment. They include survey data for the past four decades that touch upon at least some of the more basic elements of containment, including assessments of—

- major threats to national security;

Ole R. Holsti is George V. Allen Professor of Political Science at Duke University.

- the perceived intentions of the Soviet Union;
- the appropriate scope of American security commitments abroad;
- the various instruments of containment, including alliances and military and economic assistance; and
- specific undertakings by the United States in the conduct of its containment policy.[1]

The questions should, of course, be carefully crafted in order to minimize biasing responses in one direction or another. Regular inclusion of the questions in surveys (perhaps once a year), using exactly the same wording each time, would facilitate inferences about trends in public opinion. Because we are likely to be interested in more than aggregate attitudes, information about the distribution of responses by various sub-groups within the entire sample—for example, those defined by party, age, education, race, ideology, and gender—would be very useful. Because interest in and knowledge about foreign affairs is not evenly or randomly distributed throughout the population, at least occasional surveys should also distinguish between the various strata of public opinion (for example, between leaders and the mass public).

Even an accurate description of the state of public opinion on issues related to foreign and defense policy may not exhaust our needs, however. We may also wish to assess public opinion's impact on policy. In order to do so, it is essential to have information from decisionmaking groups to provide some insight into how various policymakers perceive public opinion, how (if at all) it enters into their calculations, and the extent to which it shapes or constrains their policy choices.

One might well assume that these requirements can be met rather easily. After all, containment is arguably the most persistent and important theme running through American foreign policy since World War II. Moreover, the past four decades have seen public opinion polling come of age. To be sure, several major polls missed Harry Truman's upset of Thomas E. Dewey in the 1948 presidential election, but since that time the pollsters have proven quite adept at measuring public sentiments, at least on events like elections that present respondents with clear, dichotomous choices.

Nevertheless, one must conclude that *not a single one* of the requirements spelled out above can be met in full. Among the more salient limitations are these:

● Many of the more important questions relating to containment have been included in surveys rather sporadically, for the polls tend to be more sensitive to the issue of the moment. Indeed, the public has rarely been questioned on the policy of containment itself even when it has come under attack, as it did from some quarters during the 1952 election. Even questions on NATO have been asked rather infrequently. They were included at the time the Alliance was formed, when a significant contingent of American forces was deployed in Europe, when one of the recurrent Berlin crises gave rise to the prospect of combat involving US forces, when the Mansfield Amendment and other developments made the question of reducing the level of American forces abroad a salient one, and infrequently at other times. It is much harder to find evidence on public attitudes toward such alliances as SEATO, CENTO, and ANZUS or bilateral defense agreements with Japan, South Korea, the Philippines, and others. Some polls have, however, asked about the extent of American support for allied nations should they come under attack.

● At times questions are worded in ways that are not wholly free from bias. Surveys on the appropriate level of defense spending have often been flawed in this respect.

● Even small changes in the wording of questions that are repeated at frequent intervals may pose problems for trend analyses. For example, after using a question on foreign aid for some years, in 1956 the Gallup organization tacked on the words "to prevent their going communistic" at the end of the question. Although the distribution of pro– and anti–foreign aid response that year did not vary much from those of previous years, one might infer thereby either that support for foreign aid remained steady, or that it might have fallen in the absence of an explicit cue that the program served as an instrument of containment.

• Although the situation has improved substantially during recent years, the major polls have not consistently provided information on the distribution of responses by various strata and sub-groups within the entire sample. Since Gabriel A. Almond's seminal study of *The American People and Foreign Policy*,[2] it has been customary to distinguish between various strata of the public—typically between opinion leaders, the informed public, and the mass public—and there is reason to believe that this distinction is more important on foreign policy than on other issues. However, until the first of the Chicago Council on Foreign Relations surveys in 1974, there was relatively little information about leadership views on foreign affairs. On occasion, the Gallup organization has surveyed a sample of persons listed in *Who's Who in America,* but not frequently enough to be of great value on issues relating to containment. Distinctions according to educational level—usually between those with college, high school, and grammar school educations—are often reported, but a college education may not be a wholly satisfactory surrogate measure for leadership on foreign policy issues.[3]

These shortcomings pose a number of obstacles to valid and reliable descriptions of the public mood at a given time or across an extended period. There is also some truth in John E. Mueller's observation that, because "the poll interview is a rather primitive stimulus-response social situation in which poorly thought out answers are causally fitted to questions that often are overly ingenuous," one must be cautious in analyzing such data.[4]

These difficulties, however, pale in comparison to those posed by the other requirements. In particular, information on the impact of public opinion on foreign policymaking is very scanty. Bernard Cohen has shown that the constraining role of public opinion is often asserted but rarely demonstrated or even put to a systematic test.[5] The cases where it has been tested cast doubt on the potency of public opinion as a constraint on policy-making. For example, a classic study of the public-legislator relationship revealed that the attitudes of constituents had less impact on members of the House of Representatives on foreign policy than they did on other issues.[6] Cohen's research on the foreign policy bureaucracy indicates that State Department officials have a rather modest interest in public opinion, and to the extent that they even think about the public, it is as an entity to be "educated" rather than by which to be guided.[7] With some exceptions,[8] case studies of key foreign policy decisions make no reference to public opinion. But we do not know whether that is because public opinion was irrelevant in the case under analysis, because it was excluded from the research design, or because disproportionate attention to crisis decisions tends to exclude cases in which public opinion might be expected to have a greater impact.

Given this state of affairs, it is hardly surprising that there is little agreement, even among specialists on American foreign policy, about the impact of public opinion. Is it a constraint that, over the intermediate to long run, effectively sets limits upon policymakers? Or is public opinion (to the extent that it can be said to exist at all) essentially a shapeless, malleable lump that can readily be molded through public relations activities and compliant media to meet the immediate needs of policymakers?[9] One has little difficulty in finding experts who will confidently espouse either position, as well as many in between. Or is the relationship too complex to be described adequately by theories which assume a simple, direct, and one-way flow of influence between leaders and the public on foreign affairs? Alternative and more complex models of the process are also available.[10]

There is scarcely more agreement on the important normative question about the impact of public opinion. If it does have an effect on foreign policy, is it a force for enlightenment—indeed, a necessary if not sufficient condition for sound foreign policy—as celebrated by the Wilsonians and others in the liberal tradition? Or are Walter Lippmann, Hans Morgenthau, George Kennan, and others of the "realist" school correct in describing public opinion as a barrier to any thoughtful and coherent diplomacy, hindering efforts to promote national interests that transcend the moods and passions of the moment? This issue is of more than passing interest to the student of containment because, as articulated so clearly by George F. Kennan in his seminal 'X' article, effective containment requires "caution, circumspection, flexibility and deception," as well as patience, firmness, vigilance, and a long view. He also emphasized that "such a policy has nothing to do with outward histrionics: with threats or blusterings or superfluous gestures of outward 'toughness.' "[11] Are these qualities for which the American public is noted? Indeed, are they attributes that can often be found among leaders? Once again, even a cursory search will uncover advocates for virtually every position on this issue. Indeed, the same Walter Lippmann who considered public opinion "dangerous" in 1955 had, a decade later, come to regard the public as more enlightened than the White House on the Vietnam issue.

Do these difficulties, then, suggest that "public opinion and containment" is a non-topic that is unworthy of serious inquiry? Not really. As long as foreign policy encompasses the most important issues facing the United States, as long as Soviet-American relations are the dominant question on the nation's diplomatic agenda, and as long as the nature and channels of influence and accountability between leaders and the public—that is, the very nature of democratic society—are of vital concern, the issue of public opinion and foreign policy will be important. In short, this preface is not intended to dismiss the relevance of the topic but, rather, to serve as an explicit reminder of the limitations on the analysis that follows.

Internationalism in Public Opinion

The public mood following the end of World War II was of considerable concern to policymakers and many others who worried that it might trace out a pattern resembling the period after World War I: wartime idealism and internationalism, followed soon by cynicism and disenchantment with active American involvement in efforts to create a more stable international order. This concern is reflected in the frequency with which polling organizations asked respondents a variety of questions about whether it would be better for the United States to "take an active role" in or to "stay out" of world affairs.

When confronted with that choice, a majority of the public has selected the former option in every poll conducted since the end of World War II, as table 1 shows. During and immediately after World War II, those favoring an active role usually exceeded 70 percent of respondents. The onset of the Cold War and the Korean War witnessed some reduction of approval for internationalism, but approximately two respondents in three still rejected isolationism. Public support for an active international role increased again following the Korean armistice, reaching a zenith of 79 percent in June 1965. Such data have been cited as evidence that public opinion is characterized by "a strong and stable 'permissive mood' toward international involvement."[12] Moreover, opinion polls have consistently demonstrated that respondents with a higher level of education are more likely to favor internationalism, and this relationship has usually carried over to views on more specific policies—for example, in substantially greater support for foreign aid, liberalization of trade, and assistance to allies.

However, since 1965, when public opposition to American policy in Vietnam was quite limited, there has been a rather steady decline in support for international activism, reaching, in 1978 and 1982 surveys, lows not seen since before Pearl Harbor. It is important to point out, however, that the same surveys revealed overwhelming support by *leaders*—97 percent and

Table 1.   Should the United States play an active role in world affairs, or should it stay out?: American leaders and the public, 1943–1982*

		Public (%)			Leaders (%)		
Date	Poll**	Active Role	Stay Out	No Opinion	Active Role	Stay Out	No Opinion
Mar. 1943	Gallup	76	14	10			
Feb. 1944	Gallup	69	21	10			
May 1944	Gallup	73	18	9			
Oct. 1945	Gallup	71	19	10			
Feb. 1946	Gallup	72	22	6			
Nov. 1946	Gallup	77	19	4			
1947	NORC	68	25	7			
Oct. 1947	Gallup	65	26	9			
Nov. 1948	Fortune	62	30	8			
Jan. 1950	NORC	67	24	9			
Mar. 1951	NORC	66	25	9			
Mar. 1955	NORC	72	21	7			
1956	NORC	71	25	4			
Jun. 1965	NORC	79	16	5			
Mar. 1973	NORC	65	31	4			
Dec. 1974	CCFR	66	24	10			
Dec. 1978	CCFR	59	29	12	97	1	2
Dec. 1982	CCFR	53	35	12	98	1	1

* The exact wording of the questions and response options varied somewhat from survey to survey.

** NORC = National Opinion Research Center
CCFR = Chicago Council on Foreign Relations

98 percent, respectively—for an active American role in world affairs. Although internationalism has never been evenly distributed throughout the population, this bifurcation of attitudes between leaders and the general public is almost surely greater now than at any time since 1945.

Commitments and Interventions

Because an "active role in world affairs" can encompass a wide array of specific undertakings, not all of which are part of containment, the figures in table 1 can only provide the broad opinion background against which American policy has developed. In order to gain a more precise sense of public attitudes toward containment, it is necessary to examine public responses to the specific external commitments and interventions—actual and hypothetical—that have given shape to the policy of containment during the past four decades.

Although Kennan's seminal analysis of the sources of Soviet foreign policy and their implications for relations between Moscow and Washington had reached the State Department a year earlier, 1947 marks a convenient starting point for analyzing public attitudes toward containment. The first of the three major undertakings that defined the American response to Soviet policy—the program of economic and military aid to Greece and Turkey known as the Truman Doctrine—was announced in March, followed soon by the Marshall Plan. Two years later the North Atlantic Treaty Organization was formed. Taken together, these actions constituted a significant part of what has been called "the revolution in American foreign policy."

The domestic context in early 1947 was one of rapidly changing attitudes about the prospects of cooperation with the Soviet Union. Planning for the postwar period during the Roosevelt administration had assumed that continued collaboration between the major wartime allies (the "Four Policemen") would serve as a major pillar of peace, and public attitudes tended to be consistent with that premise. Less than two years before the Truman Doctrine speech, the public was optimistic about postwar relations with the Soviet Union. In a Gallup poll taken a month after Japan's surrender, the public agreed by a margin of almost two to one (54 percent to 30 percent) that Russia could be trusted to cooperate with the United States. As late as December 1946, Gallup reported that 43 percent of the public believed that Moscow could be expected to cooperate, whereas 40 percent disagreed. Polls also indicated that the more highly educated respondents tended to be more optimistic in this respect.

Public opinion surveys revealed moderately strong but growing support for the Truman Doctrine, the Marshall Plan, and NATO. (See table 2.) Two days after President Truman's address to Congress requesting aid to Greece and Turkey, a Gallup poll revealed that those approving outnumbered opponents by a margin of 56 percent to 32 percent. At that time, public faith in the ability of the United Nations to deal with major international problems was rather high; indeed, much of the domestic criticism of the Truman Doctrine focused on the charge that the Greek-Turkish aid program would unilaterally bypass the newly created international organization. A month after Secretary of State Marshall's June 1947 speech at Harvard, the margin in support of the economic assistance program for Europe was better than two to one (57 percent to 21 percent), and within eighteen months that margin had grown to five to one (65 percent to 13 percent)—the postwar high point of support for foreign assistance. NATO elicited even more substantial and consistent approval. Polls in 1949 and 1950 showed that between two-thirds and three-quarters of respondents favored the NATO pact, whereas the opposition never reached the 20 percent level.

But if the kinds of programs that constituted the core of containment during the late 1940s had substantial public approval, not all of the real and hypothetical projects undertaken in the name of containment have garnered automatic support.

Table 2. Public opinion on various actual and proposed
          containment-related undertakings abroad, 1947–1985

Date	Poll	Issue[a]	% Favor[b]	% Oppose[c]	% No Opinion
Mar. 1947	Gallup	Aid to Greece (Truman Doctrine)	56	32	12
July 1947	Gallup	Marshall Plan	57	21	22
Nov. 1948	Gallup	To continue the Marshall Plan	65	13	22
May 1949	Gallup	North Atlantic Treaty Organization	67	12	21
May 1950	Gallup	North Atlantic Treaty Organization	74	17	9
July 1950	Gallup	Military supplies to Chiang Kai-shek government on Formosa	48	35	17
Jan. 1951	Gallup	Sending troops to Europe or keeping them at home to defend the Americas	55[d]	35[e]	10
Aug. 1950	Gallup	Support for US entry into Korean War	66	19	15
Oct. 1952	Gallup	Support for US entry into Korean War	37	43	20
Jan. 1953	Gallup	Support for US entry into Korean War	50	36	14
May 1953	Gallup	Sending troops to Indochina	12	78	10
Aug. 1953	Gallup	Sending troops to Indochina	8	85	7
May 1954	Gallup	Sending troops to Indochina	20	72	8

Date	Poll	Issue[a]	% Favor[b]	% Oppose[c]	% No Opinion
Dec. 1956	Gallup	Foreign aid to help stop communism	58	28	14
Jan. 1957	Gallup	US promise to send troops to Middle East if Russians attack there	50	34	16
Mar. 1959	Gallup	Keeping troops in Berlin even at risk of War	81	11	8
Sep. 1962	Gallup	Using armed force to overthrow Castro	24	63	13
Mar. 1966	Gallup	Support for US entry into Vietnam War	59	25	16
Feb. 1973	Gallup	Support for US entry into Vietnam War	29	60	11
Feb. 1975	Gallup	Additional aid to South Vietnam and Cambodia	12	78	10
Sep. 1973	Gallup	Reduce US troops in Europe	57	33	10
Apr. 1975	Gallup	Continue policy of helping governments that might be overthrown by communist-backed forces	53	37	10
June 1977	Gallup	Withdrawal of US troops from South Korea	40	38	22
Mar. 1981	Gallup	US support for government in El Salvador	44	47	9
July 1983	Gallup	Increasing military advisers in El Salvador from 55 to 125	24	63	13

Date	Poll	Issue[a]	% Favor[b]	% Oppose[c]	% No Opinion
July 1983	Gallup	Military assistance to friendly governments in Central America	35	55	10
Oct. 1983	Gallup	Sending Marines to Lebanon	37	51	12
May 1985	Gallup	Trade embargo on Nicaragua	46	37	17
May 1985	Harris	Invasion of Nicaragua	20	75	5
May 1985	Harris	Military aid to anti-Sandinista rebels in Nicaragua	23	73	4

a. Summary of issue rather than exact wording of question asked.
b. Includes such responses as "yes," "agree," "support," "good idea," "right thing."
c. Includes such reports as "no," "disagree," "wrong thing," "poor," "fair idea."
d. Send to Europe.
e. Keep at home to defend only North and South America.

Questions about sending American troops abroad have typically elicited much more varied patterns of response. The Korean and Vietnam Wars are, of course, the most important instances of American armed intervention. In both instances, initial bipartisan public support eroded as the prospects for early victory declined and as American casualties increased. The highly educated were most likely to approve American intervention, whereas those with only a grade school education were most critical.[13]

Reservations about deployment of American forces abroad, especially in unstable Third World areas, have persisted. Several examples will illustrate this point:

• Whereas a 1950 Gallup poll indicated a 74 percent to 17 percent margin of support for NATO, another survey by the same organization only a year later showed that only 55 percent approved sending American troops to Europe, whereas 35 percent preferred to have them remain at home to protect this hemisphere. Once forces are deployed, however, opinion often shifts. For example, a 1959 survey revealed overwhelming (81 percent) public support for keeping troops in Berlin even at the risk of war, rather than withdrawing them in the face of Premier Khrushchev's threat to alter the status of that divided city.

• As the French effort to maintain control in Indochina was reaching its climactic phase in 1953–1954, Gallup polls reported that as much as 85 percent of the public opposed sending American troops there. Despite various "trial balloons" about American intervention that were being floated in Washington during the spring of 1954, overwhelming public opposition to intervention persisted. Two polls in May indicated that opponents outnumbered supporters of such an undertaking by margins of more than three to one. Even the proposal to deploy only naval and air forces to Indochina was opposed by a substantial majority.

• Following the tumultuous events of 1956 in the Middle East, the public was rather evenly divided on the question of sending American troops should the Soviet Union attack the area, with 50 percent approving and the remainder opposing (34 percent) or expressing no opinion (16 percent).

• Less than a month before the Cuban missile crisis in 1962, less than one-quarter of the public favored using armed force to overthrow the Castro regime in Cuba.

• Even though a 1975 survey indicated fairly strong support for continuing the policy of containment (the margin of approval was 53 percent to 37 percent), a roughly comparable majority also favored a *reduction* of American forces in Europe. Support for using American troops to defend major allies should they be attacked has also tended to fluctuate rather sharply since the early 1970s. (See table 3.) Although wording differences no doubt account for at least some of the variation in responses during a specific year, there is a discernible pattern of declining support in the immediate wake of the war in Vietnam, followed by rising approval for defending Western Europe and Japan. The most recent Chicago Council survey in 1982 also reported, however, that should South Korea, Taiwan, Israel, El Salvador, or Saudi Arabia be attacked, an overwhelming majority of the public would oppose sending American troops to help them.[14]

● During the post-Vietnam period, public support for American interventions in the Third World has been decidedly lukewarm. Even the successful and low-cost invasion of Grenada elicited a less than overwhelming approval from either the public (59 percent) or leaders (62 percent).[15] Repeated surveys during the 1980s have revealed strong and growing resistance to deploying American troops or military advisers in Central America. The past few years have witnessed vigorous debates about whether perceived parallels between American involvement in Vietnam and Central America illustrate a proper appreciation of "the lessons of Vietnam" or a simplistic misapplication of them, but public opinion surveys repeatedly demonstrate that between two-thirds and three-fourths of the public fear that the situation in Central America will witness a repetition of the Vietnam War. The public also opposed the deployment of American Marines in Lebanon, with many (64 percent) expressing the fear that the situation there would turn into another Vietnam.[16]

Defense Spending

Because a substantial part of defense spending is allocated for containment, attitudes toward the Pentagon's budget provide another relevant indicator of the public mood. Questions on the issue were included in surveys rather sporadically until the late 1960s; for example, between 1953 and 1969, the Gallup poll asked about the defense budget only once—in 1960. In contrast,

Table 3. Willingness to come to the defense of Western
Europe and Japan if they are attacked*

		Public		Leaders	
Date	Poll**	Western Europe	Japan	Western Europe	Japan
1972	PA	52	43		
1974	CCFR	39		77	
	PA	48	37		
1975	PA	48	42		
1976	PA	56	45		
1978	CCFR	54	42	92	81
	PA	62	50		
	ROPER	43			
1979	PA	64	54		
1980	AP/NBC	67			
	PA	70	57		
1981	PA (Feb.)	51			
	PA (July)	53			
1982	CCFR	65	51	92	78

* Percentage of respondents who favor having the United States come
to the defense of allies.

** PA = Potomac Associates
CCFR = Chicago Council on Foreign Relations
AP/NBC = Associated Press/National Broadcasting Corporation

(Surveys within a single year are listed in alphabetical order.)

that organization polled the public at least three times on defense spending in 1983 alone.

The few surveys on the appropriate level of defense spending during the Truman and Eisenhower periods indicated an absence of public dissatisfaction. (See table 4.) In each of three
Gallup polls—in 1950, 1953, and 1960—a majority of those

with an opinion on the issue judged the budget to be "about right," and of the others, slightly more favored raising rather than lowering allocations to the Pentagon.

The absence of poll data on defense spending during the Kennedy and Johnson years makes it impossible to pinpoint a shift in mood, but it is a reasonable guess that the sharp changes in sentiment were linked to disenchantment with the Vietnam War.[17] Gallup polls in 1969, 1971, and 1973 revealed that respondents who felt that Pentagon spending was "too much" exceeded the combined total of those who judged it "too little" or "about right." Although the margin in favor of reduced defense spending varied somewhat from poll to poll during the Nixon and Ford administrations, the overall results point to substantial support for reduced defense spending.

The erosion of detente and growing concern about the magnitude of Soviet military programs during the later 1970s were reflected in a strong shift back toward support for greater defense spending, reaching a zenith during the 1980 election and the first year of the Reagan administration. Surveys of leaders and the general public revealed substantial majorities in favor of increasing allocations to the Pentagon.

The "defense consensus" was short-lived, however, despite repeated statements by President Reagan and Defense Secretary Weinberger that the job of "rebuilding America's defenses" has only begun. Evidence of a dramatic change in opinion is overwhelming; the polls since 1982 differ only on the magnitude of the shift toward a preference for reduced defense spending. Perhaps even more importantly, surveys of American leaders reveal that they also experienced a sharp shift in sentiment. Among the driving forces behind the change in mood may be a belief that the military buildup has been completed—the views of the president and defense secretary to the contrary notwithstanding—but follow-up questions in a 1985 Harris survey also document some other reasons, including massive budget deficits,

Table 4. Net attitudes favoring an increase (or decrease) in US defense spending, 1950–1985*

| Year | Surveys of the general public** | | | | | | Survey of leaders** | |
	Gallup	Harris	NORC	NYT/CBS	Roper	CCFR	CCFR	FPLP
1950	8							
1953	3							
1960	2							
1969	(44)							
1970	(41)							
1971	(39)	(34)						
1972	(28)							
1973	(34)		(27)					
1974	(33)		(14)			(19)	(48)	
1975	(32)		(14)					
1976	(14)	(2)	(3)					
1977	4	18	1					
1978		41	5		8	16	3	
1979				58	25			
1980	35	42	45	54	44			39
1981	36			43	2			

	(1)		(19)	(3)	(21)
1982	(17)				
	(25)				
1983	(31)	(14)			
	(28)	(11)			
	(16)***	21***			
		18			
1984	(35)	(7)			
1985	(29)				(63)

* Percent favoring an increase minus percent favoring a reduction; or percent stating budget is "too small" minus percent stating budget is "too large."

(Numbers in parentheses indicate net support for reducing the defense budget.)

** NORC = National Opinion Research Center
NYT/CBS = New York Times/Columbia Broadcasting System
CCFR = Chicago Council on Foreign Relations
FPLP = Foreign Policy Leadership Project

*** Surveys taken immediately after the USSR shot down Korean Airlines flight 007.

NOTE: As Bruce M. Russett ("The Revolt of the Masses: Public Opinion on Military Expenditures," in John P. Lovell and Philip S. Kronenberg, eds., *New Civil-Military Relations: The Agonies of Adjustment to Post-Vietnam Realities* (New Brunswick, N.J., 1974)) has demonstrated, questions on the defense budget are not uniformly free of bias (usually in the antidefense direction). Moreover, differences in wording or context (for example, whether the defense budget is appraised alone or within a cluster of other government programs) can have an impact on responses. Thus, the data here should be viewed with some caution. Nevertheless, they would appear adequate for tracing out broad shifts in public sentiments.

perceived waste and cost overruns in defense procurement, and weapons that often seem to function poorly.

Leaders and the General Public

Until the mid-1970s, opinion surveys rarely distinguished between leaders and the general public.[18] This limitation has been substantially reduced during the post-Vietnam period, however, as surveys of leaders have been undertaken by the Chicago Council on Foreign Relations (1974, 1978, 1982), the Foreign Policy Leadership Project (1976, 1980, 1984), Barton (1974–75), Russett and Hanson (1975), and Sussman (1976).[19]

Many of the questions posed in recent leadership surveys are not precisely the same as those asked of the general public, but they do provide some opportunities to compare public and leadership attitudes on a number of questions pertaining to containment. For example, table 1 already revealed the huge gap between leaders and the public in support for an active American role in world affairs.

The post-Vietnam leadership surveys make it possible to draw more precise comparisons of public and leadership attitudes on containment. Table 5 summarizes responses to two central questions—the importance of "containing communism" and of "defending our allies' security"—in six surveys since the end of the Vietnam War. Responses to the first item reveal a good deal of consistency over the 1974–84 period concerning the importance of containment among both leaders and the general public. Just under one-half of the leaders described containment as "somewhat important," while slightly smaller proportions rated that goal as "very important." Although the general public has been more skeptical than leaders about foreign commitments on most issues, concern for containing communism is an exception, as majorities ranging from 54 percent to 60 percent have described that goal as "very important."[20]

Reversing the finding on containing communism, results for the question of defending our allies' security indicate a

Table 5.　The importance of "Containing communism" and "Defending our allies' security" as foreign policy goals: American leaders and the general public, 1974–1984

		Leaders (%)				General Public (%)			
		Very Impt.	Somewhat Impt.	Not impt. at all	Not Sure	Very Impt.	Somewhat Impt.	Not impt. at all	Not Sure
Containing communism									
1974	CCFR*	34	49	16	1	54	27	13	6
1976	FPLP*	39	42	14	5				
1978	CCFR	45	47	7	1	60	24	10	6
1980	FPLP	41	46	11	2				
1982	CCFR	44	46	8	2	59	27	8	6
1984	FPLP	38	47	13	1				
Defending our allies' security									
1974	CCFR	47	49	2	2	33	50	9	8
1976	FPLP	37	55	4	4				
1978	CCFR	77	21	1	1	50	35	7	8
1980	FPLP	44	52	3	1				
1982	CCFR	82	16	1	1	50	39	5	6
1984	FPLP	47	49	3	1				

* CCFR = Chicago Council on Foreign Relations
FPLP = Foreign Policy Leadership Project

substantially greater sense of importance among leaders than among the general public in each of the three Chicago Council surveys. But in another respect the data are somewhat harder to interpret because of the sharp, repeated, and inexplicable differences in the Chicago and Leadership Project surveys. The one important similarity in the two surveys is that each reveals growing support over time for protecting allies.

Containment and defending allies were only two of more than a dozen foreign policy goals which respondents were asked to rate in the Chicago Council and Leadership Project surveys. These clusters of questions provide an opportunity to examine assessments of containment within the context of a richer menu of foreign policy goals. Table 6 presents responses to nine goals, combining answers into a single summary index.

Several important points emerge from these results. Although neither leaders nor the general public rated containment as a trivial goal, it did not emerge as the dominant or superordinate goal of American foreign policy. Indeed, of the five items dealing with military-strategic issues, arms control was consistently given a higher priority by leaders and the public in both surveys—even in 1980, when strong majorities favored increasing the defense budget (see table 4). This view was shared by those who stated that "matching Soviet military power" is a "very important" foreign policy goal; 84 percent of them favored arms control agreements with the Soviet Union.[21] It is also evident that a variety of economic issues—including energy, hunger, and Third World poverty—have come to be viewed as of at least equal, if not greater importance than containment.[22] In the absence of directly comparable data from the period between the Truman Doctrine and the end of the war in Vietnam, it is impossible to offer confident assessments about changes and continuities in leadership attitudes on containment, but the evidence in tables 5 and 6 strongly suggests that both leaders and the public perceive a richer set of challenges to and opportunities for American diplomacy than did their

Table 6. The importance of several goals of American foreign policy: American leaders and the public, 1974–1984*

Goals	Leaders						The Public		
	1974 (CCFR**) (FPLP**)	1976 (FPLP**)	1978 (CCFR)	1980 (FPLP)	1982 (CCFR)	1984 (FPLP)	1974 (CCFR)	1978 (CCFR)	1982 (CCFR)
Containing communism	.59	.63	.69	.65	.68	.63	.72	.77	.77
Defending our allies' security	.73	.67	.88	.71	.91	.73	.63	.73	.74
Protecting weaker nations against foreign aggression	.60	.53	.63	.58	.70	***	.53	.63	.63
Matching Soviet military power	***	***	***	***	.73	.63	***	***	.69
Maintaining a balance of power among nations	.73	.69	***	.76	***	.68	.65	***	***
Worldwide arms control	.93	.82	.89	.74	.92	.83	.82	.82	.81
Securing adequate supplies of energy	.88	.85	.94	.88	.86	.92	.88	.90	.85
Combatting world hunger	.88	.72	.83	.73	.82	.76	.79	.78	.78
Helping to improve the standard of living in LDCs	.81	.65	.81	.68	.77	.78	.66	.62	.63

* Responses scored as follows: "Very important" = 1.00; "Somewhat important" = 0.50; "Not at all important" = 0.00; "Not sure" not scored. The index ranges from 0.00 to 1.00.

** CCFR = Chicago Council on Foreign Relations; FPLP = Foreign Policy Leadership Project

*** Question not included in that survey.

counterparts during much of the Truman-Eisenhower-Kennedy-Johnson era.

Finally, and perhaps most importantly, there is substantial evidence of deep cleavages on foreign policy issues that encompass, but also go beyond, attitudes on containment. Surveys of both the general public and leaders have revealed the existence of at least three quite distinct ways of thinking about international relations and America's proper role in world affairs. (See table 7.) Although the labels used to describe these belief systems vary from study to study, their essential characteristics are quite similar.[23]

● The Cold War Internationalists—also described as "conservative internationalists" and "the security culture"—are inclined to believe that the international system remains bipolar. A relentless Soviet drive for international supremacy, buttressed by a rapid military buildup which exceeds any reasonable defensive needs, is thus the primary threat. In order to meet the Soviet challenge, it is vital that the United States and the West maintain a high level of military capabilities, a determination to match or exceed increases in Soviet force levels, and a willingness to use military power if needed to forestall Soviet adventures and to maintain the credibility of containment and deterrence.

● Variously described as "liberal internationalists," "the equity culture," and "Post–Cold War Internationalists," a second group tends to view the international system and primary threats to American interests with substantial emphasis on non-military-strategic issues, including the growing gap between rich and poor nations, threats to the environment, population, resources, racial conflicts, Third World debts, and similar issues. Although not unmindful of East-West tensions, they are inclined to view problems between Moscow and Washington as tractable. Detente, arms control agreements, and similar arrangements are seen as offering the prospect for stabilizing relations between the superpowers; they may also permit some

Table 7. Some elements of three foreign policy belief systems

	Cold War Internationalism	*Post–Cold War Internationalism*	*Semi-Isolationism*
Nature of the international system			
Structure	Bipolar. Tight links between issues and conflicts	Complex and interdependent. Moderate links between issues and conflicts	Multipolar. Weak links between issues and conflicts
World order priorities	A world safe from aggression and terrorism	International regimes for coping with a broad range of issues	Top priority should be to reduce linkages, dependencies, and interdependencies
Conception of interdependence	Encompasses security issues ("domino theory")	Encompasses economic/social issues	Exaggerated by internationalism
Primary threats to the United States	Soviet and Soviet-sponsored aggression and terrorism. Military imbalance favoring the USSR	Danger of nuclear war. North-South issues (e.g., rich-poor gap)	Danger of war by miscalculating. Domestic problems
The Soviet Union			
Nature of the system	A model totalitarian state	A great power	A great power with manifest domestic problems
Driving force of foreign policy	Aggressive expansionism inherent in the Soviet system	Seeks parity with United States. Defensiveness (exaggerated view of defense needs may create further tensions)	Fear

	Cold War Internationalism	Post–Cold War Internationalism	Semi-Isolationism
Soviet-American relations			
Nature of the conflict	Conflicts of interest are genuine. Largely zero sum	Some conflicts of interest, but these are exaggerated by hard-liners on both sides. Largely non–zero sum	Few if any genuine conflicts of interest. Largely non–zero sum
The Third World			
Role in present international system	Primary target of Soviet and Soviet-inspired subversion and aggression	Primary source of unresolved social/ economic problems that must be resolved to create a viable world order	With a few exceptions, largely peripheral and irrelevant, especially to US interests
Primary US obligations	Help provide security from aggression and terrorism	Economic and other forms of non-military assistance. Play a leading role in structural systemic changes	Few, if any, obligations for either security or economic development
Prescription for American foreign policy	Rebuild military strength to regain a position of parity with the USSR. Rebuild collective security system	Stablize relations with USSR in order to free resources for dealing with North-South and other priority issues	Stabilize relations with USSR and reduce commitments and dependencies abroad

resources that have gone into arms races to be used for coping with non-military threats to national security.

● Whereas the first two schools of thought locate the primary threats to the national interest in the international system, a third group—the "semi-isolationists" or "non-internationalists"—are skeptical. They tend to doubt America's responsibility for and ability to cope with a wide range of international problems; indeed, they believe that the excessive global agenda pursued by the United States is itself a major threat to American security. By taking on the role of the world's policeman, do-gooder, or conscience, the United States has squandered its material and other resources without commensurate success. America's vital international interests are finite, as are the resources that can be expended to protect them.

Two important points emerge from these findings. In a superficial sense, internationalists no doubt continue to constitute a majority, but differences between the two schools of internationalism are so fundamental and are rooted in such significant ideological differences that, barring a major international crisis, the chasm is not likely to be bridged soon. Secondly, semi-isolationism has achieved a position of respectability probably not seen since before Pearl Harbor. Indeed, on some issues (such as trade) the isolationist position may represent the majority view.

Partisanship in Public Opinion on Containment

Speculation about partisanship, a gender gap, or a generation gap reflect an interest in how the public's attributes affect its attitudes on foreign policy. The relationship of Party and age to foreign policy views may be of special interest. Information on Party trends may provide some clues about the extent to which major aspects of containment might be a source of partisan conflict, with the prospect that containment might be more difficult to sustain when one Party replaces another in control of the White House or Congress. Thus, the composition of an opinion majority may be almost as important as its size. A 60 percent to 40 percent poll on a containment issue, in which both Republicans and Democrats are similarly divided, is likely to have different long-run consequences than a 60 percent to 40 percent split that is composed of a 90 percent to 10 percent division in one Party and a 30 percent to 70 percent split in the other. The distribution of attitudes across age groups may provide hints not only about generational differences, but also about the likelihood of change as one age cohort replaces its predecessors.

During the formative years of America's containment policy, the bipartisan cooperation between the White House and Congress that made possible aid to Greece and Turkey, the Marshall Plan, and the North Atlantic Treaty Organization was also reflected in public opinion on these undertakings. As indicated earlier (in table 2), each of these striking departures from traditional foreign policies had rather solid public support. Equally important is the fact that Democrats and Republicans differed little with respect to any of these key elements of containment. (See table 8.) Issues relating to the Far East tended to be more contentious and placed greater strains on bipartisan cooperation, especially after the Truman-MacArthur dispute. The president's decision to fire MacArthur, culminating a conflict that reflected some fundamental differences in the appropriate conduct of containment, was not popular among Democrats (opposed, 53 percent to 30 percent), independents (51 percent to 30 percent), or (especially) Republicans (72 percent to 17 percent).[24] But surveys on other issues found limited partisan differences; for example, the decision to resist aggression in Korea, the move to aid the Chinese government in Taiwan, and the proposal to send American forces to Indochina as the French effort there was collapsing found Republicans and Democrats about equally supportive or critical. To be sure, by 1952 polls revealed that the Korean War—"Truman's War," as it was often called by critics—had lost far more support among Republicans than among Democrats, but sharp partisan divisions did not persist into the Eisenhower years. Even though in 1960 the defense

Table 8.   Partisanship on selected foreign and defense policy issues: The general public, 1946–1985

Date, Poll	Issue*		Responses by Party Affiliation (%)		
			Repub.	Demo.	Indep.
Feb. 1946	Role U.S. should play in world affairs	Active	72	72	NR
Gallup	(Active—Stay out—No opinion)	Stay out	23	22	NR
		N.O.	5	6	NR
Mar. 1947	Aid to Greece (Truman Doctrine)	Approve	56	56	NR
Gallup	(Approve—Disapprove—No opinion)	Disappr.	31	32	NR
		N.O.	13	12	NR
July 1948	US policy toward the Soviet Union	TS	73	70	NR
Gallup	(Too soft—Too tough—About	TT	3	4	NR
	right—No opinion)	AR	14	14	NR
		N.O.	10	12	NR
Feb. 1950	Defense budget	TM	16	12	18
Gallup	(Too much—Too little—About	TL	22	25	24
	right—No opinion)	AR	46	46	40
		N.O.	16	17	18
July 1950	Military supplies to Chiang Kai-shek	Should	48	50	NR
Gallup	government on Taiwan	Shd. not	39	32	NR
	(Should—Should not—No opinion)	N.O.	13	18	NR
July 1951	Sending US troops to Europe or keep-	Europe	53	61	49
Gallup	ing them at home to defend the	Home	39	30	38
	Americas (Europe—At home—No opinion)	N.O.	8	9	13
May 1954	Sending US troops to Indochina	Approve	18	22	17
Gallup	(Approve—Disapprove—No opinion)	Disappr.	76	70	72
		N.O.	6	8	11
Dec. 1956	Approve foreign aid to help stop	Yes	59	58	58
Gallup	communism	No	28	28	28
	(Yes—No—No opinion)	N.O.	13	14	14
Jan. 1957	Promise to send US troops to Middle	Approve	53	47	52
Gallup	East in case of Russian attack there	Disappr.	34	36	32
	(Approve—Disapprove—No opinion)	N.O.	13	17	16

Date, Poll	Issue*		Responses by Party Affiliation (%)		
			Repub.	Demo.	Indep.
Mar. 1960	Defense budget	TM	19	20	16
Gallup	(Too much—Too little—About	TL	15	24	23
	right—No opinion)	AR	51	42	44
		N.O.	15	14	17
Jan. 1963	Foreign aid	For	54	59	61
Gallup	(For—Against—No opinion)	Against	35	28	28
		N.O.	11	13	11
Jan. 1973	Was US policy in Vietnam a mistake?	Yes	54	64	NR
Gallup	(Yes—No—No opinion)	No	35	26	NR
		N.O.	11	10	NR
Sep. 1973	Reduction of US troops in Europe	Should	54	61	56
Gallup	(Should—Should not—No opinion)	Shd. not	36	31	34
		N.O.	10	8	10
June 1977	Withdrawal of US troops from South	F	32	47	36
Gallup	Korea	O	51	30	41
	(Favor—Oppose—No opinion)	N.O.	17	23	23
Mar. 1981	US role in El Salvador	Help	44	19	25
Gallup	conflict**	Stay Out	19	33	34
	(Help gov't—Stay out—Don't know)	DK	6	6	5
Sep. 1981	Defense budget	I	73	49	57
Harris	(Increase—Decrease—Keep	D	9	20	15
	same—Not sure)	KS	15	25	26
		NS	3	6	2
Mar. 1982	Defense budget	TM	18	43	39
Gallup	(Too much—Too little—About	TL	27	16	18
	right—No opinion)	AR	46	32	36
		N.O.	9	9	7
July 1983	Is El Salvador likely to turn into a sit-	V	27	48	41
Gallup	uation like Vietnam?	F	33	30	32
	(Very—Fairly—Not very—Not at	NV	26	13	14
	all—No opinion)	Not	8	3	6
		N.O.	6	6	7

Date, Poll	Issue*	Responses by Party Affiliation (%)			
			Repub.	Demo.	Indep.
Oct. 1983	On sending Marines to Lebanon	Mistake	36	61	50
Gallup	(Yes, Mistake—No—No opinion)	No	53	29	36
		N.O.	11	10	14
Jan. 1985	Defense budget	I	21	19	16
NYT/CBS	(Increase—Decrease—Keep	D	16	32	27
	same—No opinion)	KS	60	47	52
		N.O.	3	2	5
Jan. 1985	Defense budget	TM	29	60	49
Gallup	(Too much—Too little—About	TL	15	7	10
	right—No opinion)	AR	49	27	35
		N.O.	7	6	6
Apr. 1985	Proposal to reduce defense spending	Approve	56	76	65
Gallup	as a way of reducing the deficit	Disappr.	36	19	30
	(Approve—Disapprove—No opinion)	N.O.	8	5	5
May 1985	Trade embargo against Nicaragua	Approve	65	26	45
Gallup	(Approve—Disapprove—No opinion)	Disappr.	16	58	38
		N.O.	19	16	17

*   Summary statement of the issue rather than the exact wording of the question asked. Response options are given in parentheses below the issue and in abbreviated form to the left of the percentage distribution of responses.

**   Percentages exclude those who have not heard of the situation in El Salvador.

NR   Not reported.

budget had become a controversial issue (with charges that a complaisant administration had permitted a dangerous "missile gap" to develop), a Gallup poll revealed that differences attributable to Party loyalties were insubstantial. The absence of strong partisan cleavages extended into the early years of the Vietnam War, majorities within both Parties expressing strong support for the policies of the Johnson administration.[25]

For two-and-a-half decades spanning the Truman, Eisenhower, Kennedy, and early Johnson administrations, then, whatever differences divided the American public on foreign policies rarely fell along a cleavage defined by partisan loyalties. Indeed, during the pre-Vietnam period the distribution of attitudes among supporters of the two major Parties was sufficiently similar that the self-identified political "independents" usually stood on one side or another of the Democrats and Republicans rather than between them.

The decade since the end of the Vietnam War has witnessed a striking revival of partisan differences on a broad range of issues relating to containment. During the years immediately following the 1975 withdrawal of the last Americans from Saigon, pollsters generally concentrated on domestic issues (like inflation, unemployment, and crime) because these appeared to be of the most immediate public concern. Even the controversial question of how the United States should respond to events in Angola did not elicit a probe by the Gallup organization. Table 8 thus includes relatively little evidence about issues relating to containment during the Ford and Carter years.

Data on foreign policy attitudes have become more plentiful during the 1980s, however, and they reveal clearly that partisan differences are sharp and persistent, and that these differences encompass most containment-related issues. Moreover, the cleavages are not limited to the public but are equally pronounced among American leaders (see table 9), with Republican support for containment roughly double that of Democrats.

Table 9.   Partisanship on containment: American leaders, 1976–1984

Date, Poll	Issue		Responses by party affiliation (%)		
			Repub.	Demo.	Indep.
Mar. 1976	Containing communism (as a foreign	VI	58	24	39
FPLP	policy goal)	SI	34	46	43
	Very important—Somewhat impor-	NI	5	21	11
	tant—Not at all important—Not sure)	NS	2	8	7
Mar. 1976	Defending our allies' security (as a	VI	46	28	37
FPLP	foreign policy goal)	SI	49	61	53
	(Very important—Somewhat impor-	NI	3	5	5
	tant—Not at all important—Not sure)	NS	3	6	5
Mar. 1976	The U.S. should take all steps includ-	Agree	50	20	35
FPLP	ing use of force to prevent the spread	Disagree	50	78	64
	of communism	N.O.	0	1	1
	(Agree—Disagree—No opinion)				
Mar. 1980	Containing communism (as a foreign	VI	57	30	40
FPLP	policy goal)	SI	37	54	47
	(Very important—Somewhat impor-	NI	5	14	11
	tant—Not at all important—Not sure)	NS	1	2	2
Mar. 1980	Defending our allies' security (as a	VI	52	40	41
FPLP	foreign policy goal)	SI	46	56	54
	(Very important—Somewhat impor-	NI	1	2	4
	tant—Not at all important—Not sure)	NS	1	2	1
Mar. 1980	The U.S. should take all steps includ-	Agree	53	24	36
FPLP	ing the use of force to prevent the	Disagree	46	74	62
	spread of communism	N.O.	2	2	2
	(Agree—Disagree—No opinion)				
Mar. 1984	Containing communism (as a foreign	VI	63	23	33
FPLP	policy goal)	SI	34	56	53
	(Very important—Somewhat impor-	NI	3	20	13
	tant—Not at all important—Not sure)	NS	0	1	1
Mar. 1984	Defending our allies' security (as a	VI	57	45	44
FPLP	foreign policy goal)	SI	42	52	53
	(Very important—Somewhat impor-	NI	2	3	2
	tant—Not at all important—Not sure)	NS	0	1	1
Mar. 1984	The U.S. should take all steps includ-	Agree	56	19	30
FPLP	ing the use of force to prevent the	Disagree	43	81	69
	spread of communism	N.O.	1	1	1
	(Agree—Disagree—No opinion)				

FPLP = Foreign Policy Leadership Project

The bifurcation along partisan lines is sufficiently great that, unlike during the pre-Vietnam period, recent responses of political independents typically fall between those of Democrats and Republicans. With the possible exception of some agreement on the need to reduce defense spending, evidence neither from leaders nor from the general public suggests that a convergence of foreign policy views across political Parties will be easily achieved. Not the least reason for this diagnosis is evidence that partisan differences are buttressed by hardening ideological cleavages. The evidence on this score at the leadership level is rather strong,[26] and the same dynamics may also be found among the general public.[27]

Generations and Containment

A generational interpretation of American foreign policy views appears to offer an attractive way to account for periodic shifts in public attitudes on foreign affairs. It seems to provide an explanation for the long-term cycles in which public moods have been described as swinging between internationalism and isolationism at intervals of approximately a generation in length throughout the history of the republic.[28] It is also consonant with the observation that members of each generation view the world in the light of the critical events that mark their coming to maturity.[29]

The generational hypothesis seemed especially pertinent in the aftermath of the Vietnam War, giving rise to several analyses that depicted domestic cleavages on the war in generational terms.[30] Among the earliest and most visible opponents of the war were students at Berkeley, Harvard, and other campuses. These and other critics rejected many of the intellectual underpinnings of containment, notably the relevance for the conflict in Southeast Asia of the lessons of the pre–World War II era about the futility of appeasement and the premise that the war in Indochina presented a threat similar to that posed by Stalinist Russia during the late 1940s. Hence, several analysts depicted the foreign policy debates of the late 1960s and early 1970s as pitting the theories and values of the "Munich generation" against those of the "Vietnam generation." Former National Security Adviser Zbigniew Brzezinski summarized the argument in this way:

> There is a tendency in America to be traumatized by international difficulties. The generation of the Nineteen-forties was always thinking about the failure of the League of Nations. I'm talking about leadership groups now. The leadership of the sixties was always thinking about Munich. Now there is a generation worried by Vietnam, with consequences of self-imposed paralysis, which is likely to be costlier in the long run.[31]

Finally, the generational hypothesis seems particularly pertinent to the present topic because the policy of containment seems to evoke more of the putative differences between age groups than other foreign policy issues. For these reasons it appears especially appropriate to ask whether the "successor generation"—those for whom Vietnam was the great foreign policy drama (or trauma) of their formative years and who are assuming increasingly important responsibilities in various American institutions—differs significantly from older groups in viewing the international arena and America's proper role in it.

The major problem with the generational thesis is that hard evidence to support it is rather scarce. Even during the midst of the Vietnam War, the allegedly "dovish" younger generation provided stronger support than other age groups for the George Wallace–Curtis LeMay ticket. Public opinion polls of the post-Vietnam period also reveal few if any striking age-based differences on foreign and defense issues (see table 10). Even when small differences appear, they do not consistently fit the pattern implied by the "Munich generation versus Vietnam generation" thesis. For example, a Gallup poll in 1975 asked respondents whether the United States should continue a policy of protecting other nations against a communist takeover. There were virtually no differences in levels of support among the three

Table 10. Generations on containment: The American public, 1973–1985

Date, Poll	Issue*		Responses By Age of Respondents (%)			
			18–29		30–49	50 & over
			18–24	25–29		
Mar. 1971 Gallup	Defense budget (Too much—Too little—About right—No opinion)	TM	57		49	46
		TL	10		11	11
		AR	27		33	31
		N.O.	6		7	12
Jan. 1973 Gallup	Was US policy in Vietnam a mistake? (Yes—No—No opinion)	Yes	55	49	56	68
		No	36	44	32	20
		N.O.	9	7	12	12
Sep. 1973 Gallup	Reduction of US troops in Europe (Should—Should Not—No opinion)	S	58		60	60
		SN	33		28	28
		N.O.	9		12	12
Apr. 1975 Gallup	Should US maintain its policy of containment? (Should—Should Not—No opinion)	S	57	58	57	47
		SN	35	31	35	41
		N.O.	8	11	8	12
Nov. 1982 Gallup	Defense budget (Too much—Too little—About right—No opinion)	TM	49	45	41	35
		TL	15	19	16	17
		AR	25	29	32	34
		N.O.	11	7	11	14
July 1983 Gallup	Proposal to increase US military advisers in El Salvador (Favor—Oppose—No opinion)	F	23	27	24	25
		O	68	63	63	59
		N.O.	9	10	13	16

Date/Poll	Question (Response options)					
July 1983 Gallup	Should US provide military aid to friendly governments in Central America? (Provide aid—Not become involved—No opinion)	Aid	36	32	40	32
		NI	57	58	51	57
		N.O.	7	10	9	11
July 1983 Gallup	Is El Salvador likely to turn into a situation like Vietnam? (Very likely—Fairly likely—Not very likely—Not at all likely—No opinion)	V	33	37	43	42
		F	39	41	31	25
		NV	16	15	14	18
		Not	6	4	4	7
		N.O.	6	3	8	8
Sep. 1983* Gallup	Defense budget (Too much—Too little—About right—No opinion)	TM	42	43	35	36**
		TL	24	16	23	21
		AR	29	33	39	38
		N.O.	5	8	3	5
Oct. 1983 Gallup	On sending Marines to Lebanon (Yes, Mistake—No—No opinion)	M	56		51	50
		No	35		37	37
		N.O.	9		12	13
Jan. 1985 Gallup	Defense budget (Too much—Too little—About right—No opinion)	TM	49		46	44
		TL	13		11	8
		AR	34		36	38
		N.O.	4		7	10
May 1985 Gallup	Trade embargo on Nicaragua (Approve—Disapprove—No opinion)	A	40		48	46
		D	36		36	38
		N.O.	24		16	16

* Summary of the issue rather than exact wording of the question asked. Response options are given in parentheses below the question.

** 50–64 age group. Respondents 65 and over responded as follows: Too much (22%); Too little (19%); About right (38%); and No opinion (11%).

youngest age groups, and respondents over the age of fifty expressed somewhat *more*, rather than less, skepticism. Surveys during the 1980s dealing with such controversial issues as the proper level of defense spending and the appropriate American role in Central America also fail to reveal any sharp age-based discontinuities.

Perhaps the search for cleavages between age groups among leaders rather than among the general public might prove more fruitful. Vietnam protests were more often found at the "elite" universities than at state and community colleges or non-educational settings. As revealed in table 11, however, responses by American leaders to three central questions—on the importance of containing communism, with force if necessary, and that of defending allies—reveal relatively minor differences across four age groups. Again, those differences which do emerge do not always conform to the pattern of "young doves" versus "old hawks." For example, members of the World War II generation were *least* prone to agree with the proposition that "the U.S. should take all steps including the use of force to prevent the spread of communism." That three leadership surveys taken at four-year intervals yielded essentially similar negative evidence adds to skepticism about the generational thesis.[32]

In summary, there is little in these survey results to indicate that the inevitable replacement of one generation by its successor will yield significant changes in public opinion toward containment policy. Attitudes toward containment are unlikely to remain frozen over any extended period of time, but generational differences may not be the most fruitful place to look for the dynamics of change.

Conclusion

"Realist" foreign policy analyses place primary emphasis on the nature of the international system and the challenges emanating from it. In this respect, Kennan's 'X' article was fully within the realist tradition as it focused on the Soviet challenge and the forces driving Russian foreign policy. But in his superb analysis of containment, Professor John Lewis Gaddis demonstrates that

changes in doctrine and strategy have been sensitive also to domestic factors, especially beliefs about the resources available
for defense.[33] To the extent that public opinion enters into his
analysis, it is often in connection with leaders' efforts to shape
public attitudes; for example, Gaddis cites with sympathy
George Kennan's strong objections to the open-ended commitments of the Truman Doctrine speech, rhetorical excesses allegedly arising from a need to arouse emotional support in a
recalcitrant Congress and an apathetic and ill-informed public.

Two areas suggest themselves for further observations
about public opinion and containment. The first relates to the
future of containment, the second to the impact of public opinion on containment policy during the past four decades.

The first area is the easier of the two because conclusions
are embedded within the survey data themselves. Although we
have not begun to exhaust either the substantive issues or the
types of analyses that might lead to useful generalizations, at
least several tentative conclusions about the future of containment may be offered:

● There has been remarkable continuity and consensus on
the *ends* of foreign and defense policy related to containment.
Such general values as "peace," "strength," "active international
role," and the like have usually evoked positive and relatively
stable responses from the public. This consensus has been even
more characteristic of the more attentive and informed strata of
the public.

● However, public attitudes toward the *means* of implementing containment have been much more volatile. Foreign assistance, once quite popular, has in recent years consistently
been rated as the least popular and most expendable government
program. Security commitments to allies, interventions (especially in Third World areas), and other specific undertakings to
implement containment have also brought forth quite varied
responses.

Table 11.   Generations on containment: American leaders, 1976–1984

Date, Poll	Issue		Responses by generations* (%)			
			Vietnam	Interim	Korea	WWII
Mar. 1976 FPLP	Containing communism (as a foreign policy goal) (Very important—Somewhat important—Not at all important—Not sure)	VI	39	37	38	40
		SI	44	43	44	40
		NI	12	15	13	14
		NS	5	6	5	6
Mar. 1976 FPLP	Defending our allies' security (as a foreign policy goal) (Very important—Somewhat important—Not at all important—Not sure)	VI	45	39	32	33
		SI	50	55	61	56
		NI	3	4	4	6
		NS	2	3	4	6
Mar. 1976 FPLP	The U.S. should take all steps including the use of force to prevent the spread of communism (Agree—Disagree—No opinion)	Agree	44	39	27	28
		Disagree	55	60	72	71
		N.O.	1	2	1	1
Mar. 1980 FPLP	Containing communism (as a foreign policy goal) (Very important—Somewhat important—Not at all important—Not sure)	VI	36	39	42	43
		SI	48	50	49	44
		NI	15	10	8	11
		NS	1	2	1	2
Mar. 1980 FPLP	Defending our allies' security (as a foreign policy goal) (Very important—Somewhat important—Not at all important—Not sure)	VI	44	45	40	44
		SI	51	52	55	53
		NI	3	2	4	3
		NS	1	1	1	1

			Vietnam	Interim	Korean	World War II
Mar. 1980 FPLP	The U.S. should take all steps including the use of force to prevent the spread of communism (Agree—Disagree—No opinion)	Agree	34	40	37	33
		Disagree	65	58	61	65
		N.O.	1	2	2	2
Mar. 1984 FPLP	Containing communism (as a foreign policy goal) (Very important—Somewhat important—Not at all important—Not sure)	VI	37	41	40	36
		SI	50	48	45	51
		NI	13	11	14	13
		NS	1	1	2	2
Mar. 1984 FPLP	Defending our allies' security (as a foreign policy goal) (Very important—Somewhat important—Not at all important—Not sure)	VI	51	51	47	41
		SI	46	47	50	56
		NI	4	2	2	2
		NS	0	1	2	2
Mar. 1984 FPLP	The U.S. should take all steps including the use of force to prevent the spread of communism (Agree—Disagree—No opinion)	Agree	38	35	34	27
		Disagree	60	65	64	72
		N.O.	2	0	1	1

*Generations: Vietnam, born since 1940; Korean, born 1933–1940; Interim, born 1924–1932; World War II, born before 1924

• Survey data seem to show that the past two decades have witnessed a significant breakdown in consensus on many important elements of containment, among both the general public and leaders. However, the sources, the dynamics, and even the existence of those changes have generated spirited debates. Hence, the core question is not whether the nation is currently divided on many key foreign policy issues but, rather, whether this condition represents a significant change from earlier periods of the post–World War II era. Is it appropriate to describe the two decades following World War II as "the age of consensus,"[34] or is that merely an exercise in nostalgia? Was the Vietnam War the primary source of dissension, or was a post–World War II consensus breaking down well before Vietnam became a controversial issue? Did changes in public opinion originate primarily from disillusionment with (and perhaps an excessive tendency to generalize about) the containment policies that were perceived as having ultimately led to the Vietnam quagmire, or were attitudes among the general public essentially reflecting a collapse in consensus first at the leadership level and then among the attentive public?[35] These questions illustrate rather than exhaust some of the controversies concerning continuity and change in public attitudes toward foreign and defense policy.

• Evidence that differences in the public's foreign policy attitudes are becoming increasingly rooted in partisanship and ideology would appear to make the prospects for the early emergence of a post-Vietnam foreign policy consensus rather dim. A comparable lack of agreement on most issues among leaders is especially significant in assessing the prospects for forging a consensus, at least in the near future.

Any assessment of public opinion and containment would be incomplete unless some attention were directed to the thorny question of public opinion's ultimate impact on policy. As indicated in the preface to this paper, the impressive range of views on the matter is not matched by systematic evidence linking foreign policy leaders, the bureaucracy, the attentive public, and the media to public opinion.[36] Indeed, it is probably the paucity of hard evidence on the question that sustains such diverse conclusions.

There is no shortage of evidence that most post–World War II presidents have followed Theodore Roosevelt in thinking that the White House is "a bully pulpit," whether it is used "to scare the hell out of them" in order to gain support for aid to Greece and Turkey, to warn against the dangers of "unwarranted influence, whether sought or unsought, by the military-industrial complex," or to drum up support for assistance to the contras in Nicaragua. It is equally evident that such efforts have not been equally successful. Perhaps Daniel Yankelovich is correct in asserting that the relationship between leaders and the public has changed—"farewell to 'the President knows best,' " as he put it[37]—but it is far from clear that this new relationship represents a permanent change in the equation.

The more difficult question concerns the influence, if any, in the other direction,[38] where the evidence is even skimpier and more anecdotal. Did President Kennedy genuinely believe that he would be impeached should he fail to force removal of Soviet missiles from Cuba, as he said, or was he merely seeking to bolster decisions arrived at for reasons that had nothing to do with public opinion? How much did growing public impatience lead the Carter administration to embark on the ill-fated effort to free American hostages in Iran, or the Reagan administration to withdraw US Marines from Lebanon?

In the absence of substantial evidence, it is probably appropriate to maintain a posture of skepticism about public opinion strongly influencing foreign policy decisions. Perhaps part of the reason for the shortage of data on the question of impact arises from different concerns of the public and the policymakers. Whereas the public is mostly interested in the *ends* of foreign policy, policymakers are concerned primarily with *means*, which often involve highly specific and technical issues that have little meaning for the public.[39] For example, the public may express strong support for preventing further Soviet expansion while at the same time having little interest in or knowledge of strategies and tactics for pursuing that goal. (That may, of course, change when American casualties are at issue.) On the other hand, most policymakers have probably accepted containment as a "given" and are actively involved in debating the means.

Finally, one might ask to what extent the anticipation of public disapproval has acted to prevent action. There is substantial evidence that during the 1980s a majority of the public has consistently opposed American military involvement in Central America. Would the Reagan administration have intervened more directly in El Salvador or Nicaragua in the absence of such attitudes? Solid evidence about contemporary non-events is, to understate the case, rather hard to come by. Yet it is precisely such hard-to-answer questions that lie at the heart of this topic. Unfortunately, while this essay has explored some interesting issues on public opinion and containment, the most compelling questions must be left unanswered.

Notes

Research for this paper was supported in part by National Science Foundation grant No. SES–83–09036. The assistance of Daniel

Harkins, Arturo Borja, Charles Sowards, and Maija Holsti is gratefully acknowledged. For helpful comments on an earlier draft of this paper, I am greatly indebted to Robin Dorff, Daniel Harkins, and Bruce Kuniholm.

1. The term *containment* means different things to different people. Thus, there is still an active debate about "what Kennan *really* meant" in 1946–47, to say nothing about the much more acrimonious debate about the appropriate scope of containment today. Participation in those controversies is beyond the scope of this paper; the discussion that follows will take a broad view of containment as involving commitments by the United States to sustain the security of other nations. Restrictions on what containment entails are imposed by limits on relevant public opinion data rather than by definition.

2. Gabriel A. Almond, *The American People and Foreign Policy* (New York: Praeger, 1960 (originally published in 1950)).

3. William C. Rogers, Barbara Stuhler, and Donald Koenig, "A Comparison of Informed and General Public Opinion on U.S. Foreign Policy," *Public Opinion Quarterly* 31 (1967), pp. 242–52.

4. John E. Mueller, *War, Presidents and Public Opinion* (New York: Wiley, 1973), p. 265.

5. Bernard Cohen, *The Public's Impact on Foreign Policy* (Boston: Little, Brown & Co., 1973).

6. Warren E. Miller and Donald E. Stokes, "Constituency Influence in Congress," *American Political Science Review* 57 (1963), pp. 45–46.

7. Cohen, *The Public's Impact on Foreign Policy.*

8. See James N. Rosenau, *National Leadership and Foreign Policy* (New York: Random House, 1961); Cohen, *The Political Process and Foreign Policy: The Making of the Japanese Peace Settlement* (Princeton: Princeton University Press, 1957); and Raymond A. Bauer, Ithiel de Sola Pool, and Lewis A. Dexter, *American Business and Public Policy: The Politics of Foreign Trade* (New York: Atherton Press, 1963).

9. David Paletz and Robert Entman, *Media Power Politics* (New York: Free Press, 1981).

10. See Elihu Katz, "The Two-Step Flow of Communication: An Up-to-date Report on an Hypothesis," *Public Opinion Quarterly* 21 (1957), pp. 61–78; and Rosenau, *National Leadership and Foreign Policy.*

11. George F. Kennan (writing as 'X'), "The Sources of Soviet Conduct," *Foreign Affairs* 25 (1947), p. 575.

12. William R. Caspary, "The Mood Theory: A Study of Public Opinion and Foreign Policy," *American Political Science Review* 64 (1970), p. 546. Although Caspary's study was published in 1970, he reports data on internationalism/isolationism only through 1953.

13. Mueller, *War, Presidents and Public Opinion.*

14. John E. Rielly, ed., *American Public Opinion and U.S. Foreign Policy 1983* (Chicago: Chicago Council on Foreign Relations, 1983), p. 31.

15. Gallup poll in November 1984 and the FPLP survey in March 1984. As early as 1965, according to Gallup, only 52 percent of the public supported the American intervention in the Dominican Republic.

16. Gallup polls in March 1981; March, June, and July 1983; and May 1984 on Central America; and in October 1984 on Lebanon.

17. For more evidence on the persisting effects of the Vietnam War, see Ole R. Holsti and James N. Rosenau, *American Leadership in World Affairs: Vietnam and the Breakdown of Consensus* (London and Boston: Allen & Unwin, 1984); Rielly, ed., *American Public Opinion and U.S. Foreign Policy 1975,* p. 17; and Rielly, ed., *American Public Opinion and U.S. Foreign Policy 1983,* p. 31. A different interpretation of the breakdown in the foreign policy consensus is developed by Mueller in "The Cold War Consensus: From Fearful Hostility to Wary Contempt," mimeograph, 1984. Mueller emphasizes the correlation between perceptions of Soviet threat and consensus, arguing that the former was the adhesive that maintained the consensus.

18. Herbert McCloskey, Paul J. Hoffman, and Rosemary O'Hara, "Issue Conflict and Consensus Among Party Leaders," *American Political Science Review* 54 (1960), pp. 406–27, is a notable exception.

19. See Rielly, ed., *American Public Opinion and U.S. Foreign Policy 1975, . . .1979,* and *. . .1983;* Allen H. Barton, "Consensus and Conflict Among American Leaders," *Public Opinion Quarterly* 38 (1974–75), pp. 507–30; Bruce M. Russett and Elizabeth C. Hanson, *Interest and Ideology: The Foreign Policy Beliefs of American Businessmen* (San Francisco: Freeman, 1975); and Barry Sussman, *Elites in America* (Washington: Washington Post, 1976).

20. This is one of many questions on which wording might make a significant difference. Specifically, would respondents have attributed greater importance to containment had the question been worded differently: "containing Soviet expansion"? By 1974, the United States was well on the way to normalizing relations with the largest communist nation—China—and by 1980, some leaders who were most "hawkish" in their assessments of the Soviet Union were calling for an alliance between Beijing and Washington to counter Moscow (Holsti and Rosenau, *American Leadership in World Affairs,* p. 215).

21. Rielly, ed., *American Public Opinion and U.S. Foreign Policy 1983,* pp. 14–15.

22. The importance attached by the public to "combatting hunger" and "helping to improve the standard of living of LDCs" may seem startling in view of the finding in poll after poll that for some time a great majority of Americans have wanted to reduce if not eliminate foreign aid programs. Perhaps the explanation of this seeming anomaly is that many in the public see little connection between foreign economic aid and these two goals. In this respect, leaders are strikingly different, since they are overwhelmingly in favor of economic assistance programs.

23. Michael Mandelbaum and William Schneider, "The New Internationalisms: Public Opinion and Foreign Policy," in Kenneth A. Oye, Robert J. Lieber, and Donald Rothchild, eds., *Eagle Entangled: U.S. Foreign Policy in a Complex World* (New York: Longman, 1979); Holsti and Rosenau, *American Leadership in World Affairs;* and Michael A. Maggiotto and Eugene Wittkopf, "American Attitudes Toward Foreign Policy," *International Studies Quarterly* 25 (1981), pp. 601–31.

24. H. Schuyler Foster, *Activism Replaces Isolationism* (Washington: Foxhall Press, 1983), p. 112. For evidence of partisan differ-

ences on foreign policy immediately following Truman's dismissal of MacArthur, see George Belknap and Angus Campbell, "Political Party Identification and Attitudes Toward Foreign Policy," *Public Opinion Quarterly* 55 (1951–52), pp. 601–23.

25. For the most detailed assessment of public support for the Korean and Vietnam Wars, see Mueller, *War, Presidents and Public Opinion*. Sidney Verba, *et al.*, in "Public Opinion and the War in Vietnam," *American Political Science Review* 61 (1967), pp. 317–33, report that even after the Vietnam War became controversial, Party identification was not an important determinant of attitudes on the war.

26. Holsti and Rosenau, *American Leadership in World Affairs*, pp. 151–53, 209.

27. Schneider, "Conservatism, Not Interventionism: Trends in Foreign Policy Opinion, 1974–1982," in Oye, Lieber, and Rothchild, eds., *Eagle Defiant: United States Foreign Policy in the 1980s* (Boston: Little, Brown & Co., 1983).

28. See Frank L. Klingberg, "The Historical Alternation of Moods in American Foreign Policy," *World Politics* 4 (1952), pp. 239–73; Klingberg, "Cyclical Trends in American Foreign Policy Moods and Their Policy Implications," in Charles W. Kegley, Jr., and Patrick J. McGowan, eds., *Challenges to America: United States Foreign Policy in the 1980s* (Beverly Hills: Sage, 1979); and Jack E. Holmes, *The Mood/Interest Theory of American Foreign Policy* (Lexington: University Press of Kentucky, 1985).

29. Karl Mannheim, *Essays in the Sociology of Knowledge,* ed. by Paul Kecskmeti (London: Routledge and Kegan Paul, 1952), p. 291.

30. See Graham T. Allison, "Cool It: The Foreign Policy of Young America," *Foreign Policy,* No. 1 (Winter 1970–71), pp. 144–60; Michael Roskin, "From Pearl Harbor to Vietnam: Shifting Generational Paradigms and Foreign Policy," *Political Science Quarterly* 89 (1974), pp. 563–88; and Russett, "The Americans' Retreat from World Power," *Political Science Quarterly* 90 (1975), pp. 1–21.

31. Zbigniew Brzezinski, quoted in Elizabeth Drew, "A Reporter at Large (Brzezinski)," *New Yorker,* 1 May 1978.

32. The negative evidence on the impact of generation is not confined to the issues identified in tables 10 and 11. For evidence on other foreign policy issues, see Holsti and Rosenau, *American Leadership in World Affairs,* pp. 153–63, 209.

33. John Lewis Gaddis, *Strategies of Containment* (New York: Oxford University Press, 1982).

34. Stanley Hoffmann, *Primacy or World Order* (New York: McGraw-Hill, 1978).

35. Schneider, "Public Opinion," in Joseph S. Nye, Jr., ed., *The Making of America's Soviet Policy* (New Haven: Yale University Press, 1984).

36. In addition to the studies cited in the preface of this paper, others which have tried to assess the impact of public opinion include Richard Fagen, "Some Assessments and Uses of Public Opinion in Diplomacy," *Public Opinion Quarterly* 24 (1960), pp. 448–57; and Leila Sussman, "FDR and the White House Mail," *Public Opinion Quarterly* 20 (1956), pp. 5–16.

37. Daniel Yankelovich, "Farewell to 'President Knows Best,' " *Foreign Affairs* 57 (1979), pp. 670–93.

38. The Chicago Council on Foreign Relations surveys reveal that neither the public nor leaders believe that public opinion plays a very significant role in policymaking. In three surveys undertaken at four-year intervals, between 19 percent and 26 percent of the public rated public opinion as a "very important" factor, whereas even fewer leaders (15 percent to 20 percent) gave it that rating. On the other hand, both the public and leaders consistently ranked public opinion at the top of factors that *should* be more important in policymaking.

39. Adam Yarmolinsky, "Confessions of a Non-User," *Public Opinion Quarterly* 27 (1963), pp. 543–48.

5

Containment and the National Security Policymaking Process

Lynn E. Davis

I N "THE SOURCES OF SOVIET CONDUCT," George Kennan
described the "political personality" of Soviet power,
suggesting "that Soviet policies will reflect . . . a cautious,
persistent pressure toward the disruption and weakening of all
rival influence and rival power." He then recommended that
"the main element of any United States policy toward the
Soviet Union must be that of a long-term, patient but firm and
vigilant containment of Russian expansionist tendencies."
This "firm and vigilant containment" should be "designed to
confront the Russians with unalterable counter-force at every
point where they show signs of encroaching upon the interests
of a peaceful and stable world." Kennan was confident that
Soviet pressures against the West could be contained "by the

Lynn E. Davis is Director of Studies at the International Institute for Strategic
Studies and Editor of the Institute's journal, *SURVIVAL*.

adroit and vigilant application of counter-force at a series of constantly shifting geographical and political points, corresponding to the shifts and maneuvers of Soviet policy."[1]

In the late 1940s, Americans began to view with alarm the consolidation of Soviet power in Eastern Europe and the expansion of communist parties in Western Europe. What Kennan did was formulate an overall concept—containment—to guide American policy toward the Soviet Union.[2] Containment was general in nature. Kennan did not attempt to define precisely how the United States should respond to the "shifts and maneuvers of Soviet policy." He did not stipulate in the 'X' article whether the response should be political-diplomatic or military, implying that it would depend on the circumstances. Through the American policymaking process, the policy of containment would be applied and translated into specific actions.

The extensive literature on the American policymaking process is useful in defining what must be analyzed in order to understand why specific national security policies emerge. Ideas, personalities, and organizations are each important. Achieving a consensus is always difficult, because power is decentralized throughout the US government and many individuals and organizations have a stake in the policy outcomes. Efforts to bring coherence and discipline to the process are often thwarted by the sheer complexity of the issues.[3]

Since 1947, the American policy of containment has been defined through two different policymaking processes: one involving strategic planning, the other focusing on responses to specific events and crises. The Truman administration, in its NSC–68 study in 1950, used the strategic planning process, as did the Nixon administration in 1969, the Ford administration in 1976, the Carter administration in 1977, and the Reagan administration in 1982. Each of these administrations undertook, through an interagency study, to define an overall policy toward the Soviet Union. The studies were intended to re-examine American policies for peace and war and to address future requirements for both nuclear and conventional military forces.

Each of these interagency groups began by re-affirming the policy of containing Soviet expansion. But they had difficulty moving from agreement on this overall strategic objective to specific policy recommendations. As a result, they produced only very general guidelines, similar to those put forth by Kennan. Few specific actions followed. President Truman and the Defense Department were reluctant to fund the substantial increases in defense expenditures called for in NSC–68. The Nixon administration, in NSSM–3, went no further than to outline criteria for its doctrine of sufficiency with regard to strategic nuclear forces. President Ford undertook his study in the last months of his administration, presumably to give guidance to his successor, but President Carter rescinded Ford's decision document, calling for his own comprehensive review of US military strategy. After a number of damaging leaks and considerable controversy within the Department of Defense, the Carter study (PRM–10) produced only a set of very general objectives. President Reagan's study was primarily a response to congressional criticism that his administration's proposals for an increase in defense expenditures were not based on an overall strategy.

Participants in these studies found them useful in focusing attention on the most critical issues and in illuminating differences of views within the bureaucracy. In each case, the president was involved and reviewed the results. But each of these administrations ultimately defined its containment policy in response to specific events and crises.

This paper describes how the policy of containment was applied and refined in the following five cases: South Korea in 1950, Vietnam in 1964–65, Angola in 1974–75, the Horn of Africa in 1978–79, and Afghanistan in the 1980s.[4] What ideas did American policymakers have in each case about how to contain Soviet expansion? Which issues were in dispute, and how were they resolved? Were the policies that emerged affected by the characteristics of the policymaking process? Finally, what aspects of the process should be taken into account in refining American containment policy for the future?

Ideas and Issues: The Consensus On Objectives

The objective of containing Soviet expansion achieved a remarkable consensus among Americans. As a concept—to apply counterforce at signs of Soviet encroachment—it was simple and compelling. Kennan believed that containment should focus on the Soviet Union, but following Mao's victory in 1949, President Truman extended its coverage to the People's Republic of China. Gradually, the policy of containment expanded to encompass any communist expansion around the world.

Following the North Korean invasion of South Korea in June 1950, American policymakers agreed unanimously that the United States should respond. They assumed that the North Koreans would not have acted without instruction from the Soviet Union. According to the American Embassy in Moscow, the North Korean action represented "a clear-cut Soviet challenge" which the United States needed to answer firmly and swiftly because it constituted a direct threat to American leadership of the free world against Soviet communist imperialism. Any delay could suggest to the Soviets the possibility that they could precipitate further actions (for example, against Indochina) with impunity. Truman's advisers viewed the North Korean attack as a "valuable opportunity to act" and believed that the United States "needed to draw the line somewhere."[5]

Similarly, policymakers agreed in the 1960s that the policy of containment should be applied in South Vietnam, for the United States faced an "externally directed and supported communist insurgency." Preventing a communist South Vietnam was necessary, according to an interagency memo in November 1964, to "protect [the] U.S. reputation as a counter-subversion guarantor, to avoid [the] domino effect especially in Southeast Asia, [and] to keep South Vietnamese territory from Red hands."[6]

Following the Vietnam War, a debate arose in the United States over whether or not to apply the policy of containment to the expansion of communist influence in the Third World via either the Soviet Union or surrogates like Cuba. In the cases of Angola in 1975 and the Horn of Africa in 1978, differences existed as to whether the events in question affected American strategic interests or were of only regional importance. Responding to Soviet and Cuban assistance to the MPLA rebels in Angola, Secretary of State Henry A. Kissinger said that the United States would not remain "indifferent while an outside power embarks upon an interventionist policy—so distant from its homeland and so removed from traditional Russian interests." [7] Later, following substantial Soviet aid to the Somali government and the deployment of over 12,000 Cubans in Ethiopia, the Assistant for National Security to President Carter, Zbigniew Brzezinski, argued that "if Soviet-sponsored Cubans determined the outcome of an Ethiopian-Somali conflict, there could be wider regional and international consequences . . . greater regional uncertainty and less confidence in the United States." [8]

Although these arguments for expanding the policy of containment to cover indirect Soviet threats were rejected, Americans in 1979–80 agreed that the policy should be applied when the Soviet Union itself intervened militarily in Afghanistan to restore a pro-Soviet regime. President Carter stated, "The Soviet invasion is the greatest threat to peace since the Second World War. . . . There is no doubt that the Soviets' move into Afghanistan, if done without adverse consequences, would have resulted in the temptation to move again and again until they reached warm water ports or until they acquired control over a major portion of the world's oil supplies." [9] Concerned that the use of military force in Afghanistan foreshadowed Soviet expansion into Southwest Asia, the Carter administration responded with punitive sanctions (the grain embargo and the boycott of the Olympics), military aid to Pakistan, hints of defensive arms sales to China, and military steps to deter future Soviet aggression beyond Afghanistan.

In each of these cases, the arguments and rationale for the objectives of containment were similar to those of George Kennan in 1947. Almost unanimous support existed for the application of the policy to overt political and military expansion by the Soviet Union through the mid-1960s. After the Vietnam War, Americans were divided over whether, and if so how, to respond to Soviet and Cuban activities in the Third World. But as an overall set of objectives to guide US policy toward the Soviet Union, containment remained attractive.

Ideas and Issues: The Differences Over Means

Problems nevertheless arose in translating the general policy into specific actions. In our five cases, policymakers were not necessarily directly concerned with the part of the world where the Soviet Union showed signs of encroaching. Recall the famous speech by Secretary of State Acheson in 1950 in which he defined the defense perimeter of the United States to exclude Taiwan and Korea. Again, in 1954 the United States decided not to intervene in South Vietnam following the French defeat, the Joint Chiefs of Staff arguing that Indochina was devoid of decisive military objectives. Similarly, the Nixon administration had given very little attention or priority to events in Southern Africa, and the Carter administration had not reacted to the installation of pro-Soviet Marxist regimes in Ethiopia in 1977 or Afghanistan in 1978.

The events in these parts of the world became important because of what they seemed to mean for future Soviet actions, and in particular for Soviet plans for expansion. Washington's problem was to define a policy for Korea, Vietnam, Angola, the Horn of Africa, and Afghanistan which would influence Soviet behavior elsewhere and in the future. The policies also had to demonstrate both strength (to deter future Soviet expansion) and restraint (to avoid provoking a superpower confrontation). As a result, disputes arose over how containment should be applied in the specific circumstances—over the *means* to implement containment—which were resolved through the policymaking process.

In the case of the Korean War, policymakers in Washington differed with General Douglas MacArthur over whether the United States was becoming too involved politically and militarily in Korea, given other more vital US interests in Europe. How far should the United States apply its power in Korea? Should the United States simply "contain" the North Korean attack, or should it take the opportunity to regain territory from communist control and "reunify the country"? Following General MacArthur's military successes, and on the basis of the widespread assumption that the Chinese would not intervene, a consensus developed on the latter "reunification" approach—but once the Chinese intervened, the United States returned to the former "containment" policy.

In Vietnam, everyone supported the overall goal of an independent, noncommunist government in South Vietnam. Learning lessons from Korea, policymakers agreed that the means applied should neither threaten the existence of North Vietnam nor provoke Chinese intervention. In 1964–65, the principal issue was whether to bomb North Vietnam and, if so, with what specific military objectives. Most participants in the debate favored limited reprisal raids against Vietcong infiltration targets, although the Joint Chiefs of Staff recommended a "hard-fast bombing campaign" against an extensive list of military facilities, including airfields and bridges near the Chinese border. President Johnson decided in 1965 to begin a restrained bombing campaign against the North to stave off the collapse of the South Vietnamese government. (Bombing also seemed to offer the possibility of sapping the will of Hanoi, gaining some leverage to push reforms in the South Vietnamese government, countering potential Chinese expansion, improving the prospects of the pacification program, and demonstrating American political resolve.) Once it became clear that the bombing campaign would not succeed in any of these objectives quickly, if at all, American combat forces were introduced with little further debate. By changing the means used, the United States thus implicitly changed its objective in South Vietnam from denying the enemy victory to inflicting defeat on the enemy. But there was some dissent. Director of Central Intelligence John McCone argued that, for the United States to succeed, commitment of American combat troops would have to be accompanied by major air attacks against North Vietnam. George Ball argued that neither bombing the North nor committing American combat forces would ensure a viable noncommunist South Vietnam, adding that a Vietcong victory would not produce falling dominoes in the rest of Asia anyway.

The internal US debates on Angola, the Horn of Africa, and Afghanistan also focused on the utility of the various means available for responding to Soviet and Cuban actions. Lacking public support for military intervention, the United States had very few options, which offered little prospect for success. Nevertheless, Kissinger recommended giving the rebels in Angola $28 million in covert aid. To deter an Ethiopian invasion of Somalia, Brzezinski favored sending a carrier battle group to the Persian Gulf. In the first case, Congress objected to what appeared to be an open-ended commitment to the rebels with clear parallels to the 1964 Gulf of Tonkin Resolution; in the second case, the Departments of both State and Defense opposed any demonstration of military force, arguing that it would be perceived as a bluff and, if the Ethiopians went ahead and invaded Somalia, as a defeat for the United States.

In defining a response to the Soviet invasion of Afghanistan, most officials agreed that economic sanctions would have little effect on the Soviet economy or on Soviet actions in Afghanistan. The issue was whether the United States and its allies should nevertheless impose a grain embargo so as to make the Soviets pay some price and, thereby, to deter future Soviet expansion. US steps to deter Soviet military actions against Pakistan were also generally agreed upon, but differences arose over the size of the military aid package. Some people argued that a substantial increase in aid would tie the United States too closely to Pakistan, reducing the United States' ability to pressure the government there to forego the development of nuclear weapons. Playing the China card was attractive for many reasons, but some participants objected to moving too quickly because of the potential problems for US relations with Taiwan as well as with other US friends in Asia.

President Carter declared in January 1980 that an attempt by any outside force to gain control of the Persian Gulf would be regarded as an assault on the vital interest of the United States and repelled by any means necessary, including military force. Major differences arose over how to design a credible military strategy using the forces available to the United States. Some policymakers were attracted to strategies of horizontal and vertical escalation, while others argued for the creation of a Rapid Deployment Force and an expansion of US airlift capability. Subsequently, the Reagan administration expanded US conventional military capabilities, established the Central Command, and designed a strategy involving both a defense against Soviet aggression in Southwest Asia and the threat of global escalation.

The Policymaking Process: Executive and Congress

The disputes which arose in these cases over the means of implementing containment were resolved through the policymaking process. The process, because of its characteristics, was far less important to policy outcomes than the ideas policymakers had about whether and how to contain Soviet expansion.

The structure of the policymaking process differed, of course, according to the style of the individual presidents. But in each case, the major actors involved in defining responses to Soviet actions met both formally within the National Security Council structure and informally, their views transmitted to the president through options papers, personal memoranda, and private conversations. In the case of Korea, the departments initially drafted the interagency papers; the NSC staff transmitted these to the president and his decisions back to the departments. During and after the war in Vietnam, the interagency process became more formal and structured, the NSC staff directing and taking responsibility for drafting the decision memoranda.

As a result, each president in our five cases had the views and recommendations of his advisers as he faced critical decisions. In a memorandum transmitted to President Truman in September 1950 on "United States Courses of Action With Respect to Korea," the Departments of State and Defense outlined the considerations involved in deciding what objectives the United States should seek to achieve in Korea and whether to take military action north of the 38th parallel. An interagency group prepared a memorandum in November 1964 outlining the arguments and three possible options for bombing North Vietnam. George Ball separately sent to President Johnson his recommendation for a US disengagement. The 40 Committee reviewed the CIA proposal for covert aid to the rebels in Angola, as well as the recommendation from the Assistant Secretary of State for African Affairs, Ambassador Nathaniel Davis, not to support any group but instead to work with the Organization of African Unity, Portugal, and the Soviet Union in solving the factional dispute, avoiding a superpower confrontation. President Carter heard the arguments of the Departments of State and Defense as well as his Assistant for National Security Affairs before deciding not to intervene in the Horn of Africa; he considered a variety of options as he designed the American response to the Soviet invasion of Afghanistan. Differences of view arose and major debates ensued in all these instances, but decisions were ultimately made through consensus and compromise. Only one official resigned: Ambassador Davis, over the issue of covert aid to the rebels in Angola.

It is also fair to conclude that, in these cases, the policymakers received fairly accurate, insightful, and timely intelligence. Although the intelligence community failed in 1950 to predict the timing of Chinese intervention in the Korean War, it consistently raised the possibility. In the case of Vietnam, the CIA was pessimistic about the prospects of affecting the political and military situation in the South, either by bombing the

North or by committing American combat forces. Soviet activities in Angola, the Horn, and Afghanistan were catalogued in detail. Policy decisions were not constrained in any major way by the lack of critical intelligence.

In these cases, the American policymaking process demonstrated certain recurring tendencies and attributes often described in the scholarly literature. First, in the course of debate, distinctions among the options tended to blur; a consensus often formed on particular recommendations prior to their transmittal to the president, so that in the end all the arguments seemed to favor one course of action. Although a variety of options were analyzed before the US decision to bomb North Vietnam, for example, a consensus formed early in favor of the middle course: taking some action but not the extensive bombing campaign recommended by the Joint Chiefs of Staff. In the end, nearly everyone except George Ball supported this course, even the JCS, who viewed the reprisal attacks as the first step in their effort to increase military pressure on the North.

Second, the policymaking process was also characterized by the tendency to postpone decisions, to take only incremental steps, and to let events compel American action. For instance, the debate over whether to cross the 38th parallel in Korea was finally resolved when General MacArthur pursued the North Korean Army, arguing that it was necessary as a response to hostile fire. Similarly, bombing of North Vietnam came as a response to the Vietcong attack on Pleiku.

Third, even when presidential advisers pressed their views forcefully, the presidents in these instances were able to ensure that decisions reflected their own international and domestic priorities. In the case of Korea, Truman acted decisively to quiet his opposition on the right and to avoid responsibility for "losing another country to communism." Johnson, in seeking to maintain support for his Great Society program, moved slowly to involve the United States in Vietnam and then prosecuted the war without calling up the reserves or mobilizing American public opinion. Ford was anxious to act in Angola, viewing it as an important test case of American will and commitment following the fall of Saigon. Carter was reluctant to oppose communist expansion in the Third World, until the outright Soviet invasion of Afghanistan forced him to reconsider Soviet intentions.

Fourth, personalities played an important role. In each case, a few people tended to dominate: General MacArthur and Dean Acheson in Korea, McGeorge Bundy and General William Westmoreland in Vietnam, Henry Kissinger and Senator Dick Clark in Angola,[10] Zbigniew Brzezinski and Cyrus Vance in Ethiopia and Afghanistan. Their personalities were certainly a factor, though it is difficult to determine exactly what difference they made in the policies which emerged.

Fifth, these cases demonstrate that, since the 1960s, the Assistant to the President for National Security Affairs has become a very powerful figure, not only in coordinating the recommendations of the departments and presenting options to the president, but also in proposing and supporting specific policies. McGeorge Bundy was instrumental in selling Johnson on the bombing campaign in North Vietnam and was responsible for drafting the memoranda leading to the decision to introduce American combat troops. Henry Kissinger, although Secretary of State at the time, acted in his previous role of Assistant to the President in defining the options for US policy toward Angola and in gaining the support of Secretary of Defense James Schlesinger and President Ford in favor of covert aid to the rebels. Brzezinski failed to achieve a consensus in favor of an American military intervention in the Horn of Africa in 1978, but only after the Secretaries of State and Defense and the Chairman of the Joint Chiefs of Staff objected. He was more effective in orchestrating the various political and military responses to the Soviet invasion of Afghanistan.

Sixth and finally, organizational pressures and perspectives operated in each case. The military commander in the field played a critical role in the decisions to commit American forces in both Korea in 1950 and Vietnam in 1965. Ambassador Maxwell Taylor was instrumental in the decisions to expand the American role in South Vietnam. The State Department, particularly its regional bureaus, was very influential in the early stages of these crises, being responsible for defining the immediate American response. But over time, influence in each case tended to move away from those in the State Department and even those in the field, moving to those with responsibility for overall Soviet-American relations, particularly to the NSC staff. This shift is not particularly surprising, given the importance of the crises internationally and domestically to each president.

At the same time, the organizational interests were not pursued with the simplicity that writers on bureaucratic politics sometimes suggest. The Joint Chiefs, for example, consistently called upon the president to put aside his "self-imposed" restrictions in Korea and Vietnam and undertake bolder policies. But they were sensitive to the implications of becoming overly committed, given American vital interests in other parts of the world. And in Angola, the Horn of Africa, and Afghanistan, the military advised caution and restraint.

But if the policymaking process was not especially critical to the containment policies that emerged in these cases, the crises and American responses to them have had major effects on the process. Events in Korea in 1950 demonstrated that the president needed to be able to act quickly and decisively; therefore, war had the effect of giving presidents more authority in national security affairs. Truman decided to commit US airpower and to resupply South Korea, informing the Congress two days later. He deployed American troops and conducted the war without any formal congressional authorization. Similarly, on the basis of the Tonkin Gulf Resolution, Johnson proceeded to expand the Vietnam War by bombing the North and committing over 500,000 American soldiers. But Vietnam ultimately had the effect of reducing the authority and prerogatives of the president. In 1973, Congress passed the War Powers Resolution "to ensure that the collective judgment of both the Congress and the President will apply to the introduction of the United States Armed Forces into hostilities, or into situations where imminent involvement in hostilities is clearly indicated by the circumstances, and to the continued use of such forces in hostilities or in such situations." In 1975, Senator Clark, by amendment to the International Security Assistance and Arms Export Act, banned covert assistance to anti-Marxist guerrillas in Angola. Subsequently, the Congress has used its authorizing power to exercise influence over the formulation and execution of US national security policy and has sought to retain for itself the power to block or veto Executive branch action.[11]

The Policymaking Process in the Future

Americans have made the goal of containing Soviet expansion the cornerstone of postwar US security policy. It is difficult to see this changing. As the "political personality" of Soviet power has not changed significantly since Kennan defined the containment policy in 1947, no alternative exists by which the United States can protect its interests and democratic values. The debate can, however, be expected to continue over whether the policy should apply to Soviet Third World expansion through either military aid or surrogates. Such a debate is currently underway to determine US policy toward Central America. Americans can also be expected to disagree, as they have in the past, over the appropriate means of implementing containment. The ideas that policymakers hold about whether and how to implement the containment policy can also be expected to continue to be more important than the characteristics of the process by which the policies are made. The process will, however, be critical in resolving the differences in views and in building consensus for specific decisions.

Although presidents will continue to organize their NSC structures according to their own styles, the policymaking processes of past administrations have exhibited more similarities than differences. The particular characteristics of the policymaking process will not be very influential as long as the NSC structure ensures that the president receives the advice of all his principal advisers, that his international and domestic priorities are served, that a range of options are defined with none arbitrarily eliminated, that agency views are effectively coordinated, and that decisions are taken and implemented. The role of the Assistant to the President will be crucial in making the NSC structure function effectively, and his own policy preferences can also be expected to be very influential.

The future role of the Congress in defining US containment policy is more difficult to predict. The Executive branch has had responsibility for making and implementing decisions, but the Congress has tended to play an important role when the consensus on these decisions has broken down, as it did concerning Vietnam in 1968 and Angola in 1975. The Congress will certainly play a more important role than it did in Korea or in the initial decisions on Vietnam. Its role will ultimately depend upon the degree of consensus which exists among the American public on the policies and objectives of the administration. In the case of Afghanistan, for example, Americans favored a strong US response, but also appreciated the limits on what the United States would be able to do: the Soviet Union was not likely to withdraw in the face of American pressures. Given this consensus, Congress played a fairly small but quite supportive role in the actual definition of the American response. In contrast, a consensus does not exist today as to whether the United States should apply containment to Central America or what methods it should use if it does so. In this case, the Congress is playing a very important role—primarily by restraining the various initiatives of the Reagan administration to involve the United States militarily and to apply pressure on the Nicaraguan government.

What aspects of the policymaking process need to be taken into account in fashioning an effective strategy of containment in the future? Most important will be the ideas the policymakers hold about whether to apply the policy of containment to individual Soviet actions and about the appropriate means to implement that policy. The role of the policymaking process will be to ensure that the president hears the views of his advisers and that decisions are taken and implemented. Whether decisions will be successful will depend importantly on the support of the American people and their representatives in Congress. Only in small part will the process affect the outcome.

Notes

1. George F. Kennan (writing as 'X'), "The Sources of Soviet Conduct," reprinted in *American Diplomacy 1900–1950* (Chicago: University of Chicago Press, 1951), pp. 113, 114, 119.

2. The policy of containment called for American "counterforce" when the Soviet Union showed "signs of encroaching." A different set of problems and issues have arisen for the United States when the Soviet Union has taken steps to re-assert its control in Eastern Europe: in 1956 in Hungary, in 1968 in Czechoslovakia, and in 1980 in Poland. In these cases, the United States confronted Soviet violations of human rights and opposition to democratic values and institutions, not Soviet efforts to expand the USSR's sphere of influence.

3. The discussion which follows draws on the analysis of the American policymaking process by Warner Schilling in his introduction to *Strategy, Politics, and Defense Budgets* (New York: Columbia University Press, 1962), pp. 5–27. See also, Morton Halperin and Arnold Kanter, "Introduction," in *Readings in American Foreign*

Policy: A Bureaucratic Perspective (Boston: Little Brown and Co., 1973), pp. 1–42; Graham Allison, "Conceptual Models and the Cuban Missile Crisis," *American Political Science Review* 63 (September 1969), pp. 689–718.

4. The analysis of the individual cases is drawn from the following: *Foreign Relations of the United States, Korea, Vol. VII, 1950; The Pentagon Papers, The New York Times,* 1971, pp. 315–458; Robert Litwak, *Detente and the Nixon Doctrine: American Foreign Policy and the Pursuit of Stability, 1969–1975* (Cambridge University Press, 1984), pp. 175–190; Raymond Garthoff, *Detente and Confrontation* (Washington: The Brookings Institution, 1985), pp. 630–653, 887–965.

5. See *Foreign Relations of the United States, Korea, Vol. VII, 1950,* pp. 139–149, 157–161.

6. *The Pentagon Papers,* p. 374.

7. Quoted in Litwak, *Detente and the Nixon Doctrine,* p. 185.

8. Quoted in Garthoff, *Detente and Confrontation,* p. 649.

9. Quoted in ibid., p. 972.

10. Clark, Chairman of the Senate Subcommittee on Africa, authored the amendment which ended covert US aid to Jonas Savimbi of UNITA in his fight against the soon-victorious MPLA.

11. For a discussion of the changing role of Congress, see William Bader, "Congress and the Making of US Security Policies," *Adelphi Papers,* Number 173, Spring 1982 (International Institute for Strategic Studies), pp. 14–21.

6

Containment and the National Economy

William H. Becker

W E CANNOT THINK ABOUT past or future implications of containment without also considering the national economy. George Kennan saw the relationship between the economy and containment in terms of the perennial strategic issue of matching ends with means. He believed that the United States' great economic strength could be used to help achieve national security and a postwar world suitable to protecting American interests. Intuitively, many of the policymakers who followed Kennan recognized the essential relationship between economic capabilities and strategy.

In the last forty years, however, American strategists' interpretations of these capabilities and of containment have varied. John Lewis Gaddis sees an administration's definition of economic capabilities as determining the way in which it

William H. Becker is Professor of History at George Washington University and also holds an appointment in the School of Government and Business Administration.

perceives the country's interests and the threats to those interests. Strategists with expansive views of the economy have tended to adopt what Gaddis calls "symmetrical" approaches to containment, that is, policies that define interests and threats broadly and adopt a variety of military and diplomatic responses. Those with more limited views of the country's economic capabilities have, in Gaddis' interpretation, adopted "asymmetrical" approaches to containment, relying on a few selected means of responding to more narrowly defined foreign threats.[1]

Perceptions of economic capabilities, however, have not been the only determinants of differing American approaches to containment since the 1940s. Equally important was how well postwar administrations managed the domestic economy, that is, how their perceptions of economic capabilities (and needs) translated into fiscal and monetary policy. Also important were responsibilities for the international economy, willingly taken on with the United States' leadership of the International Monetary Fund and World Bank, and in its successful efforts to liberalize trade. These responsibilities required the government to develop an explicit international economic policy, so one of the great tasks of postwar administrations became the need to balance domestic and international aspects of economic policy.

Balancing the needs of various economic constituencies had a profound, though hardly obvious, impact on foreign policy. It was not an easy task in a political system open to pressure from well-organized economic interest groups quick to react to policies detrimental to their interests. Yet in an increasingly interdependent world economy, domestic policy affected international conditions, and the economic policies of one administration inevitably altered, for better or worse, the economic context inherited by those that followed. In short, the perceptions of economic capabilities so essential to fashioning an administration's strategy of containment were largely determined by the economic achievements or failures of its predecessor.

The growing interdependence of the world economy since 1945 is in large part a result of the multilateral exchange, capital, and trade policies promoted by the United States since the end of World War II. Containment played its part by justifying the need to rebuild potential economic competitors on grounds of national security. Kennan viewed the United States' unprecedented economic power in 1945 as unusual and unsustainable. The Marshall Plan made it US policy to revitalize Western Europe, as was later done with Japan, and American leverage in the world economy was reduced as these major industrial areas recovered. There is nothing to lament here, for it was in America's strategic and economic interest to have prosperous and stable allies;[2] but the conduct of American foreign policy became more complex, as did the management of domestic and economic policy. Our allies' economies were closely tied to our own, so managing the domestic economy required attention to the impact of our policies on them. Further complicating the situation was the United States' commitment to promoting economic development in less-developed countries, which required consideration for yet another set of variables.

Since 1945, the United States has helped achieve unprecedented growth and prosperity in the industrialized world and some progress in at least a few developing countries. Yet containment, and the sustained commitments to international leadership it required of the United States, has created monumental and growing problems for domestic and international economic policy. Despite the obvious successes of containment, this paper argues that the United States has not fully adapted to the new economic environment it was most responsible for creating. The United States has not been successful in balancing domestic economic policy with foreign economic policy, and failures which became apparent in the 1960s led to a debilitating inflation in the 1970s. More profoundly, it may well be that the way in which the Reagan administration has reduced inflation in the 1980s will lead to a lessening of American economic capabilities in the 1990s, thereby limiting the options for containment in the future.

Truman, Eisenhower, and Postwar Conservatism

In retrospect, the Truman and Eisenhower years seem halcyon compared to the troubled twenty-five years since 1960. Truman and Eisenhower had conventional views of domestic economic policy. Neither was caught up in the excitement Keynesianism created among economists, and both adhered to what would become the postwar conventional wisdom of fiscal policy. As a matter of course, they attempted to balance the budget in "normal" times. Only in extreme circumstances would the government alter spending or taxes to cope with recession or boom, and there was great reluctance to change fiscal policy in anticipation of a recession. To be sure, as Gaddis shows, NSC–68 included a sophisticated rationale for increased defense spending based on Keynesian notions of an expanding economy. But when the war in Korea intervened, Truman responded rather conventionally in financing that war through increased taxes.

Truman and Eisenhower nevertheless did reflect a new consensus that went beyond the traditional conservative view of economic policy. They understood that, left alone, the economy would not necessarily stabilize itself near full employment. This was one of the great lessons of the 1930s. Managing the growth of aggregate demand became an accepted responsibility of the government's budget making. But Keynes' ideas were modified to fit the conservative economic views of the Truman and Eisenhower administrations. Both aimed for growth and stability, but without dramatic changes in policy that might alter the private economy's structure or the role of government. Fear that government spending might get out of hand and lead to inflation was strong in both political parties in the 1950s, and Eisenhower adjusted spending accordingly. For its part, monetary policy was very much in step with fiscal policy. The Federal Reserve had only gained independence from the administration after a bruising battle with President Truman. By the end of the 1950s, however, the Fed had enough independence to make monetary policy an important independent component of any effort to achieve economic stability.[3]

The economy performed well in the first fifteen years after 1945. There was no slide back into the depression of the 1930s, and the recessions of 1949, 1954, 1958, and 1960 were fairly mild. With the exception of the Korean War years, inflation remained low compared to rates in the 1970s. Output in 1960 was 134 percent higher than before the Great Depression, and real disposable income was up 44 percent. Defense spending had increased the ratio of federal expenditures to GNP above pre–World War II levels, but not by much (9.6 percent in 1960 versus 8.4 percent in 1939).[4]

Economists disagree about the reasons for the steady performance of the economy in the 1950s. Some attribute the relative success to "conservative" or "business" Keynesianism on the part of government. Others, such as Herbert Stein, Chairman of the Council of Economic Advisers in the Nixon years, see a vigorous private economy as the major reason, with government policy at least not hindering an economy which was mainly driven by pent up demand from the war and public and private needs still unmet from the 1930s.[5]

But there was another reason for the success of the 1950s. The full economic implications of America's commanding new role in the world had not yet been felt. The Truman and Eisenhower administrations, for one thing, were unable to live up to their own rhetoric about freer trade. Congress modified the liberalizing effects of the 1947 General Agreements on Tariffs and Trade by adding "escape clauses" and "buy American" provisions to later trade legislation. The system of fixed rates and free convertibility of currencies established at Bretton Woods in 1944 did not fully take effect until 1958, after Europe had substantially recovered from the war. Until that time, the British and Europeans maintained a system of exchange controls that sharply restricted investments and purchases in dollars.[6]

Yet the costs of containment were beginning to appear in the 1950s in the form of large balance-of-payments deficits. These resulted from the expenses of carrying out the Marshall

Plan, rearming NATO, keeping occupation troops abroad, and aiding underdeveloped countries, as well as from foreign direct investments of US corporations. Although the deficits grew worse after exchange restrictions were ended in 1958, they were in one sense a positive sign. They suggested the return of European economic strength and a normalization of world trade, and they increased international liquidity. But the Eisenhower administration was concerned. Unchecked, such payments deficits would erode the United States' ability to provide economic and military aid. The administration sought to make the Europeans pay more for their own defense and cooperate with the United States in providing multilateral aid to less developed countries through the Organization for Economic Cooperation and Development (OECD), formed in October 1960.[7]

The Fall of 1960 saw perhaps the most disturbing sign of problems to come, a bidding up of the price of gold on the private market. This reflected concern over the dollar, the principal reserve currency of the Bretton Woods system, which was a result of the large US balance-of-payments deficits. Many of the dollars that went abroad did not end up in central banks as reserves, but in the hands of foreign investors and multinational corporations. These increasing pools of dollars became a threat to the exchange system based on a fixed ratio between the dollar and gold.[8]

Expansive Containment in the 1960s

President Kennedy took office facing a crisis over the dollar. His administration developed a series of temporary responses to the problem and plunged ahead with ambitious programs for both the domestic economy and American foreign policy, adopting what Gaddis would have called a symmetrical approach to geopolitical strategy. At home and overseas, Kennedy wanted to regain momentum after what he considered the sluggishness of the Eisenhower years. In trying to do so, the administration confronted the profound difficulty of expanding beyond the economy's resources. It paid little systematic attention to the need to integrate domestic and international economic policies, a failing which became more flagrant in the Johnson administration.

Kennedy's ambitious plans for containment included building a strategic missile system, increasing the number of troops in Europe, and developing "special forces" to allow the United States greater flexibility in meeting foreign threats. The president also began spending to put a man on the moon, while at the same time increasing foreign aid 50 percent above its 1950 levels. At home, Kennedy immediately turned to economic problems. Unemployment was high (6.7 percent) and the growth of GNP relatively slow (2.2 percent) when he entered office. The new president promised more jobs and important social programs to help the poor, who had been ignored during the Eisenhower years.

These new domestic and foreign policies required increases in spending. An expansive fiscal policy was put in place to support growing defense and domestic programs, the latter growing even more rapidly when Lyndon Johnson launched the Great Society. The Kennedy people were not economically naive. The president's economists realized that they had to stimulate supply as well as demand, so they also pushed through an investment tax credit that would help stimulate growth.[9]

Eisenhower's 1960 budget was balanced, generating a small surplus for the year. Two years into the Kennedy presidency, the budget was in deficit: $7.1 billion for 1962. Kennedy wanted to raise taxes, but was dissuaded by economic advisers who worried about precipitating a recession while unemployment continued at high levels. In fact, the president's economists convinced him of the need for a tax *cut,* converting him to the neo-Keynesian idea of a "full-employment budget," that deficits were necessary to sustain employment even when the economy was not in a recession. This philosophy represented a significant departure from the Truman and Eisenhower approach; in effect, it provided a justification for deficits under almost any circumstance. The Congress was not so quickly converted to the new interpretation of Keynes, but the tax bill did pass in January 1964 as part of the emotional tribute paid to the assassinated president.[10]

Commitment to full employment and to something of a perpetual boom had an impact on monetary policy, too. Kennedy and his advisers advocated an easy money policy in order to make capital available for investment. Although there were skeptics in Congress, constant pressure arose from agriculture and the construction industry to keep interest rates down, giving the Federal Reserve the difficult task of trying to balance an expansive fiscal policy with a restrictive monetary policy.[11]

Kennedy's economic advisers had convinced him of their ability to "fine tune" the expansion underway in 1963, that they could calibrate the expansion to reduce unemployment while keeping deficits in hand. But Lyndon Johnson, for political reasons, ignored the counsel of the economic advisers he inherited from his predecessor. A year after Kennedy's death, inflation was beginning to become an obvious problem. And by the end of 1965, the Vietnam War had begun to increase government spending significantly. In the next year, Johnson's Great Society programs also began to add to the totals. Johnson refused to increase taxes to help pay for the war, for fear that the Congress would demand an accompanying cut in his cherished social program. The Federal Reserve tightened monetary policy in 1966, but relented under pressure from both the Congress and the White House. Inflation rose to almost 5 percent in 1968, forcing Johnson to support a tax cut, while the Federal Reserve again tightened monetary policy.[12]

Inflation now began to have damaging effects both at home and abroad. It had a major impact on America's foreign economic policies, on its role as the leader of the postwar multilateral world order, and ultimately on its place in the international economy. Inflation was a clear manifestation of an inability to manage the relationship between economic policy and the demands of containment. The inflation that began under Johnson continued under Nixon, even though he entered office with Johnson's restrictive policies already in place, and became a critical national issue in the Ford and Carter years.

At home, American exporters were among the first to suffer from the effects of inflation. But trade relations had been a problem since the early 1960s. The Kennedy administration had gone forward with a liberalization of trade in the Trade Adjustment Act of 1962, which gave the president broad powers to negotiate reciprocal tariff reductions in what became the "Kennedy Round" of GATT (General Agreement on Tariffs and Trade) discussions. Kennedy's policy was to integrate the US economy with the recovered economies in Japan and Western Europe, but the negotiations took longer than expected. The primary difficulty was over agricultural exports, with the French in particular concerned about protecting their own farmers. Negotiations on industrial tariffs went more smoothly but had unforeseen consequences for the United States. By the time lower rates went into effect in the late 1960s, US rates of inflation had undermined America's competitive trade position. Furthermore, the inflow of foreign goods, without the offsetting benefits of increased exports, led to stronger calls for protection.[13]

The Kennedy and Johnson administrations also supported an increase in aid to Third World countries as part of a more activist policy of encouraging growth and modernization. According to the theory fashionable in the early 1960s, such changes would lead ultimately to more stable societies. An enhanced US government role aiding Third World countries, especially in Latin America, induced American-based multinational corporations to increase their direct investments there, but these new investments focused on industrial plant rather than raw materials. Kennedy and Johnson considered this change a mixed blessing, since it worsened the American balance-of-payments problem and drew investment away from the domestic economy. The corporations were attracted to lower foreign wage rates, an inducement to go abroad that grew as inflation intensified in the

United States. International capital markets expanded in these years, too, partly in response to the needs of the multinationals. As a result, the 1960s were also a period of great growth abroad for major American banks.[14]

However, international concern over the dollar was the most serious sign that domestic and foreign economic policies were not effectively synchronized. Since the Bretton Woods agreements of 1944, the American dollar had been both the "key" currency against which other currencies were valued and the major reserve currency. In theory, foreign central banks preferred to keep dollars instead of gold because dollars could be held in the form of interest-earning government securities. The dollar had also been the major "vehicle" currency, used as the pound had been in the nineteenth century for international transactions. The total number of dollars in circulation increased dramatically alongside the growth of international trade, and a large dollar market developed in Europe, where no US government controls restricted foreign borrowers. This Euro-dollar market was significantly larger than the monetary reserves of the United States and the major foreign central banks.

Free from state control, either European or American, this mass of circulating dollars put great pressure on the Bretton Woods exchange system. The French were the most critical of this state of affairs because, they charged, it allowed the United States to "export" its inflation; and it was true that expansive US domestic and foreign policies had pumped more dollars into the international monetary system than was necessary even to service increased international trade. President Johnson pressured central banks, nevertheless, to continue accumulating dollars so as to preserve the system of fixed-rate convertibility. But Nixon, unable to resist the pressure against the dollar, in 1971 suspended convertibility, a development one observer called "America's monetary Vietnam."[15]

By the end of the 1960s, therefore, the heavy deficits the United States incurred to finance its expansive economic and containment policies had inexorably weakened the domestic economy and reduced its position in the international economy. Some erosion was inevitable because of the unusual position the United States enjoyed at the end of World War II. But domestic inflation weakened the US trade position and undermined the country's leadership of the international exchange system. Richard Nixon thus inherited both serious problems and reduced economic capacity to deal with them. While he and Kissinger had a better sense of economic limits and saw the need to come up with a less expansive strategy of containment than Johnson's, Nixon was unable in practice to exercise the necessary discipline. His political victory in the presidential election of 1972 required an expanding economy, but the long-run costs were heavy at home and abroad. As a result, he left his successors an economy even more troubled than the one he inherited from Johnson.

Misaligned Policies in the 1970s

President Nixon and Henry Kissinger reoriented American foreign policy. Much has been made of their realism and commitment to a sophisticated balance of power as the expression of US containment. But the economic side of the Nixon foreign policy was no less important than the strategic. Nixon endorsed a more nationalistic role for the United States in the international economy. His administration recognized the great costs to domestic prosperity of the United States' preeminence in the international economy and made adjustments to reduce them. That changes appeared necessary was in large part the result of the success of containment and of the United States' achievements rebuilding Europe and Japan. Unhappily, while Nixon's perceptions of the need for change were accurate, the policies he adopted only worsened domestic economic problems, especially inflation.

Lyndon Johnson had left office with a stringent monetary policy and a belated commitment to fiscal restraint, both of which slowed inflation a little. The budget actually showed a surplus in 1969, and there was also a small surplus in the basic balance-of-payments account, the first since World War II. These achievements, however, came at a high cost. Over-extended debtors, especially farmers and small businessmen, were strained by the tight money policy of the Federal Reserve, and unemployment increased. When Republicans did not do well in the congressional elections of 1970, Nixon advocated an expansion of the economy and a less restrictive monetary policy. What followed was an overt manipulation of the business cycle for political benefit.[16]

The results of Nixon's economic expansion were predictable. Inflationary pressures increased at home, and abroad there was a flight from the dollar which challenged the maintenance of the fixed exchange system. Nixon responded with the announcement of a "New Economic Policy" in August 1971. The president presented his program as a means of correcting the failings of the international monetary system, which he portrayed as having victimized the United States. Dollar convertibility was suspended, supposedly temporarily, but in effect for good. The dollar was allowed to float downward in international exchange; Nixon argued that an overvalued dollar had been detrimental to domestic industry, making American goods expensive abroad, limiting exports, and inducing American corporations to invest abroad. To help arrest the deteriorating balance of trade, the president imposed a 15 percent surcharge on imports.[17]

These new policies marked an important change in the United States' conception of its role in the international economy. An overvalued dollar had aided European and Japanese recovery, as had openly discriminatory trade policies directed toward the United States. At the same time, America had absorbed the bulk of the military costs of defending Europe and Japan. Unless the United States devalued the dollar, it would be condemned to serious national and international economic maladjustments, particularly if countries with a surplus in trade continued to refuse to revalue *their* currencies.[18]

The Nixon policy found wide acceptance in the United States, even though there was skepticism about the temporary wage and price controls imposed as part of the new program. American trade did improve, helping industry and its workers. Moreover, many of the larger corporations that had increased their direct investment in foreign manufacturing facilities preferred the new policy to restrictions on the export of capital.

America's European and Japanese allies were not so pleased with the new US posture, especially since exports were more significant to their economies than they were to the US economy. Nixon's new policy presented them with unhappy choices. One response might have been to form an independent monetary and trading bloc, but that was impractical in view of their dependence on the United States for defense. In any case, Washington would probably not have accepted such an openly hostile response. Another option was to revalue their currencies upward against the dollar, but to do so would have reduced their export capabilities, increasing unemployment at home. Ultimately, the Europeans and Japanese were forced to revalue their currencies, and the revaluation did lead to unemployment. Some of the Europeans, especially the Germans, were able to handle the situation fairly well because they had a large number of foreign workers who could be sent home. For others, the British in particular, American devaluation only exacerbated domestic economic problems.[19]

Nixon's new policy turned out to be a domestic political success but an economic disaster. To be sure, wage and price controls temporarily held in check the inflationary effects of an expansive fiscal and monetary policy, and an openly mercantilist approach to trade, exchange, and foreign investment did increase agricultural, manufacturing, and capital exports. But once the 1972 election was over, the president relaxed wage and price controls, and the oil price shocks of 1973–74 intensified the upward pressure. Prices took off, doubling in 1973 and then doubling again in 1974. As inflation mounted, the Federal

Reserve raised interest rates. In 1974, investment slowed, real GNP declined two percentage points, and unemployment reached 7.2 percent. Abroad, inflation increased in the other major industrial countries, spurred by rising oil prices and Nixon's relaxation of controls on the export of capital. American banks became major actors in the Euro-dollar market, which tripled in size between 1971 and 1975.[20]

Devaluation clearly appeared to help trade in manufacturing and agricultural goods. So, too, did a 1970 trade bill that equipped the president with a new arsenal of retaliatory measures. Acrimonious trade discussions followed, éspecially with the Japanese, who nevertheless made concessions in the "Tokyo Round" of GATT negotiations completed in 1977. US exports increased in the 1970s, helped by the devaluations and the aggressive trade stance.[21]

But the inflation of the 1970s had a negative overall impact on American industry. For one thing, high interest rates kept investment down, which meant that American factories operated with older equipment and were slow to adopt state-of-the-art technology. US spending for industrial-related research and development was lower than that in the other major industrial countries. To be sure, research and development rates were part of a larger problem of military research and the numbers of engineers syphoned off from private industry for military and space projects, but an inflationary atmosphere was not conducive to changes in that unfortunate pattern.[22]

In effect, Nixon and Kissinger had retreated from the leadership position the United States had created for itself after World War II. No longer was the United States to accept the costs of its economic preeminence by maintaining the fixed exchange system and tolerating barriers to American trade. Europe and Japan had recovered, and the United States was going to follow a more nationalistic international economic policy. The problem with the new Nixon approach, however, was its failure to balance international with domestic economic policy. The floating dollar, which in effect allowed for a long-term devaluation, adversely affected the trade posture of America's European and Japanese allies, leading to increases in unemployment abroad. In addition, Nixon's domestic expansion led to inflation both at home and abroad. The removal of restrictions on overseas operations of American banks only added to foreign inflation already exacerbated by sharp increases in the price of oil.[23]

Perhaps most surprising, both Gerald Ford and Jimmy Carter adopted the Nixon strategy. Each continued to let the dollar depreciate while following expansionist monetary and fiscal policies at home. Nixon left his unelected successor with more than a political mess. Inflation was high (9.1 percent in 1975), and most indicators pointed toward a serious recession. Unemployment was at 9 percent and real business fixed investment dropped by more than 15 percent in 1975. Ford moved quickly to expand the economy, approving a very large tax reduction and increasing federal spending by 19 percent, leading to a $71.2 billion deficit for fiscal 1975. Monetary policy was also eased. Ford was lucky in that good harvests kept food prices down and oil prices only increased moderately. But despite the improvement, there were still troublesome signs in 1976: high levels of unemployment and a slowing in the growth of GNP. Worried as he was about inflation (which had been brought down to 5.5 percent), Ford resisted pressures for further expansion.

Carter made an issue of Ford's restraint in the 1976 presidential campaign, even though the administration ran a deficit of $66.4 billion in fiscal 1976,[24] and once elected, Carter found it difficult to resist constituencies hostile to restrictions on monetary policy. Carter's economic policies benefited, as had Ford's, from the dollar's devaluation, since exports held up. And both administrations benefited from inflation's erosion of OPEC's oil prices, at least until the second increase in oil prices (of 120 percent) of December 1978 to April 1980.

The new president exhibited a deep ambivalence in domestic economic policy. Carter worried much about the unemployed, yet became increasingly concerned about inflation; his policy cycled rhythmically between phases of expansion and sudden restraint, accumulating deficits that reached $60 billion for fiscal 1980. In August 1979 the president appointed Paul Volcker chairman of the Federal Reserve. Volcker quickly tightened monetary policy, and in March 1980 the administration imposed direct controls on credit to help dampen inflation. Foreign governments had forced the United States temporarily to stop the dollar's slide in value in the fall of 1978, but the joint plan of the Fed and Treasury to stop the dollar's decline did not last. Alarmed at the prospects of a recession in 1980, the Carter administration resumed a looser monetary policy.[25]

Carter's domestic economic policies had a negative impact on America's European and Japanese allies. Prices continued to rise abroad, and foreign critics maintained that the United States exported inflation by its expansive policies at home and the growing involvement of American banks in the Euro-dollar and petro-dollar markets. Continuing devaluation of the dollar through the floating exchange rate system reduced foreign countries' abilities to export, thereby increasing rates of unemployment among the United States' industrial allies.

But there were more serious challenges to Carter's inept handling of the balance between domestic and international economic policies. Crises in the exchange markets were an important measure of discontent. Gold prices exploded in 1979, as foreigners dumped dollars for gold. Fears arose that the dollar's role as a reserve currency would end, leading to a catastrophic liquidation which would shake the foundations of international finance. The German and French governments made their unhappiness obvious by a revival of interest in a continental monetary union, which would have allowed them to avoid the dollar—at least in theory—and they openly discussed the need for a new international reserve currency.[26]

At the same time, the Europeans increased their trade with the Soviet Union and Eastern Europe. The Carter administration was incensed at this turn of events, especially after the Russian invasion of Afghanistan. But increasing trade with the communist bloc, however much it weakened containment, was a sensible response to the more nationalistic economic policies introduced by Nixon and followed by his successors. In an important sense, the Nixon-Ford-Carter approach to international economic policy gave the Soviet Union a wedge to work against the Western Alliance. While a more nationalistic approach to the world economy had theoretically reduced the costs of American international leadership, it thus weakened the economies of our allies and strained the Alliance.[27]

The Nixon-Ford-Carter administrations brought about an important change in the United States' role in the world economy. They asserted the need for the United States to cut its costs as leader of the international economic system—indeed, Nixon explicitly wanted the United States to gain greater benefits from the system—and its allies had no choice but to acquiesce in the new role the United States set for itself. There was some justice in the United States' view that the international economic system was detrimental to America, especially in view of the reluctance of the Europeans and the Japanese to increase their contributions to their own defense. Most troubling, however, was the United States' stimulation of worldwide inflation, a result of the United States' inability to restrain its own expansive domestic economic policy.

Nixon, Ford, and Carter lacked the kind of political self-assurance that would have allowed them to resist the short-term advantages of rapid expansion. All three knew better. Nixon, in particular, was sensitive to the need to balance ends with means; it formed the cornerstone of his and Kissinger's strategy of containment. But he was unable to balance the needs of domestic with foreign economic policy. On the whole, his successors did no better. Ford's policies led to a boom that benefited Carter. Carter ran large deficits to accommodate his own expansive domestic program. As we shall see, Reagan has had similar blind spots, barring a clear view of the interrelationship between domestic and international economic policy. To be sure, he inherited from Carter and his two predecessors a series of domestic and international economic problems that limited his policy options. But his unusual response to this situation may well create even more serious problems for the future.

Reagan: Maximum Containment on Borrowed Resources

Unlike his three immediate predecessors, President Reagan has approached containment symmetrically. He has defined threats and interests broadly. To meet the perceived needs of containment, the current administration has undertaken an unprecedented military buildup: real defense spending has increased 60 percent since 1981.[28] And Reagan has matched his broad definition of containment with an appropriately expansive vision of the economy. Supply-side economics maintains that economic growth will generate sufficient revenues to help pay the huge costs of the military expansion, with the rest of the costs paid for by paring down a bloated government.

The Reagan administration appears more like Kennedy's than any other postwar government. It has the same heightened view of the United States' role in the world and of the need to protect that position. Reagan and his advisers exude the same kind of optimism about the ability of the US economy to provide the resources required to sustain the administration's vision of containment. Kennedy wanted to get the country moving again after a sluggish decade; Reagan wants to unleash the United States from the military and economic restraints of the 1970s.[29]

After five years, Reagan appears to have achieved some success. GNP is growing steadily if modestly, and inflation has slowed significantly: the projected US rate for 1985 is 3.9 percent. US allies have been mollified; they no longer believe that American economic policies are savaging their economies. The projected 1985 inflation rate is also down in the other major industrial countries: to 2.3 percent in West Germany, to 1.9 percent in Japan, to 6 percent in France, and to 5.5 percent in Great Britain. Unemployment, however, remains relatively high in most of these countries, as in the United States. In West Germany, for example, it has been about 9.5 percent.

Yet Reagan's domestic accomplishments have been achieved at a high price. The deficits and the overvalued dollar make the current situation untenable. Moreover, Reagan's policies exhibit the same failure to balance domestic and international economic policy that has marked every administration since Kennedy's. Unlike its three immediate predecessors, however, the Reagan administration also seems to lack the traditional conservative sense of balancing ends with means. And some critics question whether the administration even has a coherent foreign economic policy.[30]

In any case, Reagan clearly has reversed the economic strategy developed by Nixon and followed by Ford and Carter. Under Reagan, the United States has again assumed the heaviest cost for maintaining containment and for the functioning of the international economy. This reversal is paired with a domestic economic policy that departs sharply from that of other postwar administrations, marked by a restrictive monetary policy and an expansive fiscal policy. Reagan's tax cuts and sharply rising military spending have led to unprecedented deficits. But tight money (thanks to Paul Volcker) has kept interest rates relatively high, attracting foreign capital which in turn has helped finance the deficit. As a result, GNP has continued to grow, because capital remains available at "reasonable" rates for productive investment.

Reagan's overvalued dollar is the key factor in the current situation. Comparatively good interest rates and modest economic growth have kept the dollar high in international exchange, allowing imports to rise markedly. European and Japanese export growth has stimulated those economies, lessening some of the unemployment problems Europe and Japan faced in the 1970s. Increasing imports, along with lower oil prices, have reduced inflation in the United States.

On the face of it, Reagan has achieved a better balance between domestic and international economic policy than his immediate predecessors. But the administration's achievements are based on untenable economic circumstances. The unusually large deficits are a matter of growing public and business concern, deepened by a recognition that the overvalued dollar has allowed the United States to run unprecedented peacetime deficits and that decline in the dollar would increase interests rates in the United States, slowing economic activity. There has been a gradual weakening of the dollar during 1985; a precipitous drop might lead rather quickly to a serious recession. A decline in the value of the dollar also might increase inflation, as imports would be reduced. Estimates are that a 30 percent decline in the value of the dollar could push inflation up five percentage points, into the neighborhood of double digits. Moreover, unemployment has remained fairly high in the face of the large deficits, despite the fact that new jobs have been created at about the same rate as during the Carter administration. The result of a decline in the dollar could therefore be a renewal of the "stagflation" that first appeared as a serious problem in the 1970s. Over the longer term, capital formation would be retarded, and though exports would increase, they would have to be higher than imports to help finance the heavy interest burden from the foreign-held debt.[31]

The real problem with the dollar has been its effect on imports. Increased imports do reduce inflation, but the unusually strong dollar has had a very negative impact on American agriculture and industry. Estimates are that the overvalued dollar accounts for a 40 percent price disadvantage for American exporters. Agricultural exports for the first quarter of 1985 were 35 percent below 1981 levels. The family farm is being decimated by the current inability to compete abroad, for many farmers are unable to pay for land and equipment they bought or mortgaged in the inflationary 1970s. Similarly, industrial exports have been curtailed, and the growing competition with foreign goods in the American market is compounding the situation. There are 1.8 million fewer jobs in manufacturing in 1985 than there were in 1979, while industrial production increased only 1.3 percent in the last year.[32]

Fewer family farms might lead to larger and more efficient agricultural production units; but family farming has been relatively efficient, and the United States has been committed to protecting family-based farming as a matter of social policy since the 1930s. Then there was very little else for farmers to do but farm, and the case is not much different in the 1980s. The number of industrial jobs is declining, and although there is growth in the service sector, many new jobs are of lower status and pay considerably less than either farming or traditional industrial jobs.

At the same time, the Reagan administration has contributed to the decline of basic American industries. In the super-competitive atmosphere created by cheap imports, hard-pressed industries are unlikely to invest in new plants and technology, making future competition more difficult and future job growth unlikely. Reaganomics has not contributed to an increase in the historically low rate of savings in the United States; Americans saved about 1.9 percent of income in 1985 while the Japanese saved about 16 percent.

And the accumulating deficits are not likely to be offset by future economic growth. When the dollar falls in value, the United States will have to absorb more of its fiscal deficits itself. Taxes will have to rise and spending (including that for the military) decline, perhaps even in the face of a recession, making an economic downturn potentially serious.

The Reagan policies might very well have other unintended results. They have already stimulated protectionist sentiments in the Congress and hostility toward allies, especially the Japanese. Protectionist measures, depending on their harshness, could be harmful to the United States (by raising inflation) and to our allies (by curtailing their exports). The latter would increasingly turn toward the Soviet Union and the Eastern bloc. Protection would lead to worldwide retaliation. The less-developed countries, dependent on exports, would be hard hit. The sharp recession of 1981–82 created a serious debt crisis in Latin America. Mexico and a few other major debtors were rescued with short-run assistance, and the recovery of 1983–84 improved the situation as exports increased. But a sharp round of protectionism would jeopardize the fragile economies of countries seriously in debt and heavily dependent on exports. A new crisis in the international financial system could emerge, threatening some of the United States' largest banks.[33]

In short, the Reagan policies seem to have achieved some worthy short-term objectives, but at potentially high future costs. And it is these future costs that may very well undermine Reagan's own goals of self-sustaining growth at home and military strength abroad.

The Future Economics of Containment

George Kennan saw containment as requiring a clear vision of American interests and steady pursuit of them over the long term. Kennan's ideas were formed in the context of, and meshed nicely with, the United States' postwar commitment to a multilateral world economy based on the World Bank, the International Monetary Fund, and free trade. Containment has been a success, if in a somewhat qualified sense. The Soviet Union has not expanded in the way Kennan and others feared it might in the late 1940s, while peace has been maintained between the two superpowers, although at the cost of a huge arms race. Prosperity has been achieved for the noncommunist industrial world and unprecedented levels of economic growth for some formerly underdeveloped countries.

But containment has occasioned costs as well, especially to the American national economy. These costs have been incurred in large part because of the US inability to balance the needs of domestic economic policy with those of international economic policy. In the next decade, the social, economic, political, and diplomatic costs of such failures seem destined to increase. Paying the price for Reagan's policies may weaken the US economy, making containment more difficult in the 1990s.

Notes

1. John Lewis Gaddis, *Strategies of Containment: A Critical Appraisal of Postwar American National Security Policy* (New York, 1982), pp. vii–x, 354–57.

2. Ibid., pp. 36–39.

3. Herbert Stein, *Presidential Economics: The Making of Economic Policy from Roosevelt to Reagan and Beyond* (New York, 1984), pp. 80–83, 93–94, 119–20.

4. Ibid., pp. 86–87.

5. Ibid., p. 87; see also Robert M. Collins, *The Business Response to Keynes, 1929–1964* (New York, 1981); and Michael D. Reagan, *The Managed Economy* (New York, 1963).

6. Burton I. Kaufman, *Trade and Aid: Eisenhower's Foreign Economic Policy, 1953–1961* (Baltimore, 1982), p. 58; David P. Calleo, *The Imperious Economy* (Cambridge, Mass., 1982), pp. 17–18. An abbreviated statement of Calleo's argument appears in "Since 1961: American Power in a New World Economy," in William

H. Becker and Samuel F. Wells, Jr., eds., *Economics and World Power: An Assessment of American Diplomacy Since 1789* (New York, 1984), pp. 391–457.

7. Kaufman, *Trade and Aid,* pp. 179, 182–88, 192–96.

8. Calleo, *The Imperious Economy,* pp. 19–20.

9. Ibid., pp. 9–14; Stein, *Presidential Economics,* pp. 89–113; George P. Shultz and Kenneth W. Dam, *Economic Policy Beyond the Headlines* (New York, 1977), pp. 200–203.

10. Calleo, *The Imperious Economy,* pp. 12–13; Stein, *Presidential Economics,* pp. 108–13; James Tobin, *The New Economics One Decade Older* (Princeton, 1979), pp. 1–39.

11. Stein, *Presidential Economics,* pp. 101–02.

12. Calleo, *The Imperious Economy,* pp. 26–44; Stein, *Presidential Economics,* pp. 115–22.

13. Edward L. Morse, *Foreign Policy and Interdependence in Gaullist France* (Princeton, 1973), pp. 77–83; John W. Evans, *The Kennedy Round in American Trade Policy: The Twilight of GATT?* (Cambridge, Mass., 1971), pp. 265–79; Wilbur F. Monroe, *International Trade Policy in Transition* (Lexington, Mass., 1975), pp. 94–99.

14. Calleo, *The Imperious Economy,* pp. 15–17; Mira Wilkins, *The Maturing of Multinational Enterprise: American Business Abroad from 1914 to 1970* (Cambridge, Mass., 1974), pp. 327–73; see also Robert A. Packenham, *Liberal America and the Third World: Political Development Ideas in Foreign Aid and Social Science* (Princeton, 1973).

15. Calleo, *The Imperious Economy,* pp. 45–61.

16. Ibid., pp. 62–78; Stein, *Presidential Economics,* pp. 133–207. See also Edward Tufte, *Political Control of the Economy* (Princeton, 1978); and William E. Nordhaus, "The Political Business Cycle," *Review of Economic Studies* (April 1975), pp. 169–90.

17. The ideas for Nixon's new economic policy were drawn from a study on America's competitive position supervised by Peter

G. Peterson and published by the government as *The United States in the Changing World Economy* (Washington, 1971).

18. Calleo, *The Imperious Economy*, pp. 62–78.

19. Ibid., pp. 45, 62–64.

20. Ibid., pp. 105–17; Nordhaus, "The Political Business Cycle."

21. Calleo, *The Imperious Economy*, pp. 105–17.

22. On the impact of the military on industry, see Seymour Melman, ed., *The War Economy of the United States: Readings in Military, Industry, and Economy* (New York, 1971); for a discussion of industry's problems see Barry Bluestone and Bennett Harrison, *The Deindustrialization of America: Plant Closings, Community Abandonment, and the Dismantling of Basic Industry* (New York, 1982), pp. 140–92.

23. Calleo, *The Imperious Economy*, pp. 118–38.

24. Ibid., pp. 140–44; also Stein, *Presidential Economics*, pp. 212–16, 236–37.

25. Calleo, *The Imperious Economy*, pp. 141–50.

26. Ibid., pp. 139–53; also Stein, *Presidential Economics*, pp. 216–33.

27. Calleo, *The Imperious Economy*, pp. 144–46.

28. "Pentagon Spending is the Economy's Biggest Gun" *Business Week*, 21 October 1985, pp. 60–64.

29. Stein, *Presidential Economics*, pp. 235–62.

30. C. Fred Bergsten, "The State of the Debate: Reaganomics," *Foreign Policy* 59 (Summer 1985) pp. 137–38; Alan S. Blinder, "Once Upon a Time in Reaganomics Land. . .," *Business Week*, 7 October 1985, p. 16.

31. Bergsten, "The State of the Debate," pp. 136–37; "The New Trade Strategy," *Business Week*, 7 October 1985, pp. 90–96.

32. Bergsten, "The State of the Debate," pp. 136–38.

33. Ibid., p. 139.

7

Economic Containment

Angela E. Stent

T HE CONVICTION THAT IT IS both desirable and possible to
contain the Soviet Union by retarding its economic development has been a key element of American policy since the
end of World War II. The logic is as follows. The Soviet Union
is weaker economically than the United States and wants to
import Western manufactures to improve its economic performance. Denying it advanced industrial goods will slow development of its industry (and therefore its military-industrial complex), enhancing America's national security by ensuring a
weaker Soviet economy. A secondary aspect of economic containment has been the belief that economic leverage can be used
in the pursuit of political ends.

These two premises and the policies they have produced
have been a subject of constant controversy, not only in the
United States but also within the NATO alliance. One part of
the controversy centers on the effectiveness of economic containment: Since, it is asked, the Soviet Union has managed to
attain military parity with the United States, can economic containment be said to have worked? Another aspect arises out of
the rather confused way economic measures have been used for

Angela E. Stent is Director of the Russian Area Studies Program and an Associate Professor at Georgetown University.

both political and economic ends: Since the goals of American economic containment policy are multiple and sometimes unclear, how can one ascertain whether they have been achieved?

Despite the controversy, economic containment retains a distinct attraction for policymakers. After all, the United States is the mightiest economic nation on earth and produces goods that the Soviets need. In the rather meager arsenal of levers available for us to use in dealing with our chief antagonist, this one seems an effective means of influencing Soviet developments. Moreover, when the militarily powerful Soviets take actions that outrage us morally or seem to threaten Western security, the economic weapon is one of the safe and acceptable means of reacting that we have.

Economic containment in the postwar era has had three major components. The first, no longer totally operative, is economic warfare, the attempt to weaken the overall economic performance of the Soviet Union in both civilian and military sectors. The second is the strategic embargo, designed to deny goods (increasingly in high technology areas) that could be used specifically to build up the Soviet military. The third element of US policy has been economic leverage, the use of economic means to restrain Soviet political behavior.[1]

This paper focuses on how America's economic containment policy has evolved since 1945 and what economic and political effects that policy has had on the USSR.

The Evolution of US Policy in the Postwar Era

Prior to the Second World War, American economic policy toward the USSR was mixed. Initial government opposition to the Bolshevik seizure of power, with its cancellation of czarist debts and withdrawal from World War I, was followed by a period of enthusiastic business participation in the Russian economy in the 1920s. It was Stalin's policy of autarky, rather than US reservations, that reduced US economic ties with the Soviets during the 1930s. There has always been a belief on the part of some US businessmen that the Soviet Union offered a vast potential market to US entrepreneurs. As *Fortune* argued in 1945,

> Our businessmen are both perplexed by the thought that Russia's huge economic potential will bring it neck-and-neck with us in another twenty years, and bemused with the business possibilities in helping it reach that point. . . . Russia holds for us a fascination that engages our respect. . . . Russians are remarkably like us in recognizable traits—our common expansiveness as heirs to a spacious land, our kindred feelings for machines.[2]

Although this was written a few months before the end of wartime collaboration between Washington and Moscow, these sentiments have been echoed many times in subsequent business discussions. The US government was always more skeptical than the private sector about the possibilities for trade, largely because there seemed little that the United States wanted to purchase from the USSR.

At the end of World War II, there was a debate about whether or not the United States should pursue a policy of economic cooperation with the Soviet Union. Behind this debate were disagreements over whether trade could be used as a political lever and whether the United States was threatened with a postwar economic depression which Russian orders would help avert. While Averell Harriman, the US Ambassador in Moscow, favored offering postwar economic aid to the USSR, his counselor, George F. Kennan, disagreed. Kennan was unconcerned about a US depression and skeptical of the value of extending trade and credits to the Soviets; he supported the cutoff of Lend-Lease in May 1945.[3] His position was that economic assistance to the Soviets would not elicit political concessions and that the USSR would use US trade and credits to build up its military-industrial infrastructure to the detriment of US national security. Kennan advocated a long-term strategy of economic denial to the USSR on security grounds. Yet he was well aware of the difficulties of securing agreement in

Washington on such a policy. In 1949, he criticized some government officials who "have an idea that if you can only lure the Russians . . . into some sort of a flexible free trade system, you will thereby put salt on the feathers of the Russian tail and the bird will appear to be much more tame and amenable."[4]

The debate about whether to pursue a policy of economic inducement or denial continued until late 1947, when both the Executive and Congress endorsed restrictions on economic ties with the USSR in view of the Soviet takeover of Eastern Europe and the growing tensions in US-Soviet relations. Since Washington feared that the United States might soon be involved in a war with the Soviet Union, economic warfare seemed appropriate: obviously, nothing should be done to strengthen overall Soviet warmaking capacity. The key decision was taken in 1947, when the National Security Council decided that "US national security requires the immediate termination, for an indefinite period, of shipments from the United States to the USSR and its satellites of all commodities which are critically short in the United States or which would contribute to the Soviet military potential."[5] The following month, the order was expanded to cover items of indirect military significance. The US military, favoring economic warfare, linked the granting of Marshall Plan aid to an embargo against the Soviets.[6] But even then, there was agreement that trade controls should not be so stringent as to cause the Soviets to limit their supply of strategic materials to the United States.[7]

Until the Nixon era, US economic containment was enshrined in two pieces of legislation. The first was the Export Control Act of 1949, which emphasized the danger to US national security of exporting materials without regard to their potential military significance and empowered the president to exercise trade controls. It was the first comprehensive system of export controls ever adopted by Congress in peacetime.[8] The second was the Mutual Defense Assistance Control Act of 1951 (known as the Battle Act), which recognized that economic warfare would succeed only if American allies cooperated. It empowered the president to terminate all forms of military, economic, and financial assistance to any nation that knowingly sold embargoed goods to a prohibited destination, thereby providing for US sanctions against NATO allies. In order to multilateralize and coordinate the strategic embargo aspect of economic warfare, the United States formed the Consultative Group–Coordinating Committee (CoCom) in 1949, an organization of NATO states minus Iceland and plus Japan.[9]

By 1951, American economic warfare policy was enshrined in various pieces of legislation. The premise was that any assistance in building up the Soviet economy by the sale of Western goods with direct or indirect military application represented a danger to US national security. The essence of US policy was the desire to weaken the Soviet economy through denial and to contain Soviet power by retarding the growth of the military-industrial infrastructure that would permit Soviet foreign expansion. Moreover, Washington recognized that its policy would be ineffective if it did not secure allied cooperation. The United States therefore used a mixture of positive (Marshall Plan aid) and negative (Battle Act) incentives to achieve this cooperation. There was little attempt during these years at the height of the Cold War to use trade as a political weapon to moderate either Soviet domestic or foreign policy. The overriding importance of denial for national security reasons took precedence over more carefully calibrated attempts at linkage.

Despite various liberalizations of the CoCom lists in the 1950s, US policy remained essentially unchanged until the Kennedy administration began to retreat from economic warfare. After 1963, economic containment policy moved toward mixing the strategic embargo with agricultural sales and positive economic-political linkage as the administration reconsidered the entire premise of US economic warfare policy. Walt Rostow, then head of the Policy Planning Staff in the Department of State, wrote,

> The major issues of our trade control policy are
> political—not strategic, economic or commercial. From
> the standpoint of the USSR, the political significance of
> the U.S. restrictive policies has been out of all proportion
> to their impact on the Soviet economy or strategic posi-
> tion.... They serve as a symbol of U.S. unwillingness to
> grant the USSR full respectability as an equal in the
> postwar world order.... Trade denial has also come to be
> an important symbol of our cold war resolve and purpose
> and of our moral disapproval of the USSR.[10]

Here was a recognition, echoed in other documents from the
Kennedy administration, that economic warfare had had a limited economic effect.

Nevertheless, in 1962 the Kennedy administration had decided to risk a major allied confrontation by seeking to prevent
its Alliance partners from selling the USSR large-diameter
pipe—a commodity not on the CoCom list—for the construction
of the Soviet–East European Friendship oil pipeline. This effort
echoed earlier economic warfare policies, and in many ways
foreshadowed the 1982 gas pipeline sanctions. The official motivation was to bolster Western security by preventing the construction of a pipeline that would enhance the Soviet military
posture in Eastern Europe. Another reason was the desire to retard the growth of the Soviet energy industry, under the fear that
a flood of Soviet oil would "drown" the West and make it too
dependent on Soviet supplies.[11] In addition, there may have
been concern on the part of the Western oil industry that Soviet
competition would threaten its business. Also, because the
United States was angry that its European allies had begun to increase their trade with the Soviets, the administration sought to
arrest this new economic flow. The effort partly succeeded, in
that it forced West Germany to comply with the embargo. But
other NATO allies refused to cancel contracts, and the embargo
may have forced the Soviets to improve their capacity to produce large-diameter pipe. Certainly, though the Friendship pipeline was completed, the West did not drown in Soviet oil.

Ultimately, in fact, Kennedy's broader policies were moving away from economic warfare. A few weeks before his assassination, he announced the first wheat sale to the USSR in the postwar era, justifying it as good for "the American farmer, the American exporter, [and] the American citizen concerned with the strength of our balance of payments."[12] Suddenly, domestic economic interests seemed to have superseded national security. There was, however, also some attempt to justify wheat sales on political grounds. The State Department argued that a wheat sale "would advertise the superiority of our agricultural system over the communist system in a most dramatic fashion. . . . It would be a further step toward reduction of East-West tensions."[13] Thus, it was claimed that wheat could be used as a political lever, whereas large-diameter pipe could not; American wheat sales apparently did not threaten national security, whereas European industrial equipment sales did. Although wheat does not in fact help directly to build up Soviet industry, this argument was greeted with skepticism by America's allies, who argued that grain was, if anything, more important than large-diameter pipe for the survival of the Soviet economy.

This dual policy of the Kennedy administration—combining strategic embargoes with grain sales and the use of trade for political purposes—continued in the Johnson administration. In 1965 President Johnson created a special committee on US trade relations with East European countries and the Soviet Union, instructing it to explore "all aspects of expanding trade" in support of the president's policy of bridge building. Although the main elements of policy did not change in this period, there was increased emphasis on the use of "peaceful" trade as a positive political lever.

The major change in American economic policy toward the USSR, downplaying the strategic embargo and emphasizing the political and economic significance of trade, came during the Nixon presidency. Although the strategic embargo remained in force, there was considerable liberalization of export controls. In 1969, the Export Control Act was renamed the Export

Administration Act, symbolizing the movement away from embargoes to a cautious expansion of exports. The assumption was that trade should be encouraged unless it could detrimentally affect US security, with the burden of proof on the opponents of East-West trade rather than its proponents.

US policy changed because Europe had recovered and was no longer receiving Marshall Plan aid, and it was much harder for the US to exercise leverage over its allies on East-West trade questions. The Europeans and Japanese had begun to expand their trade with the USSR, and there was fear that US business was losing opportunities in the East.

Another major reason for the change, however, lay in the requirements of detente. In his memoirs, Henry Kissinger claims that initially both he and the president opposed liberalizing trade with the Soviets until they showed foreign policy restraint. Indeed, he criticizes those in the State Department who believed that more trade would lead to better Soviet behavior.[14] Kissinger's grand design involved linking trade and politics, using trade incentives to reward Soviet behavior after rather than before Soviet policies were implemented.[15] Nevertheless, despite Kissinger's insistence that trade be linked only to Soviet foreign policy, he did discuss the question of Jewish emigration with the Soviets. According to his account, he secured an informal agreement that the USSR would permit a certain number of Jews to emigrate in return for a trade treaty that included Most-Favored-Nation status. From Kissinger's point of view, the Jackson-Vanik amendment torpedoed his attempts at linkage by denying the Soviets MFN status until they made the promise formal.[16] Senator Jackson and his supporters disagreed.

Whatever the precise sequence of events, the Nixon-Kissinger linkage strategy was never given a chance to work. The Stevenson amendment, which set a limit of $300 million on official credits for the Soviets, may have been more important than Jackson-Vanik in torpedoing the US-Soviet trade treaty. Although there was some liberalization of trade and the Soviets were able to secure a few major gains like the notorious 1972 grain deal, the administration's inability to secure congressional support of the new policy hampered any major trade expansion. By 1974, therefore, US economic containment (with the exception of the strategic embargo) had been diluted. The principle of economic-political linkage was partially implemented, but Executive-Legislative battles made a consistent set of new guidelines impossible.

President Carter, therefore, inherited a mixed situation. Trade had been liberalized, but it had also been more directly linked to Soviet political behavior. Carter continued both of these lines, first encouraging economic relations and later hinting that the issue of a US-Soviet trade treaty might be revived in Congress.[17] On the other hand, since human rights was a cornerstone of his administration's foreign policy, Carter was committed to linking trade to Soviet internal behavior far more broadly than was Nixon. Samuel Huntington of the National Security Council developed a sophisticated plan for the use of both economic carrots and sticks in dealing with the Soviets. Where Nixon and Kissinger had favored positive linkage, the Carter White House believed in using both positive incentives and trade denial.[18] Indeed, Carter imposed trade sanctions on the Soviets for their treatment of dissidents (Scharansky and Ginzburg) as well as for their invasion of Afghanistan. Yet the Carter sanction policy was erratic, as its fluctuating policies on energy technology transfer show,[19] and its inconsistencies caused problems with both allies and the American business community.

After the Soviet invasion of Afghanistan, the Carter administration began to move US policy back toward economic warfare. It took a more consistent stand on East-West trade, imposing a grain and technology embargo on the USSR and trying to enlist NATO allies in this cause. It also secured an agreement within CoCom for a "no exceptions" policy for the USSR.[20] Although most US officials agreed that these sanctions would not lead to the withdrawal of Soviet forces, they wanted to show the USSR that there could be no more business as usual.[21] In some ways, these US actions marked a return to the idea that economic warfare should be used to express the United States' "moral disapproval" of the Soviets, even if it did not retard their economic development.

The inconsistencies of US economic containment have hardly been resolved in the Reagan era. During the 1980 election campaign, Ronald Reagan argued both for a tougher technology transfer policy toward the Soviets and for removal of the grain embargo, claiming that the embargo had hurt US farmers while not affecting the Soviets because they had merely purchased grain elsewhere. In fact, there is evidence that the grain embargo *did* impose considerable economic costs on the USSR, and that the main reason for the Reagan pledge was domestic politics, just as had been true of John F. Kennedy's initial grain agreement. And like Kennedy's, the dualism of Reagan's economic containment has caused problems both domestically and abroad.

The argument for selling grain to the USSR while restricting a wide variety of technology has been two-fold: "Grain, the Soviets can get in other places, if they want it.... The other element is that grain [sales] will result in the Soviet Union having to pay out hard cash."[22] This justification has been greeted with skepticism. US grain sales may save the Soviet economy $30 billion annually by enabling Moscow to avoid costly new investments.[23] But at the same time, the Reagan administration has returned more fully than any of its predecessors to an economic warfare policy reminiscent of the Cold War years. It has broadened the definition of military relevance by including certain items which, it argues, could make an indirect contribution to Soviet warfighting capability. Domestically, technology transfer laws and procedures have been tightened, and the United States has sought, though with only limited success, to secure CoCom agreement on larger embargo lists.

Another feature of Reagan's partial economic warfare policy has been the use of economic coercion against American allies who do not share Washington's approach to East-West economic relations. In 1982, the administration imposed extra-territorial sanctions on European states that had contracted to sell compressor components for the Urengoi natural gas pipeline from western Siberia to Western Europe.[24] The sequence of events was similar to that in 1962, but this time a more inde-pendent West Germany did not comply. The United States put forward familiar arguments: that the Europeans would become dangerously dependent on Soviet gas supplies, and that the So-viets would gain hard currency enabling them to purchase tech-nology from the West to build up their military-industrial infrastructure. Europe rejected the arguments and cited US grain sales as proof of American double standards.

In the end, the conflict was resolved by Secretary of State George Shultz, and a series of allied studies was carried out to harmonize East-West trade policies.[25] Although the United States failed to prevent the construction of the Urengoi pipeline and did not change its allies' policies on East-West trade, Wash-ington retained strict controls on energy trade with the USSR. Moreover, the US sanctions, by delaying some of the gas con-tracts, were partially successful. Because the gas market sof-tened, Europe contracted to take only 26 billion cubic meters (bcm) of Soviet gas as opposed to the 40 bcm originally envisaged.[26]

Reagan has avoided the use of trade inducements to alter Soviet political behavior. Considering the Kissinger-Nixon link-age policy naive, administration officials express skepticism that trade carrots could ever affect Soviet behavior. Instead, the ad-ministration has pursued trade denial as the only acceptable means of deterring future Soviet behavior or reacting to Soviet moves.

Thus, by 1984, the United States had almost come full cir-cle from the early years of the Export Control Act and the Battle

Act. There was partial economic warfare, in that the administration wanted to weaken the entire Soviet economy rather than only its military sector, and arguments against economic ties with the Soviets were based on national security grounds as well as political disapproval. In 1985, it appeared that the United States might be moving away from this tougher policy of economic containment in its efforts to seek a dialogue with the new Soviet leadership; but many inside the Reagan administration still opposed any liberalization.

The Domestic Politics of US East-West Trade Policy

It has become a cliche to remark that what is good for US domestic politics—the institutionalized separation of powers that ensures democracy—is potentially damaging for foreign policy. To have any hope of success in their foreign relations, nations obviously need a coherent international strategy. Yet it is worth emphasizing this point in trying to understand the difficulties of coming up with an effective trade policy. Since the early Cold War years, the United States has not been able to formulate or implement a consistent long-term economic policy toward the Soviet Union because of the cacophony of inputs from officials, politicians, and interest groups who enter into policymaking. Often these individuals and the institutions they represent have disagreed on matters of principle. At other times, they have used the question of economic ties with the Soviet Union to fight domestic political battles that have nothing to do with East-West trade. Either way, the ability of the United States to conduct a rational, consistent, and effective policy has been impaired.

The first major problem that has beset East-West trade policy has been rivalry within the Executive branch for policy control. The National Security Council and the Departments of Defense, Commerce, State, Energy, Agriculture, and the Treasury have all had a hand in policymaking and have increasingly disagreed over what US policy should be. Traditionally, the Departments of Commerce and Agriculture have taken the most forthcoming attitude toward trade with the Soviets; the State

Department and Security Council have been concerned with the political implications of such trade as part of overall diplomacy toward the USSR; and the Defense Department has taken a much more restrictive attitude, focusing on the danger to national security of such commerce.[27] The Department of Defense has taken a stronger role in the Reagan administration, but it has not always been able to tighten restrictions on economic relations with the USSR. Moreover, in recent years there have been conflicts *within* these various departments over East-West trade, further complicating the procedure. Because of the cumbersomeness of policymaking and the inbuilt rivalries between various parts of the Executive branch, economic policy toward the USSR is often hostage to bureaucratic squabbles, frustrating those affected by that policy—the business community, America's allies, or the Soviet Union—and leaving loopholes from which the USSR can and does benefit. The question of who has ultimate responsibility for trade policy remains unanswered.

Another problem is the role of Congress. Sometimes, Congress and the administration have agreed on economic policy toward the USSR. But at other times, Congress has blocked administration attempts either to liberalize or to tighten policy. During the 1950s the Executive and Congress agreed on East-West trade policy, but as presidential authority weakened and Congress became more assertive, problems like those posed by the Jackson-Vanik and Stevenson amendments increased. In this case, a Democratic Congress that had previously criticized the Executive for too restrictive a policy toward the USSR decided to thwart White House policy. Yet the Democrats also opposed a policy of detente which paid no attention to human rights. Moreover, since trade is one of the few available weapons, Congress has often been quick to impose economic sanctions as a response to Soviet actions. To some extent, congressional actions were a product of opposition to the administration's handling of the Vietnam War, making US-Soviet trade hostage to struggles that had little to do with the merits of economic ties.

Recently, the division between a Republican-controlled Senate and a Democratic-controlled House also delayed renewal of the Export Administration Act.

Interest groups have also had some influence on the evolution of US policy, although they have had far less impact than the Executive or Legislative branch of government. The business community has from time to time lobbied for increased East-West trade, but with surprising reticence compared to lobbying efforts on other aspects of US foreign trade policy. US business groups have been deterred from vigorous lobbying for US-Soviet trade because of the political stigmas attached to such advocacy and the risk of provoking consumer boycotts of their products at home. In addition, the cost of doing business with the cumbersome Soviet bureaucracy has dampened the pursuit of Soviet markets. The farm lobby has been less reluctant to campaign for exports to the USSR because its activities generally have received official encouragement. The Carter grain embargo is the one exception. Finally, organized Labor—particularly the AFL–CIO—has consistently opposed a policy of liberalized trade with the USSR and enthusiastically supported boycotts and sanctions against Moscow.

Economic Containment and US Allies

Since the beginning of postwar economic containment, it has generally been assumed that such a policy could only be effective if the United States secured its allies' cooperation. Since the era of detente, it has become equally clear that America's allies do not share Washington's belief in the desirability or efficacy of economic containment apart from the limited strategic embargo. Some people within this country have argued that, failing allied cooperation, Washington should impose an economic containment policy unilaterally.[28] But most experts recognize that without allied cooperation, a restrictive policy is impossible, so they continue to seek European and Japanese cooperation.

European willingness to support the US attitude toward economic ties with the USSR ended along with the continent's recovery from economic devastation and reliance on Marshall Plan aid. The last European statesman to support across-the-board restrictions was Konrad Adenauer, who complied with the 1962 pipe embargo and criticized Kennedy for selling grain to the USSR.[29] Western Europe and Japan are far more trade-dependent than the United States, and even though trade with the Soviets constitutes only a small percentage of the total, it is disproportionately important for certain sectors of their economies (particularly the steel, machine-tool, and chemical industries).[30] Moreover, the Europeans and Japanese see a healthy economy as vital to national security, whereas American officials have traditionally given security a much narrower military definition. Thus, from our allies' perspectives, the contribution to national security that comes from a healthy export sector—including non-military exports to the USSR—outweighs the potential danger to national security that machinery exports to the Soviets might involve. All of the United States' allies agree that no explicitly military technology should be exported to the USSR, but they favor all other industrial exports.

There is also a political dimension to this approach. Most European nations view the detente era as successful. Tending to judge Soviet behavior by what the Kremlin does in Europe, not by its activities in Afghanistan or Nicaragua, they argue that the Soviets have abided by their agreements in Western Europe despite the deployment of SS–20 missiles. Moreover, they believe that economics and politics are linked, that a cooperative economic relationship can reinforce political ties. The West Germans particularly believe that trade incentives can bring political results, as shown by the development of the inter-German relationship. The French, British, Italians, and Japanese are more skeptical about positive economic levers, but they all agree that sanctions are not an acceptable means of responding to Soviet behavior because they hurt the countries involved without affecting what Moscow does.

Furthermore, although Europe and Japan accept the necessity for a strategic embargo and have been willing to cooperate in CoCom's tightening of technology transfers, they have been unwilling to accept the broad, US-backed definition of indirect contributions to Soviet military prowess. There have been endless disagreements about the relevance of the "militarily-critical" technologies concept enshrined in US law.[31] CoCom works surprisingly well, considering that it is an informal organization with no power to impose sanctions against violators; yet it will not restrict the flow of civilian goods to the USSR unless they can be proved to have direct application to Soviet military capabilities.

Europe and Japan have particularly resisted US attempts to use industrial trade sanctions to punish the Soviets for Afghanistan, Poland, or human rights abuses. The 1982 extra-territorial pipeline sanctions, for instance, affected companies in Europe and Japan much more than in the United States; indeed, they were seen as sanctions against Western Europe rather than the USSR. The Europeans sold pipeline equipment to the Soviets, even under threat of American countersanctions against European goods coming into the United States. Arguably, America's economic containment policy in the last few years has had more effect on Western Europe than on the USSR. Certainly, those in the White House and Defense Department who favor a restrictive policy are willing to apply it to Western Europe as much as to the East, unless Western Europe is willing to alter its stance. These administration officials have already sought to limit contact among Western scientists working in what the government considers sensitive areas.

Europe and Japan reject the idea of an across-the-board policy of economic containment, apart from CoCom, arguing that it is unworkable and counterproductive. This position will probably not change, since conservative and socialist governments alike share it. As a consequence, it is possible to achieve only the lowest common denominator of allied cooperation in CoCom, and this only with considerable pressure.

The Economic Effect of Economic Containment

What effect have such fitful economic containment policies had on the Soviet economy? A careful examination of Soviet writings on Western trade restrictions reveals a dual message. On the one hand, the Soviets have always criticized them as a manifestation of the Cold War and contrary to "normal" international practice.[32] Countless articles have pointed out that US restrictions violate the Helsinki principles and are opposed by America's allies, citing particularly the pipeline embargo of 1982.[33] Soviet authors have also emphasized the clash between US business interests, which favor trade with the USSR, and those in Congress who oppose trade.[34] Since an acute consciousness of technological inferiority is a major element in Russian political culture, the Soviets go out of their way to say that they favor economic ties because trade will help the American economy. They never admit their own economic needs.

On the other hand, Soviet writers have always been quick to stress that American restrictions have not affected the USSR economically, even if they have complicated the political atmosphere. Soviet articles point to the USSR's economic progress, its economic links with other capitalist states, and its rosy prospects for future economic growth. And yet, their level of invective against US restrictions belies that tone of indifference. Moreover, the fact that the Soviets have acquired so much American technology illegally (and appear to have a special section for that purpose in the KGB) suggests that they are very interested indeed in obtaining it by whatever means possible.[35]

The policy of economic warfare—to the extent that it has been implemented since 1949—has not prevented the USSR from experiencing impressive rates of growth in the postwar era or becoming the world's largest producer of a number of key commodities, including oil and steel. Despite current difficulties, Soviet economic achievements and potential should not be dismissed. Moreover, it is likely that Soviet economic problems are more the product of the domestic system than the result of Western economic denial.

But if economic warfare has proved ineffective, most Western experts agree that the strategic embargo has had a greater impact. It may well have contributed to slower rates of technological development, and although it has not prevented the USSR's military buildup in the conventional or nuclear spheres, it may have made the buildup more costly in terms of resource diversion from other sectors.

Despite such basic agreement that CoCom restrictions have had an impact, the more difficult question is how much they have retarded Soviet growth. Some analysts contend that the Western embargo, particularly in the strategic sphere, has had a smaller impact on Soviet developments than Americans would like to believe. On one end of the political spectrum, Anthony Sutton has argued in an exhaustive examination of Western technology exports to the Soviet Union that all items—even those of strictly civilian equipment—have fueled Soviet military growth:

> We cannot make any meaningful distinction between military and civilian goods. Every industrial plant directly or indirectly affords some military capability. It is the availability of Western technology that makes Soviet industry more efficient.... The Soviet Union and its socialist allies are dependent on the Western world for technical and economic viability.... We have constructed and maintain a first-order threat to Western society.[36]

Sutton's argument—that America's strategic embargo has failed (partly due to misguided US policies) and that the West has built up the Soviet economy—has been taken up by opponents of trade with the Soviets.[37] At the other end of the political spectrum, Gunnar Adler-Karlsson's study of CoCom concludes that the Western strategic embargo did little to halt Soviet economic growth because it was not supported by the American allies or neutral countries and because the Soviets did not need

Western technology to develop their economy or their military sector.[38]

More recent analyses of the impact of Western technology and trade—and their denial—on the Soviet economy suggest that it has been marginal but not irrelevant. One detailed analysis of the Soviet economy, sector by sector, shows that Western equipment has made a very modest, even minimal contribution to the development of Soviet industry and the Soviet military.[39] However, it may have reduced bottlenecks in some sectors like energy. Morris Bornstein's study for the OECD emphasizes the USSR's difficulty in absorbing and diffusing Western technology, suggesting that such imports have a net resource-demanding effect on the Soviet economy.[40] Recent developments indicate that the Soviet Union is becoming more technologically "chauvinistic," with key officials stressing the need for the USSR to rely on its own technology.[41] Moreover, some have argued that "U.S. denials of strategic products may galvanize [the USSR] to overcome its problems in the longer run."[42] This theory stresses that the Soviets carefully study the US embargo lists and then put all their resources into producing embargoed items, with the result that US restrictions ultimately have a counterproductive effect.

The message that has recently emerged from most Western writing on this issue—one that is supported by some US government estimates—is that Western equipment and technology imports have made only a very modest contribution to Soviet economic growth. Moreover, the Soviets have cut back their imports of Western technology since 1977. The West, most scholars argue, has a very limited impact on a Soviet economy which is large, self-sufficient, and deliberately insulated from the effects of Western restrictions. Just as a strategy of trade denial has not succeeded in retarding Soviet *military* growth, so a strategy of across-the-board trade promotion would probably not have much impact on Soviet *economic* growth. The over-centralized, neo-Stalinist Soviet economic system, and not Western restrictions, is the major barrier here, a view Mikhail

Gorbachev has all but acknowledged. If so, the United States' ability to influence Soviet economic developments has probably been exaggerated.

The Political Effect of Economic Containment

Economic containment has, therefore, had only a marginal effect on the Soviet economy. But has it had any political effects? The evidence suggests not, largely because of asymmetries in the economic and political stakes involved. Because trade with the West has never played an important macroeconomic role in Soviet economic development, the United States has often found itself using relatively insignificant economic ties in attempts to force changes in Soviet behavior on core political issues (such as treatment of dissidents or actions in Poland or Afghanistan). Quite simply, the ends demanded have been out of all proportion to the means used.[43]

There are two major forms of economic linkage: negative and positive. Negative linkage, or trade denial, uses the stick retroactively.[44] Usually, the United States has used it to punish the Soviets for domestic or foreign policy actions, without demanding specific concessions in return. As a result, it is difficult to find any examples in the postwar era of when American sanctions have led to a modification of Soviet policies, even when (like the grain embargo) they may have had an economic impact. Moreover, a major problem in using negative linkage is devising a timetable that will send consistent signals. For example, President Carter imposed technology sanctions on the Soviets to punish them for their treatment of dissidents, but then removed the sanctions even though Scharansky and others were still imprisoned. Similarly, President Reagan lifted the grain embargo with the Soviets still in Afghanistan. These kinds of inconsistencies—largely the product of domestic politics—call into question the entire rationale of the exercise and lessen American credibility.

Positive linkage—using trade incentives to elicit more desirable behavior from the USSR domestically or internationally—is the other available option. Any trade carrot is, of course, a potential stick, because the Soviets realize that the incentive can be withdrawn if the requisite concessions are not forthcoming. Although the Soviets have always argued that they will never make political concessions in return for trade, postwar experience indicates that they have sometimes done so, providing the stakes were roughly commensurate and the concessions demanded did not involve core values or major questions of national security. There are examples of such trade-offs in the Soviet–West German economic relationship, involving humanitarian concessions on emigration in return for increased trade,[45] and Moscow also proved willing to liberalize Jewish emigration until the Jackson-Vanik and Stevenson amendments were passed.[46] Although the United States has rarely tried to implement a policy of positive linkage, the record suggests some reason to believe that a trade inducement strategy might produce humanitarian concessions on marginal issues.

Implications for the Future

Economic containment has been only partially implemented since the mid-1950s, and its economic and political impact has been questionable. While it may have retarded Soviet economic development in some areas, it has not prevented an impressive Soviet military buildup or considerable economic achievements in heavy industry and energy. In some ways, a refusal to sell grain to the Soviets might have been a more effective form of pressure, but since 1963 this means of US leverage has not been acceptable. The strategic embargo has prevented the transfer to the USSR of technology with direct military application, but only at the cost of constant struggles to agree on dual-use technologies, and CoCom's effectiveness has been hampered by inconsistencies in US and allied policies.

Similarly, using economic levers to produce political results has been disappointing. Yet one can still argue that sanctions have a deterrent effect. It is impossible anyway to prove the contrary, because that would involve knowing what Soviet behavior would have been without the threat of sanctions. Moreover, it is undeniable that if American politicians feel it necessary to react to Soviet misconduct, then the trade weapon is one of the few safe and domestically popular ones—as long as grain is left out. Nevertheless, recent sanctions have done more harm to the West than to the East. In the pipeline case, the economic costs imposed on the USSR may not have been worth the damage done to the Western alliance and therefore to Western security. Positive linkage may be more productive, but trade inducement is not containment, whatever its utility to a more cooperative US-Soviet relationship.

The United States has three options for the future. The first would be to return to a policy of economic warfare, including a total grain embargo as envisaged in 1949. The assumptions behind this policy would be that a weak Soviet economy is good for US security and that American policy can affect how weak the Soviet economy is. Both propositions are, of course, debatable. Should the United States decide to return to such a confrontational policy, it would provoke even more dissension within the NATO alliance and further jeopardize Western cooperation, resulting in a unilateral (and therefore ineffective) policy. It is safe to say that Washington would never be able to secure European or Japanese cooperation for economic warfare unless the USSR were to invade Western Europe or Japan. Moreover, since even the Reagan administration has not moved toward a renewed policy of economic containment—indeed, is moving away from it—it is difficult to envision any future American administration returning to economic warfare. Moreover, the broad crackdown on high technology trade between the East and the West and within the Alliance demanded by such a policy would be detrimental to US research and development.

The second option would be to continue the current mixed policy, encouraging grain sales, cautiously promoting exports of some manufactures, maintaining the strategic embargo, tightening up on high technology exports, and periodically using trade for foreign policy purposes. Acceptable domestically, this policy will secure only grudging allied cooperation. It also will provoke continued complaints from the US business community that Washington is giving business to Western Europe while not preventing the Soviets from acquiring Western technology. A Democratic administration might lean somewhat more toward encouraging trade, but in either case this mixed scenario is the most likely one for the foreseeable future.

A third option would be to assume that it is in the interest of the United States to have a stronger Soviet economy, on the premises that a fat communist is less belligerent than a thin one and that the United States could help to improve Soviet economic performance through a policy of trade inducement. Again, both propositions are debatable. A policy of encouraging grain and manufacture exports while retaining necessary strategic controls would give more business to the United States, would lead to less political conflict with US allies, and would increase cooperative channels of communication with the Soviets. To be consistent, this kind of trade promotion strategy would have to eschew economic linkage, but trade and politics might more generally reinforce each other in a policy of revived detente. It is questionable, however, whether Congress or the Executive branch would be willing to forego totally economic sanctions for foreign policy reasons.

The sobering reality is that none of these three strategies would have an appreciable *economic* effect on the USSR. They would, however, make a difference domestically and in ties between the United States and Western Europe. The major influence on Soviet economic performance in the future will be Gorbachev's economic policy, and whether he is willing and able to reform the ossified Soviet system. US economic policy can certainly affect the *political* relationship between the two nations, but it cannot determine Soviet economic policy. Some observers may continue to argue that if only we could get our allies and all the neutral countries to agree to a total economic blockade of the USSR, we could bring it to its knees. Perhaps, but the premise is based on fantasy. There has never been, nor will there ever be, worldwide agreement on economic warfare against any nation in peacetime. The best the United States can do is to reconsider whether what is achievable in economic containment is worthwhile, balancing as best it can the East-West, West-West, and domestic economic and political dimensions of the issue.

Notes

1. For a fuller discussion of these three strategies, see Michael Mastanduno, "Strategies of Economic Containment," *World Politics* 38 (No. 4, 1985), pp. 503–29.

2. "What Business with Russia?" *Fortune* (January 1945), p. 204.

3. John Lewis Gaddis, *The United States and the Origins of the Cold War* (New York: Columbia University Press, 1972), chap. 6; George F. Kennan, *Memoirs (1925–1950)* (Boston: Little, Brown, 1967), pp. 280–84.

4. Lecture by George Kennan and Lewellyn G. Thompson at the National War College, 17 September 1949, p. 24. George F. Kennan papers, Princeton University Library.

5. Report by the National Security Council, "Control of Exports to the USSR and Eastern Europe," 17 December 1947, in *Foreign Relations of the United States, 1948,* Vol. IV, p. 512.

6. Department of the Army, Memorandum, "National Security Interest in East-West Trade," 8 December 1947, Spaatz Papers, Box 28; Secretary of the Navy, Memorandum, "U.S. Government Organization for Conducting Economic Warfare," 9 April 1948, Spaatz Papers, Box 29, Library of Congress.

7. State Department, "Control of Exports to the Soviet Bloc," 26 March 1948, Harry S Truman Library, Independence, Missouri, President's Secretary's Files.

8. See Harold Berman and John Garson, "United States Export Controls—Past, Present and Future," *Columbia Law Review* 57 (No. 5, 1967), pp. 791–890, for more details.

9. See Office of Technology Assessment, *Technology and East-West Trade* (Washington: Government Printing Office, 1979), chap. VII.

10. W.W. Rostow, Memo to the Policy Planning Council, "U.S. Policy on Trade with the European Soviet Bloc," 26 July 1963, pp. 2, 5, Box 223, National Security Files, John F. Kennedy Memorial Library, Boston.

11. See Angela Stent, *From Embargo to Ostpolitik: The Political Economy of West German–Soviet Relations, 1955–1980* (Cambridge: Cambridge University Press, 1981), chap. 5.

12. Letter from John F. Kennedy to Mike Mansfield, 15 November 1963, Box 314, National Security Files, John F. Kennedy Memorial Library.

13. Comments on Question 17, "U.S. Benefit from Sale to USSR of Wheat," State Department Memorandum, 25 September 1963, Box 518, National Security Files, Kennedy Library.

14. Henry A. Kissinger, *White House Years* (Boston: Little, Brown, 1979), pp. 152–54.

15. Ibid., pp. 1270–71.

16. Kissinger, *Years of Upheaval* (Boston: Little, Brown, 1982), pp. 985–88.

17. Bruce Jentleson, "Pipeline Politics: The Complex Political Economy of East-West Energy Trade," unpublished Ph.D. dissertation, Cornell University, 1984, chap. 5.

18. Samuel P. Huntington, "Trade, Technology and Leverage: Economic Diplomacy," *Foreign Policy* 32 (Fall 1978), pp. 63–80.

19. Office of Technology Assessment, *Technology and Soviet Energy Availability* (Washington: Government Printing Office, 1981).

20. CoCom operates by having weekly meetings where exceptions to the embargo lists are discussed. Before 1979, the United States always requested the largest number of exceptions in order to export items to communist nations. After 1979, there was a general agreement that, apart from items necessary to keep pipelines to the West operating, there would be no more exception requests for the USSR.

21. According to National Security Advisor Zbigniew Brzezinski, "We had no illusions that sanctions in themselves would force the Soviets out, but we felt that the Soviet Union had to pay some tangible price for its misconduct." Brzezinski, *Power and Principle* (New York: Farrar, Straus, Giroux, 1983), p. 43.

22. President Ronald Reagan, quoted in the *New York Times,* 29 July 1982.

23. Jan Vanous, *Washington Post,* 10 October 1982.

24. Stent, *Soviet Energy and Western Europe,* The Washington Papers, no. 90 (New York: Praeger, 1982).

25. See Stent, "Technology Transfers in East-West Trade: The Western Alliance Studies," *AEI Foreign Policy and Defense Review* 5 (No. 2, 1985), pp. 44–52.

26. Stent, "The Geopolitics of Soviet Energy," Cambridge Energy Research Associates Private Report (Cambridge, Mass.), November 1985.

27. See "East-West Commercial Policy: A Congressional Dialogue with the Reagan Administration," a Study prepared for the use

of the Joint Economic Committee, Congress of the United States, 16 February 1982.

28. Statement of Charles Wolf in Senate Foreign Relations Committee and CRS, *The Premises of East-West Commercial Relations: a Workshop*, 14–15 December 1982 (Washington: GPO, 1983), p. 145.

29. See Stent, *From Embargo to Ostpolitik*, pp. 121–24.

30. For a detailed discussion of European views, see Stent, *Technology Transfer to the Soviet Union: A Challenge for the Cohesiveness of the Western Alliance*, Arbeitspapiere zur Internationalen Politik no. 24 (Bonn: Europa-Union Verlag, 1983).

31. The concept of "militarily-critical technology" was first developed in a 1976 Department of Defense report known as the Bucy Report. An unclassified version of the militarily critical technologies list (which in its classified version runs over 700 pages) can be found in Department of Defense, *The Militarily Critical Technologies List*, October 1984 (Washington: Office of the Under Secretary of Defense for Research and Engineering).

32. For instance, see A. Kozyrev, "Torgovlya Oruzhiem Kak Instrument Vneshneii Politiki SSha," *SSha: Ekonomika, Politika, Ideologiia*, No. 5, 1980, pp. 19–30.

33. O.Ye. Tishelenko, "Soviet-American Trade Today," in *USA: Economics, Politics, Ideology* (FBIS Translation), No. 11, 1984; V. Shemyatenkov, " 'Ekonomicheskaia Voina' ili Ekonomicheskoe Sorevnovanie?" *Mirovaia Ekonomika i Mezhdunarodnye Otnosheniie*, No. 3, 1985, pp. 30–40.

34. G. Bazhenov, "USSR-USA: Businesslike Cooperation," *International Affairs* (Moscow), August 1974, pp. 15–21.

35. See the new DOD study, "Soviet Acquisition of Militarily Significant Western Technology: An Update," September 1985.

36. Anthony Sutton, *Western Technology and Soviet Economic Development, 1945 to 1965* (Stanford: Hoover Institution Publications, 1973), pp. 399–400.

37. Carl Gershman, "Selling Them the Rope," *Commentary* (April 1979), pp. 35–45.

38. Gunnar Adler-Karlsson, *Western Economic Warfare 1947–1967* (Stockholm: Almquist and Wiksell, 1968).

39. See Bruce Parrott, ed., *Technology and Soviet-American Relations* (Bloomington: Indiana University Press, 1985), for a detailed sector-by-sector analysis.

40. Morris Bornstein, "West-East Technology Transfer: Impact on the USSR," *The OECD Observer* 136 (September 1985), pp. 18–22. See also, Thane Gustafson, *Selling the Russians the Rope* (Santa Monica: The RAND Corporation, 1981).

41. See Philip Hanson, "Technological Chauvinism in the Soviet Union," *Radio Liberty Research,* 30 April 1985.

42. Marshall Goldman and Raymond Vernon, "Economic Relations," in Joseph S. Nye, Jr., ed., *The Making of America's Soviet Policy* (New Haven: Yale University Press, 1984), p. 169.

43. See Stent, *From Embargo to Ostpolitik,* pp. 7–12.

44. For a fuller discussion, see Ellen Frost and Angela Stent, "NATO's Troubles with East-West Trade," *International Security* 8 (Summer 1983), pp. 179–200.

45. See Stent, *From Embargo to Ostpolitik,* for details.

46. In the later Carter years, when the promise of a trade treaty was revived, the numbers of Jewish emigrants reached an all-time high of 51,320 in 1979.

8

Alliances and Security Relationships: A Dialogue with Kennan and His Critics

Terry L. Deibel

Few informed observers would argue against the proposition that alliances, and security relationships generally, have been a major tool of American foreign policy since the Second World War. In the forty years since that conflict ended, the United States has been through at least three major periods of alliance formation, and today it remains committed to literally dozens of nations around the globe. Right now, in fact, the United States is at the crest of a major commitment expansion which began in the middle of the Carter administration and has continued and accelerated under Ronald Reagan.

Nevertheless, it is also quite clear that Americans find something unnatural and even disturbing about alliances. As a

Terry L. Deibel, Professor of National Security Policy at the National War College, is on sabbatical as Resident Associate at the Carnegie Endowment for International Peace.

nation founded upon principles of *laissez faire* economics, democratic politics, and individualist ethics, the United States tends
to approach alliance relationships in an oddly unilateralist mode.
Fortunate to have spent most of its national life protected by either its geo-technological isolation or an overwhelming preponderance of power within the international system, the United
States has grown accustomed to seeking its security in freedom
of action rather than the restraints and promises of commitment.
Whole alliance systems, including SEATO (the Southeast Asia
Treaty Organization) and CENTO (the Central Treaty Organization), have come and gone since World War II, and even the
strongest relationships, like NATO, seem continually prone to
tension and crisis.

To raise in this context the issue of alliances as instruments
of containment is to pose whole congeries of interesting yet am-
biguous questions. Many concern what is meant by *containment*
itself. If it means simply the goal of preventing direct expansion
of the Soviet state, then one could perhaps argue for the success
of American alliances, since no allied state has ever been attacked by, let alone fallen to, Soviet arms; yet one can never
prove the success of a negative proposition like deterrence, and
certainly not the causal relationship of alliance ties to that success. If, on the other hand, containment means preventing the
creation of Soviet-allied and Soviet-armed regimes or the spread
of Moscow's influence, then one has to acknowledge that the
Rio Treaty did not stop the emergence of Castro's Cuba or the
Sandinistas' Nicaragua, nor did SEATO preclude communist
control of its protocolary states in Indochina; contrariwise, withdrawal of formal alliance protection from Taiwan in 1980 has
not—at least not yet—led to its absorption by the communist
world. Clearly, the record of alliances as devices for containment is mixed and incomplete, and the analyst has to be clear
about which sort of containment alliances are to serve.

Then there is the question of what is meant by *alliances*. In
its narrowest sense, the term can be taken to mean only those
relationships in which there is a treaty obligation of protection

against attack. But to so limit the definition would leave out virtually all security commitments formed in recent years. (Excluding such informal allies would make little sense in any case, since the language even of American alliance treaties leaves the United States with a great deal of freedom of action.)[1] If alliances are defined in their broadest sense, however, one would almost need to include any country with which the United States has a defense relationship, clearly a scope too broad for meaningful evaluation.

This writer hopes to proceed through these analytical thickets in three stages. The first stage will be a look at what the father of containment, George F. Kennan, meant by the term and what role he envisioned for alliances and security commitments. Second will be a survey of what the United States has actually done in its commitment policy over the past forty years, to compare this performance with the purposes for which Kennan's or other visions of containment called. And last will be some comments about the role security relationships may be expected to play in containment strategies during the years ahead.

Alliances and the Theory of Containment

Although containment's founder never set forth in one place the full scope of his strategic vision, and in spite of shifting emphases in his thought over the years, scholars who have studied Kennan's writings maintain that his view of the concept is internally cohesive and broadly consistent over time. As reconstructed by John Lewis Gaddis,[2] Kennan's containment had three elements or stages. First (and of greatest importance by far), Kennan argued for an active US policy to maintain the world balance of power in the special circumstances following World War II. That meant preventing the Soviets from acquiring *control* of the remaining centers of world industrial capacity other than the Soviet Union and the United States, all of which had been greatly weakened by the war: the industrial heart of Europe, Japan, and the United Kingdom. Second, containment was intended to limit Soviet *influence* outside the regions Moscow already controlled, which in Kennan's time pointed to a policy aimed at dividing and weakening the world communist movement. Finally, Kennan hoped that over time the Soviet view of international politics could be modified to permit a negotiated settlement with the West and a modus vivendi between the superpowers, vastly reducing Cold War tensions and establishing a global balance which could endure without constant and intensive American involvement.

What Kennan thought of alliances as tools to implement this strategic vision is less clear and not so easily explained, since he rarely spoke directly to the issue. His early thought was, however, free of many features which predisposed others to oppose commitments. For example, in a period when isolationism was still a strong current of American thought, Kennan was urging his countrymen to take the kind of active role in world politics that formation and maintainance of alliance systems would require. At a time when great hopes were placed in the United Nations as an alternative to alliances, Kennan had grave doubts about an organization which he thought was based on the illusion that a universalistic legal scheme could do away with power realities.[3] And if others might oppose American ties to unsavory regimes which fell short of American standards of good government, Kennan was realist enough to argue that the United States should not make the domestic systems of other states a determinant of its own foreign relations.[4]

In fact, far from precluding security commitments, there were aspects of Kennan's views on US foreign policy in the late 1940s which would almost have seemed to require a role for alliances. Always concerned lest the United States overextend itself, the founder of containment said on more than one occasion that America needed allies to share the burden of free world leadership, and he also argued that a strong American defense posture was necessary to maintain allied confidence.[5] In a September 1946 lecture to the first National War College class, Kennan explicitly included alliances among "Measures Short of War" that the new US policy would need.[6] Perhaps most significant, the classic mechanism for executing containment, as stated in the famous 'X' article, was "the adroit and vigilant application of counter-force at a series of constantly shifting geographical and political points," a task that would seem to have demanded a rather extensive network of allies and bases.[7]

In the end, though, the major thrust of containment a la Kennan was against alliances as primary tools of American national security policy. On one level, this was a result of Kennan's own character and philosophical cast of mind. As his refusal to write out a comprehensive statement of containment indicates, Kennan preferred a "particularist" rather than a "universalist" approach to foreign policy;[8] he was extremely doubtful of "the ability of men to define hypothetically in any useful way, by means of general and legal phraseology, future situations which no one could really imagine or envisage."

> I had little confidence in the value of written treaties of alliance generally. I had seen too many instances in which they had been forgotten, or disregarded, or found to be irrelevant, or distorted for ulterior purposes when the chips were down.[9]

Then, too, the author of containment was a thoroughgoing elitist who imputed as little moral as political value to areas outside the five major centers of industrial power.[10] Kennan worried that if the United States started creating a structure of anti-Russian alliances, there would be "no logical stopping point until that system has circled the globe and has embraced all the non-communist countries of Europe, Asia, and Africa."[11] Alliances, in other words, would wind up associating America with the *hoi polloi* of the world, areas and peoples that Kennan really did not believe counted.[12]

But there were more substantive reasons why Kennan was unenthusiastic about security commitments as instruments of containment. At its core, Kennan's reasoning put a great premium on flexibility; the United States, he believed, had to be able to shift its counterpressure to any region where the Soviet

Union might need to be contained. He argued, therefore, for small, mobile American military forces which, despite their need for basing at various points around the world, should remain free to strike wherever needed.[13] Added to this was Kennan's affinity (as noted by Professor Gaddis) for a "strong point" rather than a "perimeter" defense.[14] Increasingly impressed over his lifetime with the relative sparsity of American resources, Kennan argued that the United States must at all costs avoid spreading itself too thinly around the world and remain able to concentrate its defensive power on certain key points essential to protecting its vital interests. An extensive system of alliances might lock the United States in, depriving it of the maneuverability needed to meet the Soviet challenge wherever it occurred.

But Kennan also opposed alliances because he deplored their emphasis on a single *means* of containment. Never believing that the threat from the USSR was primarily armed force,[15] he feared that the use of alliances would militarize US relationships with much of the world, diverting allies' energies from the tasks of political and economic reconstruction so necessary for resistance to the *real* threats of ideological subversion and political infiltration. Having a strong proprietary interest in the Marshall Plan (which he had hastily left the War College to create), Kennan feared that an emphasis on military means would absorb US resources that should have backed economic and political reconstruction.

Finally, Kennan tended to downplay the role of alliances in a successful containment strategy because of his concern about how the existence of an extensive network of American security commitments might shape the future of the international system and the American role in it. For Kennan, the whole point of American postwar policy was to restore those areas important to the balance of power to conditions of economic, social, and political health that would enable them to resist Soviet pressure on their own; his vision for the future was of a world of independent power centers, pluralistic rather than divided between the superpowers. In alliances, by contrast, Kennan saw a formula for keeping great nations in tutelage under the United States.[16] Ultimately, he feared that a militarized policy would derail the third stage of containment, that holding American military power "tightly at every point to the borders of the Soviet orbit" would make impossible the negotiations that might lead away from confrontation and into a modus vivendi with a mellowed Soviet leadership.

> I . . . wanted to hold the door open to permit the eventual emergence of large areas . . . that would be in the military sense uncommitted, as between the two worlds. In each case, I was prepared to see us withdraw our military forces if Soviet power would be equivalently withdrawn and if we could look forward to the rise, in the areas thus thrown open, of political authority independent of Soviet domination.[17]

Alliances and the Practice of Containment

Reasoning on the basis of Kennan's overall approach to world affairs and American foreign relations, then, one is left with the ironic conclusion that the author of containment disapproved of one of the primary instruments used to implement his policy. Interestingly, Kennan's difficulties with alliances grew out of fundamental differences of vision quite close to those in today's debate over containment and its future. On the one side of this debate are those who see the Soviet Union as a uniquely expansionist state, driven by ideology to conquer the world for communism, a nation which understands only force and with which no settlement will ever be possible; on the other side are those who consider the Soviet leadership to be motivated by traditional security concerns, cautious and defensive in nature, and willing to respond to positive and negative inducements in ways that permit traditional diplomacy to operate. As the chart on the following page indicates,[18] people in the first school tend to see military force as the preeminent means of containment and to argue that virtually all areas of the world are vital to the balance

Two Schools of Containment

1. *What drives Soviet expansion?*
   ideology   historical insecurity, con-
                                     spiratorial internal rule

2. *What is to be contained?*
   international communism   Soviet state power

3. *What should be the condition of the balance of power?*
   US superiority is necessary   parity is acceptable

4. *What areas are vital to the balance?*
   all areas of the world   industrial areas only

5. *Is a differentiated policy possible?*
   self-confidence and psycho-   since its resources are
   logical credibility demand   limited, U.S. must differen-
   U.S. resist even marginal   tiate between peripheral and
   changes in balance of   vital interests
   power

6. *What is the primary means of containment?*
   military   political/economic

7. *How persistent is Soviet expansionist behavior?*
   Hitlerian, total   abnormal, but limited

8. *Does the USSR have significant weaknesses, and how should
   they affect US policy?*
   definitely; should be   probably; can be used
   exploited to weaken and   through negotiations policy
   destabilize Soviet regime   to benefit stability

9. *To what kind of Soviet behavior should US policy be linked?*
   to internal liberalization   to external policies

10. *Is a settlement possible?*
    doubtful; negotiations are a   negotiations can work if
    trap for U.S.   properly handled

of power, whereas those in the second favor economic and political means of containment and contend that the United States must differentiate between peripheral and vital interests lest it overextend itself in a useless effort to stop the spread of communism everywhere. Finally, where the first school would link American policy to internal liberalization in the USSR and exploit any indication of Soviet weakness to destabilize the regime, the latter dismisses such policies as futile and dangerous, arguing instead that Soviet weaknesses provide opportunities for meaningful if limited negotiations which can be exploited by linking US policy to Soviet international behavior.

George Kennan, of course, was and remains very much of the second school and has participated in the public debate over containment during the past forty years from that perspective. He would argue, however, that containment's implementation has often been in the hands of officials of the first school, who have transformed alliances from temporary expedients into fixed elements in the diplomatic firmament: "what was conceived as an instrument became, little by little, an end in itself."[19] In that judgment Kennan is broadly accurate, but alliances are actually an adaptable instrument of policy that can be used to support either view of containment. In fact, one can identify at least three major periods of alliance creation in American diplomacy since World War II, distinguishing each according to the motives which impelled policymakers at the time, the kinds of nations involved, and the characteristics of the resulting relationships. Although Kennan opposed each group of alliances more strenuously than the last, it is worth examining these alliances in some detail to see which concept of containment they were intended to further and what can be said of their success.

The Truman-Acheson Alliances

Most of the first postwar system of American alliances should have had some chance of receiving Kennan's approval.[20] He had always maintained that to be effective, alliances must reflect "the cultivation of solidarity with other like-minded nations" and be based on a "real community of interest and outlook."[21] These conditions, the North Atlantic Treaty of 1949 and the Japan and ANZUS (Australia, New Zealand, and the United States) treaties of 1951 certainly fulfilled. Moreover, the Truman-Acheson alliances were specifically designed to achieve Kennan's first stage of containment, the protection of non-communist centers of world industrial capacity. They were, in fact, the considered and deliberate products of the broader shifts in American foreign policy that were taking place as the nation came to grips with Soviet hostility and adjusted its occupation policies in Germany and Japan accordingly.

The North Atlantic Treaty, for example, resulted from a European effort to involve the United States in the containment of a rehabilitated Germany when it became clear that that nation would have to be rebuilt quickly if Europe were to resist Soviet pressures.[22] In 1949, officials of the Truman administration were willing to give an American guarantee of European security, not primarily because they considered that guarantee necessary for deterrent purposes but because of its psychological value in maintaining the self-confidence Europe needed to continue with its economic and political rehabilitation. Kennan grudgingly agreed with this rationale but still could not bring himself to approve the treaty, in spite of his belief that the Europeans were America's "real and natural allies."[23] His main objections were the familiar ones: that the alliance would militarize the relationship with Europe, diverting local resources from economic reconstruction, and that it would freeze East-West divisions, preventing the kind of Soviet-American settlement he hoped for. In fact, Kennan argued that the European community should be strictly continental in scope so the admission of Eastern European states would be easier, and that Greece and Turkey should be kept out of NATO so the USSR would not feel encircled by the alliance. The only compact he favored the United States joining was a "world-trading, maritime bloc" including the Canadians, the British, and certain Commonwealth, Iberian, and Scandinavian countries, based on a single currency and destined for eventual federation.[24] This association apparently would have had no military character at all.

In the end, of course, Kennan's fears of NATO's long-term development turned out to be reasonably accurate. When, in 1950, North Korea's attack on South Korea seemed to demonstrate that the Soviets really might begin a third world war, NATO was transformed from a political, confidence-building measure into an alliance in being with substantial numbers of US troops and an organization headed by an American military commander. Kennan believed there was no need for NATO as a military deterrent; he remained certain that the Russians "had no idea of using regular military strength against us."[25] And when, in 1954, the European Defense Community failed and Britain moved to rearm West Germany as a member of NATO, Kennan strongly objected for the same reasons.[26]

In the Far East, the Japanese, Philippine, and ANZUS alliances were the results of similar megatrends in American policy. Prior to the Korean conflict, the United States was moving deliberately toward a Japanese peace treaty that would (as in the case of Germany) bring that nation into the Western camp. But the Truman administration, oriented to a Europe-first strategy and convinced that European commitments were all it could afford to support, was not interested in a NATO-like pact for the Pacific until the Korean conflict seemed to demonstrate the urgency of security guarantees.[27] When, in early 1951, John Foster Dulles canvassed opinion in the Pacific region on an early and lenient Japanese peace treaty, he found that the Philippines, Australia, and New Zealand demanded US commitments as protection against a rearmed Japan.[28] Indeed, those nations refused to enter into a multilateral pact with their recent enemy, with the result that the three treaties still in force were signed separately in mid-1951.[29]

In 1948, George Kennan had written that Japan and the Philippines were essential "cornerstones of a Pacific security system,"[30] but by 1951 he had found reasons to dissent from all three Pacific treaties. In his *Memoirs,* Kennan argues that the evident determination of the United States to keep its military forces in Japan and bring that nation into the Western alliance system was "among the various considerations that might have impelled Stalin to authorize" the North Korean attack.[31] Before the war in Korea, he had hoped that the United States "would eventually be able to arrive at some general understanding with the Russians, relating to the security of the northwestern Pacific area," which would have made permanent stationing of US troops in Japan "unnecessary."[32] Once the Korean War was underway, Kennan urged the United States to offer the Russians demilitarization and neutralization of both Japan and Korea as quid pro quo for a peace settlement. He felt that it would be "unnatural" for the United States permanently to hold the line in Korea, and that mutual demilitarization of Northeast Asia could be enforced by the kind of distant striking power he advocated for the American military.[33]

Those on the opposite side of today's containment debate, it can be safely assumed, would have considered Kennan's hopes for reconciliation unrealistic and his dismissal of the military threat naive and dangerous. Doubtless, they would have applauded both the formation of the Atlantic and Pacific alliances and the transformation of NATO into a deterrent force in being, regretting only that the Alliance never in subsequent years armed itself sufficiently. And in fact, by the mid-1970s Kennan himself apparently came to support both the NATO and the Japanese alliances. Although he does not endorse them explicitly, he wrote positively of the two relationships in *The Cloud of Danger,* a book otherwise filled with what his opponents in the debate would consider calls for American retreat. The book's section on Europe, for example, endorses an increase in American conventional capacity in Europe and concludes with the statement that the American stake in European security is "one of the very few really vital interests this country possesses . . .; [I] would rather see us concentrate our efforts [there] . . . than waste them on a thousand peripheral efforts [*sic*] in other parts

of the world."[34] In the same book, Kennan recommends continued close American ties with the Japanese on the slightly different grounds that Japan's great industrial power is "so tremendous a factor in world affairs" that the United States dare not
risk its alienation. "Left to themselves," he warns, "the Japanese . . . would have to give a wholly different value to their relations with their great mainland neighbors; and we could never
be sure where these new relationships would find their end-
ing."[35] While these reconsiderations may simply be the result of
20/20 hindsight or the recognition that wrecking established alliances would have quite different effects than not creating them
in the first place, they also reflect Kennan's original concerns
regarding the essential balance of power and a community of interests, thereby suggesting that his original opposition to the
NATO and Pacific treaties was more tactical than substantive.

Indeed, after some 35 years of experience with this first
group of American alliances it is difficult not to appreciate their
contribution to either vision of containment. Even those who believe that there is no serious Soviet military threat to deter can
do little more than dismiss these arrangements as wasteful on
the margins; Kennan was wrong in fearing that they would spur
military buildups that would impede economic recovery in
Europe, Japan, or the ANZUS nations. Nor have they made it
impossible to negotiate with the Russians, for example, about
European security. Indeed, one could argue that the strength of
NATO during the 1950s and 1960s made possible the 1971 Berlin settlements and the Helsinki negotiations which eventually
brought an end to successive Cold War crises in Europe—ironically by legitimizing rather than transcending the East-West division of the continent.

At the same time, the positive services of these alliances
have not been insignificant. They have provided the framework
for defense relationships among the world's leading free countries, helping (as Kennan eventually acknowledged) to protect
these major weights in the world balance of power. For those to
the right in the debate, who believe that the military threat from

the East is real, the alliances may well seem to have provided just the aggregation of military force necessary to deter attack. Those who contend that controversies within these alliances— such as the various NATO crises over nuclear forces or the current US rift with New Zealand over port visits—serve only to demonstrate collective weakness are making an argument akin to that of a patient who rejects all medication on the grounds that nothing can provide a total cure. Even less convincing is the argument that disputes on matters other than defense (such as that with Japan over trade) should cause us to act in ways that would jeopardize the security benefits these alliances provide. In short, although one cannot with certainty predict what would have happened had the Truman-Acheson system of alliances not been created, it would seem hard for those on either side of the contemporary debate not to judge those alliances successful as instruments of containment and worth sustaining for the future.

The Eisenhower-Dulles Alliances

It is doubtful that similar statements could be made about the second group of US postwar alliances, those negotiated by Secretary of State Dulles during the Eisenhower years (including the Taiwan and South Korean alliances, SEATO, and CENTO). Though these also were treaty alliances with superficial resemblances to NATO, they joined the United States to countries with whom it hardly shared a great complementarity of interests. Nor were these relatively weak, developing states intrinsically important to the world balance of power as Kennan defined it, although in the perfervid logic of the height of the Cold War they were made to seem so. Perhaps most important, the Dulles alliances were anything but deliberate manifestations of an overall strategy. For Dulles, some would argue, tactics all but replaced strategy as a guide to policy.[36]

In a sense, of course, one could see the Dulles alliance system as perfecting the containment of the USSR around its perimeter begun in the Truman years, an idea quite foreign to the "strong point" defense preferred by Kennan. Through his alliances, Dulles connected NATO with the Pacific defenses he had earlier negotiated, politically by tying the developed European and Pacific powers into SEATO and CENTO, and geographically by completing the arc of allies from South Korea, Taiwan, and the four nations of Indochina through Pakistan, to Iran, Iraq, and Turkey. But if Dulles had a strategy, it was massive retaliation, the effort to get more bang for the buck by substituting centralized nuclear power for dispersed conventional forces. And, upon close inspection, the alliances he created appear to have been tactical responses to the failure of that strategy—last-minute, crisis-driven efforts to make credible a deterrent threat that otherwise could hardly be believed.[37]

A Southeast Asian alliance, for example, was first conceived by Dulles as a prerequisite for US military intervention to save the French position at Dienbienphu. Months later, SEATO came to fruition as an American scheme to hold the line against further communist gains in Indochina after the collapse of the entire French effort and the negotiated partition of Vietnam at the 1954 Geneva Conference (the latter an outcome Dulles considered tantamount to appeasement and which he had worked frantically, though unsuccessfully, to forestall).[38] The bilateral alliance with Taiwan was signed during the first Formosa Strait crisis of 1954–55, which began with a bombardment of Quemoy just a few days before the United States and its allies met in Manila to sign the SEATO pact. Although the Eisenhower administration was deliberately vague as to precisely which of the offshore islands it intended to defend, the treaty's purpose was to dissuade the People's Republic of China from going too far in pressing its military case against the Chiang regime.[39] The alliance with Korea had been signed a year before in a somewhat similar effort to reinsure the precarious armistice which had just ended the Korean War, by making it clear (in a way the Truman administration had conspicuously failed to make clear its position before June 1950) that the United States would come to the Republic's defense in case of a second armed attack. And the Baghdad Pact, engineered by the British in 1955 as a way of maintaining their military presence and political influence in the Middle East as Nasser pushed them out of Egypt, was transformed by the United States into

CENTO after a 1958 coup in Iraq appeared to create a gaping hole in the "northern tier" containing Soviet penetration of the region.[40]

Collectively, then, the Dulles alliances represented a codification and reemphasis of deterrence, draping American protection around Third World states who could hardly be of material help (except perhaps with manpower) should a war actually come.[41] It appears that from time to time the Secretary of State harbored rather grandiose thoughts about a macro-alliance, linking all his pacts into a global structure which could maintain a precise perimeter defense against Soviet expansion. In *War or Peace* (1950) Dulles expressed admiration for the idea of a General Protocol under Article 52 of the UN Charter, a total insurance policy without territorial limit; and during the debate on the Eisenhower Doctrine he told the Senate Foreign Relations Committee that the United States might "end up with a . . . universal doctrine reflected by multilateral treaties or multilateral [*sic*] worldwide authority from the Congress."[42] As this last remark indicates, Dulles wanted to enhance the deterrent effect of his system with general congressional authorizations (such as the Formosa Resolution and Eisenhower Doctrine gave him), offering at the same time escape from the constitutional restrictions which had prevented US military intervention at Dienbienphu. But by 1959 the Congress was already becoming wary of such schemes, and in any event the idea of a single worldwide alliance seems for Dulles to have been more rationalization after the event than a conscious strategy from the beginning.

It is far from difficult, given what we have seen thus far of Kennan's views, to imagine what he thought of all this, or why. The Dulles alliances had none of the characteristics that eventually recommended the Truman-Acheson pacts to Kennan; and in the "incurable conflict between the ideal military posture and the goal of winning the political war" against the USSR,[43] the Dulles pacts had radically exacerbated the pro-military imbalance which he so deplored in Acheson's policy. Kennan spelled out the specifics of his disgust at what he called "the madness of universal involvement" in *The Cloud of Danger.* In the whole region east of Iran (including the Indian subcontinent, Southeast Asia, and the southeastern Pacific through the Philippines) Kennan could see "no vital interests of the United States anywhere," a condition he thought should preclude US "political involvement, military aid, [and] association as members of regional pacts...."[44] In particular, the United States should renounce its military relationship with Pakistan ("a matter which concerns intimately our relationship with the Soviet Union"), terminate its bases in the Philippines ("the original justification ... has now been extensively undermined"), reduce US representation on Taiwan to de facto status and cancel the defense treaty ("shabby .... but ... a step that will surely have to be taken at some point" in the developing relationship with China), and "extract ourselves, as gently and prudently as we can, from our military involvement" in Korea ("one of the two most explosive and dangerous spots" in the world).[45] As he put it in 1976, when he confessed to being "in a sense" an isolationist,

> I do not advocate that we should suddenly rat on NATO and abandon our West European allies. I don't even mean that we should do anything abruptly to curtail our commitments anywhere. To do so would be a new offence in its own right. But I do feel that we should not accept new commitments, that we should gradually reduce our existing commitments to a minimum even in the Middle East, and get back to a policy of leaving other people alone and expect to be largely left alone by them. We greatly exaggerate the hazards of doing so.[46]

It may well be unfair to impute too much to these views of 1976; they were not too far, after all, from the center of American opinion in those post-Vietnam years, and many of them found resonance in the policies of the new Carter administration. The moderate left of the containment debate today probably would refuse to follow Kennan on Korea after the experience of the Carter troop withdrawal plan of May 1977, or would feel that the Clark and Subic bases retain their importance to a minimal American military presence in the Pacific, or would argue that the American relationship to Pakistan must be considered in a new light after the Soviet invasion of Afghanistan. What is clear, however, is the predictive power of Kennan's original criteria for effective alliances. The Truman-Acheson relationships, reflecting a community of interests among like-minded states and supporting key elements of the balance of power, remain and endure. But most of the Dulles alliances are gone, overturned by world events beyond the control of American power or will, intrinsically unable to demonstrate their cost-effectiveness to the great bulk of the American people.[47]

Can one say, nevertheless, that these alliances were effective instruments of containment while they lasted? Is it possible that the very process of forming them provided some temporary deterrence, or that the local confidence they induced or the framework they provided for American aid made a difference in economic growth and political stability? Here the pattern seems mixed. Korea and Taiwan are obvious success stories, and some would argue that even the ill-fated Vietnam conflict provided critical time for the development of reasonably stable and prosperous regimes in places like Thailand, Malaysia, and Indonesia. But in the Philippines the American relationship may well have simply created the conditions for political stagnation, sowing the seeds of its own destruction. And in Iran the American embrace was obviously a long-term liability, whatever its short-term contribution to stability. Equal, if yet unconfirmed, doubts can be raised about Pakistan.

The Carter-Reagan Alliances

Those on the right in the containment debate would doubtless argue not only that the Dulles alliances were in their time successful, but also that their demise was a result not of any unsoundness of conception or lack of American power but rather of the political impact in the United States of views very much like those Kennan espoused. The third system of postwar American security commitments was negotiated in large part under the Reagan administration by those of this mindset. Interestingly, these new commitments are not at all mirror images of the kind of commitments Dulles negotiated thirty years ago; if they are creations of the right in the containment debate, they are also witness to the vast changes that have taken place in world politics and American power since the 1950s. They are creatures, in other words, not just of Iran and Nicaragua and Afghanistan, but also of Vietnam and OPEC and Watergate.

Geographically, like the Dulles pacts, the Carter-Reagan alliances center on the Third World, but in a much more diffuse and far-ranging pattern. After all, the possibility of perimeter defense has long been foreclosed by the reach of Soviet power projection forces and the Kremlin's success in penetrating the Dulles salient with proxies (like Cuba and the Vietnamese empire), allies (such as Ethiopia, Syria, and South Yemen), and even its own forces (in Afghanistan). Thus, the new pattern of commitments includes some refurbished old allies like Thailand, Pakistan, Saudi Arabia, Honduras, and Morocco, as well as new converts like Egypt, Oman, and Somalia. Central America and the Caribbean have a much higher priority now (given Soviet-Cuban penetration) and the Far East enjoys a somewhat lower visibility after the debacle of Vietnam, while the Middle East seems to remain equally critical even in the post-OPEC era. Broad congressional authority does not buttress this system, and although there is a plethora of US statements of support for individual countries, only the Carter Doctrine reminds one of the repealed Formosa and Eisenhower resolutions. No grand multilateral alliances are in prospect to rationalize this "system," which seems every bit as ad hoc and crisis-driven in origin as its predecessor. The only remembrances of Dulles' schemes are pale, proxy alliances like the Association of Southeast Asian Nations, the Gulf Cooperation Council, or the Organization of Eastern Caribbean States, enjoying only US support, not direct US commitment.

Functionally, these new commitments are also very different from those of thirty years ago. In most cases, being bilateral rather than multilateral, these ties are underpinned by no formal organizational apparatus. Lacking treaties, the new commitments are based far more than their predecessors on arms transfers and military training, economic aid, ad hoc diplomatic contact, and facilities construction or use. These commitments have to be highly discreet, both on the American side (given public and congressional skittishness about new commitments) and on the foreign side (since visible ties to the United States seem often to have destabilizing effects on Third World regimes). American physical presences in-country are austere, so the military power needed to back these new pledges must often be over the horizon or even held back home in the form of mobile conventional forces. In fact, when all these characteristics are added up, one can hardly call these new security partners "allies" in the traditional sense of the term; they are, rather, associates or "coalites," and American freedom of action with regard to them remains at a very high level. They are, in short, far weaker commitments than either of their predecessor systems.

If the Carter-Reagan alliances do not directly protect Kennan's major industrialized centers of the world balance of power, and if one rules out as impractical any perimeter containment of the Soviet Union, then it may be worth a moment to ask what function these commitments do fulfill. Although for most of these "coalites" direct attack is unlikely, the weaker Carter-Reagan ties might well perform a rudimentary deterrent function, given the superpowers' extreme reluctance to tread on each other's toes. Yet to value them for that function would require a very un-Kennanesque and intensely bipolar outlook which Dulles would have recognized as his own: namely, a belief that the balance of power is so finely poised that the United States cannot tolerate the extension to any of these areas of Soviet influence. Even so, there remain the tools of infiltration, subversion, and proxy assault, to which alliances have never been a very good counterweight, particularly in countries as unstable as most of those in this new group of security partners.

Perhaps, however, there are other purposes for these new associates. Two suggest themselves. First, the quest for the facilities and rights ("basing" is out of the question) that would be required by US forces in the event of their deployment to places of vital interest has been a major determinant of

American alliance policy since the days of Zbigniew Brzezinski's "security framework" for the "Arc of Crisis."[48] The result has been a series of what might be called "secondary" commitments, offered as quid pro quos for such access, to states
which even less than Dulles' allies share Kennan's solidarity of
interest and outlook with the United States, all ostensibly in order that the United States be really able to defend those states of
primary interest—a process Barton Gellman called "the unhappy
tendency of our strategic interests to have interests of their
own."[49] The other motivation, while apparent in outline for
some time, has only recently become obvious. It is the need,
under the so-called Reagan Doctrine, for relationships solid
enough to provide platforms for the supply of America's own
proxy warfare, whether conducted from Honduras by the contras against Nicaragua, from Thailand by the Cambodian resistance against Vietnam, or from Pakistan by the Afghan rebels
against the Soviets directly.

Kennan, needless to say, would have deplored all this. He
has never believed in destabilization, except perhaps by the sub-
tle example of a West measuring up to its own best traditions, a
possibility of which he has long since despaired. And as to the
impact of bases, he has argued that "no great country . . . could
sit by and witness with indifference the progressive studding of
its own frontiers with the military installations of a great-power
competitor." Yet, as he wrote of American policy,

> Year after year nothing would be omitted to move Ameri-
> can air bases and missile sites as close as possible to So-
> viet frontiers. . . . Time after time, as in Pakistan or
> Okinawa, the maintenance and development of military or
> air bases would be stubbornly pursued with no evidence of
> any effort to balance this against the obvious political
> costs.[50]

Even before the massive Reagan base agreement "buys" in the
Philippines, Spain, Portugal, Greece, and Turkey, Kennan was
outraged at the "tribute" exacted from the United States for such
facilities, arguing that his country should never put itself in the
position of paying "huge annual bribes as a form of hush
money" to keep foreign leaders quiet while the United States

retained installations they did not want on their territory.[51] For both these reasons, Kennan has urged American abandonment of facilities in Greece and Turkey, as well as those in the Philippines.[52]

Alliances and the Future of Containment

Although Kennan's imputed criticisms may not be surprising, it is remarkable how little contemporary controversy the Carter-Reagan commitments seem to have stirred. Perhaps, because they have not come before Congress as formal treaties, there has been no occasion for a great debate like those over NATO or the Dulles pacts. Or perhaps this set of agreements has been spared serious questioning because it seems a logical part of the widely accepted effort to restore American military power. Possibly the American people are not even aware that extensive commitments have been extended. What criticism there has been seems almost monochromatic, with isolationists and neoconservatives on the right joining liberals on the left to deplore the drain such relationships pose for American resources, to doubt these allies' ability to contribute to the common defense, and to worry about the long-run effect on American solvency.[53] Their solution is similar to or even more radical than Kennan's "pruning of unnecessary or marginal involvements and . . . paring down of America's commitments," with only a few on the right arguing for more security ties in the form of an "all-oceans alliance" or standing proxy armies overseas.[54] There is little questioning of whether alliances of this tentative kind can be effective as instruments of containment, still less discussion of what kinds of relationships might be best adapted to the security environment of the future.

Even to pose such issues leaves one gasping, especially at the end of an already too-long dissertation. On the one hand, one is tempted to say that the Carter-Reagan alliances are the best one can do, given the world of the 1980s; that the commitments they embody are an unavoidable concomitant of security dealings with the Third World, however marginal their deterrent effect; and that their drain on American resources is simply the price one pays to execute the Nixon Doctrine, in the hope that one day new "coalites" will become real additions to the West's deterrent power.[55] On the other hand, there is the nagging sense that so much instability lies between now and then, that weapons and facilities may wind up in hostile hands (like Iran's F–14s or Vietnam's Cam Ranh Bay), and that in the meantime (as Walter Lippman once suggested) the effort to contain the Soviets everywhere is forcing the United States into "dubious and unnatural" alliances which themselves impose great strains on the United States' relations with its natural allies of the Truman-Acheson years.[56] Who can believe that the Carter-Reagan alliances will last even as long as the Dulles ones? In fact, it may be that world conditions are proving Kennan right the first time, that until the developing world arrives at a greater degree of economic and political maturity, additional fixed commitments will have little utility as instruments of containment. Such, at least, are the dilemmas which history suggests attend the conduct of American alliance policy in a revolutionary era.

Notes

The author would like to thank the Carnegie Endowment for International Peace for supporting the research and writing of this paper during his year there as Resident Associate during 1985 and 1986.

1. Terry L. Deibel, *Commitment in American Foreign Policy,* National Security Affairs Monograph Series 80–4 (Washington: National Defense University Press, 1980).

2. John Lewis Gaddis, *Strategies of Containment* (New York: Oxford University Press, 1982), pp. 36–51.

3. Ibid., pp. 26, 29.

4. Barton Gellman, *Contending with Kennan* (New York: Praeger, 1984), p. 78.

5. George F. Kennan, *Memoirs: 1925–1950* (Vol. I) (Boston: Little Brown, 1967), p. 378; Gaddis, *Strategies of Containment*, p. 39.

6. Gellman, *Contending with Kennan*, p. 125.

7. Kennan (writing as 'X'), "The Sources of Soviet Conduct," *Foreign Affairs* 25 (July 1947), p. 576.

8. Gaddis, *Strategies of Containment*, pp. 27–28.

9. Kennan, *Memoirs* I, p. 408.

10. Kennan's colors in this regard showed clearly during his first trip to Latin America, where he found Mexico City "violent [and] explosive," was "appalled" by Caracas, found Rio "repulsive" and Sao Paulo "still worse," and on Lima commented only that its dirt was "untouched" since the last rain 29 years earlier! Ibid., p. 476–79.

11. Gaddis, *Strategies of Containment*, p. 72.

12. Gellman, *Contending with Kennan*, p. 54.

13. Ibid., p. 120.

14. Gaddis, *Strategies of Containment*, pp. 58–65.

15. See Gellman, *Contending with Kennan*, p. 136.

16. Kennan, *Memoirs* I, p. 464.

17. Ibid., p. 463.

18. Many of the perspectives indicated on the chart are revealed by the authors of the essays in Aaron Wildavsky, ed., *Beyond Containment: Alternative American Policies Towards the Soviet Union* (San Francisco: Institute for Contemporary Studies, 1983).

19. Kennan, *Memoirs* I, p. 428.

20. I have left the Rio Treaty out of consideration here because of its very different origins and purposes and because many of its characteristics belong more to the Dulles system than the Truman one.

21. Gellman, *Contending with Kennan,* pp. 125, 34.

22. See Alan K. Henrikson, "The Creation of the North Atlantic Alliance, 1948–1952," *Naval War College Review* 32 (May–June 1980), pp. 4–39.

23. Kennan, *Memoirs* I, p. 350.

24. Ibid., pp. 454, 411, 458. Kennan has certain personal ties with Scandinavia, where he regularly spends his summers in Norway.

25. Ibid., pp. 407–08.

26. Ibid., p. 446.

27. Townsend Hoopes, *The Devil and John Foster Dulles* (London: Andre Deutsch, 1974), p. 94. The administration refused to actively support Chiang Kai-shek's efforts in that direction, and the new NATO Council rejected the idea of a NATO-like Pacific pact in September 1949.

28. See David Lange, "New Zealand's Security Policy," *Foreign Affairs* 63 (Summer 1985), p. 1009.

29. Hoopes, *The Devil and John Foster Dulles,* pp. 105–09.

30. Kennan, *Memoirs* I, p. 381.

31. Kennan, *Memoirs: 1950–1963* (Vol. II) (New York: Pantheon, 1972), p. 39.

32. Kennan, *Memoirs* I, p. 393.

33. Kennan, *Memoirs* II, pp. 45–52.

34. Kennan, *The Cloud of Danger* (Boston: Little, Brown & Co., 1977), p. 127.

35. Ibid., p. 108.

36. Hoopes characterizes Dulles as a "man who went from the specific to the specific, without any enduring ideas to offer, and so susceptible to immersion in the twists and turns of his tactical ingenuity that he chronically lost his sense of proportion and not infrequently his sense of reality." *The Devil and John Foster Dulles,* p. 358.

37. The suspicion that the United States would not bomb Moscow if the communists engineered a coup in Iraq or infiltrated northwestern Thailand was in many ways an early version of the current credibility crisis in NATO, appropriately scaled to the lesser importance of the real estate in US eyes and the lesser vulnerability of the United States in the 1950s. But something had to be done about it, and alliance guarantees were Dulles' answer.

38. See the account of SEATO's formation in Leszek Buszcynski, *SEATO: The Failure of an Alliance Strategy* (Kent Ridge: Singapore University Press, 1983), pp. 1–42; see also Hoopes, *The Devil and John Foster Dulles*, pp. 202–44.

39. There is some possibility that Chiang's campaign for such a treaty, under way since the Korean pact and encouraged by the American military, may have provoked the crisis in the first place; and it is clear that Eisenhower used the treaty to restrain Chiang as he had earlier used the Korean pact to leash Syngman Rhee. See Hoopes, *The Devil and John Foster Dulles*, pp. 263–72.

40. While Dulles at first hung back from full membership in the pact because of his concern about its effect on moderate Arabs, the United States later eased into membership, beginning as an observer, joining the Military Planning Committee in 1957, and becoming in effect a full participant—indeed, stepping in to save the organization—during the 1958 crisis. Guy Hadley, *CENTO: The Forgotten Alliance* (Sussex, UK: Institute for the Study of International Organization Monograph No. 4, University of Sussex, 1971), pp. 1–9.

41. Gaddis, *Strategies of Containment*, pp. 152–53. Gaddis points out that Dulles' alliances actually extended US formal commitments to only four nations not already covered. Still, it seems puzzling that an administration so concerned with the limitations on US resources would have involved the country in the support of nations which could only be drains on the limited dollars available for defense.

42. Hoopes, *The Devil and John Foster Dulles*, pp. 241, 408. Indeed, after the SEATO conference, the United States seems to have intended to make the alliance part of a grand Pacific defense arrangement including Japan, South Korea, Taiwan, and the ANZUS nations in a NATO-type alliance; see Buszcynski, *SEATO: The Failure of an Alliance Strategy*, p. 42.

43. Kennan, *Memoirs* II, p. 141.

44. Kennan, *The Cloud of Danger,* pp. 92–93.

45. Ibid., pp. 92, 97–98, 104, 231, 111.

46. Interview with George Urban, September 1976, reprinted in Martin F. Hertz, ed., *Decline of the West? George Kennan and his Critics* (Washington: Georgetown University Ethics and Public Policy Center, 1978), p. 13.

47. CENTO is gone; all that is left of SEATO is the commitment to Thailand; of the bilateral pacts, only that with South Korea remains, hostage to Kennan's primary interest in Japan.

48. Zbigniew Brzezinski, *Power and Principle: Memoirs of the National Security Advisor, 1977–1981* (New York: Farrar, Straus, Giroux, 1983), pp. 443–54.

49. Gellman, *Contending with Kennan,* p. 41.

50. Kennan, *Memoirs* II, pp. 141, 143.

51. Kennan, *The Cloud of Danger,* p. 98.

52. Ibid., pp. 116–17.

53. Earl Ravenal, "The Case for Withdrawal of Our Forces," *New York Times Magazine,* 6 March 1983, pp. 58–61, 75; Irving Kristol, "Does NATO Exist?" *Washington Quarterly* 2 (Autumn 1979), pp. 45–53; Alan Ned Sabrosky, "Allies, Clients, and Encumbrances," *International Security Review* 5 (Summer 1980), pp. 117–49; James Chace, *Solvency* (New York: Random House, 1981).

54. Kennan, *The Cloud of Danger,* p. 122; Ray S. Cline, "All-Oceans Alliance," in *World Power Trends and U.S. Foreign Policy for the 1980's* (Boulder, Colo.: Westview Press, 1980), pp. 181–203; Charles Wolf, Jr., "Beyond Containment: Redesigning American Policies," *Washington Quarterly* 5 (Winter 1982), pp. 107–17.

55. Indeed, perhaps the economic growth of American-allied NICs in the Pacific has already obviated Kennan's dictum that only industrial centers can really make a difference in world power.

56. Walter Lippman, *The Cold War* (New York: Harper, 1947), pp. 29–30.

9

Military Instruments of Containment

Paul F. Gorman

I N THE ORIGINAL 'X' ESSAY, "The Sources of Soviet Conduct," George Kennan postulated containment as a means of affecting the Soviet mentality, and in particular Soviet *diplomacy:*

> On the one hand . . . [Soviet diplomacy] is more sensitive
> to contrary force, more ready to yield on individual sectors
> of the diplomatic front when that force is felt to be too
> strong, and thus more rational in the logic and rhetoric of
> power. On the other hand it cannot be easily defeated or
> discouraged by a single victory on the part of its oppo-
> nents. And the patient persistence by which it is animated
> means that it can be effectively countered not by sporadic
> acts which represent the momentary whims of democratic
> opinion but only by intelligent long-range policies . . . no

Paul F. Gorman, a retired US Army General, is Vice President for Program
Development at Burdeshaw Associates, Ltd.

less steady in their purpose, no less variegated and re-
sourceful in their application, than those of the Soviet
Union itself.[1]

But X also held out the hope that, in the long run, the willingness and ability of the United States to muster the moral and
physical resources thus "to confront the Russians with
unalterable counter-force at every point at which they show
signs of encroaching upon the interests of a peaceful and stable
world" would exert an even more powerful influence over the
Russian psyche, one which might finally lead to permanently
ameliorated relations between the United States and the USSR:

> It would be an exaggeration to say that American behavior
> unassisted and alone could exercise a power of life and
> death over the Communist movement and bring about the
> early fall of Soviet power in Russia. But the United States
> has it in its power to increase enormously the strains under
> which Soviet policy must operate, to force upon the Krem-
> lin a far greater degree of moderation and circumspection
> than it has had to observe in recent years, and in this way
> to promote tendencies which must eventually find their
> outlet in either the break-up or the gradual mellowing of
> Soviet power.[2]

Four decades have elapsed since X's views were published.
Kennan's more recent writings have expressed disenchantment
with containment on the grounds that the West, "honeycombed
with bewilderment and a profound sense of internal decay," pat-
ently lacks the moral wherewithal for persevering with such a
policy, and that there are now larger, more urgent demands
upon all nations than military confrontation—such as "an absolutely certain ecological and demographic disaster which is going to overtake this planet in the next, I would say, 60–70
years. . . ." Concerning the military instruments with which the
United States might pursue a policy of containment, especially
nuclear weapons, Kennan has written, in his *Nuclear Delusion,*

We have been putting emphasis in the wrong places. We talk of saving Western civilization when we talk of a military confrontation with the Russians—but saving it for what? In order that 20 or 30 years hence we may run out of oil and minerals and food and invite upon humanity a devastating conflict between the overpopulated and under-nourished two-thirds of the world and ourselves?[3]

And in February of this year, *The New Yorker* published a literate reminiscence of Kennan's in which he recalled that what he wanted of US policy in the aftermath of World War II was to pursue "containment"

in the sense of restoring economic health and political self confidence to the peoples of Western Europe and Japan in order that they may be resistant to local Communist pressures ... and then, when a political balance has been created, to go on to the negotiation with Moscow of a general political settlement.[4]

But my purpose here is not to enter the debate between the contemporary Kennan and X, but rather to inquire into present and future military requirements for counterforce as originally commended by the latter.

Containment and Present US Strategy

Containment is not a word prominent in the lexicon of modern US strategists, but the concept seems implicit in their formulations of *deterrence*. For some, Kennan's term may seem too passive, too much of a surrender of initiative; for others, possibly too aggressive, too intervention-prone. For example, a recent report of the Center for Strategic and International Studies, entitled *Toward a More Effective Defense,* states,

At the broadest level, U.S. military forces have three major missions: to deter nuclear attacks on the United States and its allies, to deter and, if necessary, defend against an attack on Western Europe, and to project U.S. military power where necessary to defend vital interests and support U.S. foreign policy in other parts of the globe.[5]

In the recently released study by the staff of the Senate Armed Services Committee, *containment* is not listed among the functions of the Department of Defense:

> In fulfilling U.S. national security objectives and in implementing U.S. defense strategies, the Department of Defense has six major missions, three of which are worldwide in nature and three of which are regional. The major worldwide missions are:
>   *nuclear deterrence*—essential equivalence with the strategic and theater nuclear forces of the Soviet Union;
>   *maritime superiority*—controlling the seas when and where needed.
>   *power projection superiority*—deploying superior military forces in times of crisis to distant world areas which are primarily outside the traditional system of Western alliances.
> The major regional missions are:
>   *defense of NATO Europe,* including both the northern and southern flanks;
>   *defense of East Asia,* particularly Northeast Asia; and
>   *defense of Southwest Asia,* especially the region's oil resources.
> While DoD has other regional missions (e.g., Western Hemisphere and Africa), these relatively smaller, while important, missions are included in the mission of power projection superiority.[6]

Similarly, Secretary of Defense Weinberger, in a 9 October 1985 address to the National Press Club on the topic "What is our Defense Strategy?" never used the word *containment,* but talked *in extenso* of *deterrence.* Secretary Weinberger described the "pillars of our defense policy for the 1990's" as—

- SDI and nuclear deterrence.
- Conventional deterrence and uses of force.
- A strategy for reducing and controlling arms.

Nonetheless, Weinberger stressed the continuity of the present administration's approach with our strategy since 1945, and in so doing, echoed X's aspirations for exerting a fundamental and benign influence over the thinking of Soviet leaders:

> What is our strategy? Deterrence for the 1990's: the safest, strongest possible deterrent.
>
> What is our aim? Freedom and peace, the protection of our vital interests and those of our allies at the lowest possible risk of nuclear war, indeed of any war.
>
> What is our hope? That over time, our determination to deny the Soviet Union any significant exploitable military advantage against our vital interests will persuade them to consider more attractive alternative uses of their resources and their energy. We have no illusions that Soviet leaders will be persuaded by our words, or by any short-term demonstration of our commitment. But we do believe that over time, if we have and use our firm long-term resolve to maintain a vigorous and effective deterrent, we can not only keep the peace, but move the Soviet Union toward *peaceful competition....*

Although our modern strategists do not use the word *containment,* their strategies and goals seem to embody the concept. What is defense of the Asian rimlands if not containment? We seek to deter, an essentially psychological objective. The modern parallels with X's thinking are plain.

As a matter of fact, despite some rather tense interludes, war has *not* broken out between the United States and the USSR in the years since X wrote. It is significant that only in Afghanistan have Soviet ground forces extended their control over people and territory where they had no troops in 1947; even in Afghanistan, it is possible to argue that their control is only temporary. But if US containment policies have worked in that sense, they have by no means influenced the Soviets to move away from their reliance on a massive military establishment supported by a top-priority defense industry. As Secretary Weinberger noted, the Soviets continue to allocate proportionally three times more from their Gross National Product than the

US government does for defense; they have been regularly spending upwards of 16–20 percent of GNP, we 6–7 percent. And in the meantime, the Soviets, through aggressive (and skillful) diplomacy, independently or through surrogates, and backed by impressively growing sea and air power, have established their presence and influence far beyond their position at the end of World War II. To use Secretary Weinberger's construct, the Soviets have resorted to not-so-peaceful competition with some modest success, notably in Cuba, Nicaragua, Peru, Syria, Ethiopia, and Angola. And although these successes have been accompanied by occasional setbacks, Soviet leaders have transformed Stalin's beleaguered communist homeland into a world power. The prospect seems to be for more, not less, of this behavior, and Weinberger's hope for a less militarized USSR seems no closer to fulfillment than X's.

Future Requirements for Counterforce

But what of future containment? As X reminded us repeatedly, containment is a function of *counterforce*. How should one think of the notion of counterforce in the waning 1980s and the 1990s? The answer lies in considering the sort of international behavior which might call for forceful counters from the United States or its allies, and then in anticipating the kinds of instruments we should have on hand to deter such behavior, or to react to it.

As recent public debates make evident, no aspect of defense policy is fixed or assured. But it seems likely that any future confrontation with the Soviets will take place in an era of essential nuclear parity between the United States and the USSR. This relationship forms the strategic backdrop, a setting we ought to be careful to preserve because it has reduced Soviet interest in armed action against the United States, just as Kennan predicted. In the second place, it was not the American militarism Kennan so deplores (if indeed such an influence were operative) which led to NATO, but the insecurity and historic anxieties of European allies. Hence, we shall have to maintain some forces in Europe so long as the Europeans perceive a need for our presence. In this respect, the relentless military buildup in Eastern Europe scarcely reassures the Western allies. It calls for continued efforts on our part to maintain a credible defensive posture, both to deter intimidating uses of such force and to maintain confidence within the Western coalition.

But neither an exchange of nuclear weapons nor a westward march by the Warsaw Pact seems very probable. What sorts of military confrontations, then, are US forces more likely to face? Both the United States and the USSR will probably continue to go to some lengths to avoid a direct clash. But neither power can expect to act militarily without engaging to some degree the interests of the other, and in that sense all uses of military force heighten the risk of superpower war.

The record since X wrote supports the contention that *low intensity conflict* is more probable that *high intensity conflict*. By *conflict* I mean the use of violence for political purposes. *Intensity* refers to the means of violence, and to the nature and extent of consequent casualties and destruction.

From the perspective of the United States, high intensity conflict describes the relatively unconstrained use of available military forces and weapons, including nuclear, chemical, biological, or other weapons capable of affecting large numbers of people or broad expanses of territory. Mid intensity conflict implies limitations on the use of weapons of mass destruction but assumes employment of conventional military forces and weapons in a given region with extensive destruction and heavy casualties among participants. Low intensity conflict, in contrast, refers to situations in which the perpetrators of violence resort to coercive crime, sabotage, subversion, terrorism, or guerrilla warfare, and the United States limits its military response either to direct action by its Special Operations Forces, to advising or supporting a threatened ally, or to positioning US forces to deter escalation of the conflict by third nations.

From the perspective of the assisted ally, this latter kind of conflict (for example, an invasion by neighbors or an extensive counterinsurgency campaign) may require the commitment of all its available military resources and involve extensive destruction and casualties; from its point of view, in other words, the conflict may be of mid or high intensity. Nonetheless, the terminology is useful for those charged with planning and programming the US forces which must implement containment worldwide. This is so because—

(1) Low intensity conflict is the form of political violence most likely anywhere in the world, and the roles which the USSR and the United States are likely to play, or to have thrust upon them, will probably pit them against each other on opposite sides of violent confrontations.

(2) US industry has moved over the past forty years from a position of substantial industrial independence to far-reaching dependencies on Third World suppliers of semi-conductors, castings, vacuum tubes, fasteners, and fossil fuels. During the same two score years, we have developed a new societal relationship with the Third World, especially with Latin America, as important to our future as was the importation of slaves centuries earlier. Therefore, low intensity conflict can engage US strategic interests in ways which Kennan and his generation did not have to contemplate.

(3) Congressional and public attention, and DOD expenditures, tend to be directed toward preparation for less probable, albeit more dangerous, higher intensity conflict. In short, we spend more seriously to deter mid and high intensity conflict.

(4) Low intensity conflict often requires distinctive material, or forces structured and trained differently from those for higher intensity conflict. We have not raised and trained such forces in sufficient strength, or maintained what we have in a state of adequate readiness, to constitute an effective deterrent against Soviet adventurism in the Third World.

(5) Although the United States has a consensus, or doctrine, for reacting to threats of high intensity and mid intensity conflict, we are sorely confused and divided over how to handle low intensity conflict, especially in the Third World. This lack of national policy probably constitutes our gravest weakness and is a principal invitation to our adversaries.

It is useful to graph the spectrum of conflicts, comparing their relative risks or costs with intensity (as done in figure 1).

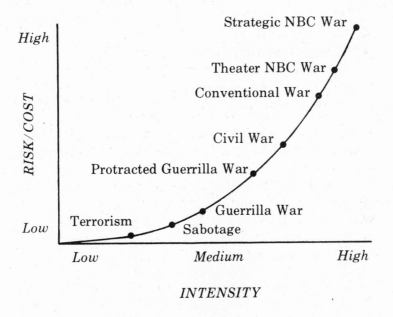

Figure 1
Spectrum of Conflict

For a Soviet, Cuban, or Bulgarian strategist, this portrayal should convey the message that if political objectives can be achieved by recourse to low intensity conflict, that is the lower-risk, lower-cost course of action. And in fact, their clear preference for low intensity conflict can easily be inferred from their past behavior.

The US strategist might more usefully plot conflict *probability* versus intensity, as in figure 2. Were the US national security community seriously interested in applying the notion of containment to low intensity conflict, it would have to deal

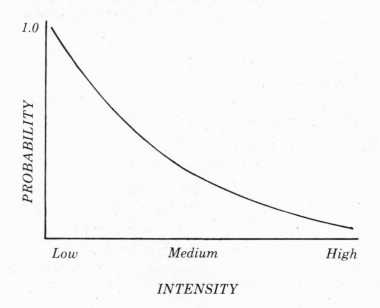

Figure 2
Probability versus Intensity
of Conflict

promptly with the problem posed by the fact that we have structured our general purpose forces for mid and high intensity conflict, assuming that forces so structured also have utility in conflict at the low end of the spectrum. In my judgment, this assumption is incorrect and can lead to tragic misestimates, even to strategic vulnerability—to flawed judgments of the sort that the United States made in Southeast Asia and the Soviet Union made in Afghanistan.

Capabilities for Third World Combat

To illustrate this last point, figure 3 lists military force functions in low intensity conflict, arranged on the Probability-Intensity

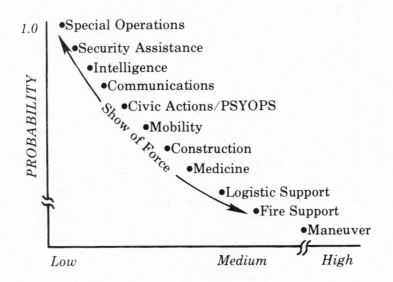

Figure 3
Force Functions

graph roughly in the order in which they might be called into play as the intensity of conflict increases. These force functions describe many of the military tools of national policy; the capability adroitly to perform them is *sine qua non* for future containment. Moreover, all the functions cited depend upon additional capabilities to project and to support forces abroad, and therefore assume intercontinental airlift and maritime power.

The broader strategic context in which these force functions are employed usually includes a "show of force" by our extensive and far-reaching maritime power, a demonstration—designed to deter escalation—that we can meet any challenge at whatever scale or intensity the situation may demand. A show of force is effective only when it is clear that the United States could, and might, resort to firepower. But we should be clear that air and land forces can also "show" our determination, and that in certain circumstances a humble engineer company is more effective than a carrier battle group off the coast.

Significant progress has been made in setting up special operations forces, and in training them for specific missions in low intensity conflict. The United States has been slower to establish such forces than the British, Israelis, or West Germans. Aside from the Ranger assault on the airfield at Grenada, US Special Operations Forces have fortunately received little publicity; but they have already proved to be useful to the Commander-in-Chief in a number of other instances, and they have therefore no doubt come to figure in the calculus of the Soviets. If we can resist our propensity to equip and train these forces for unconventional warfare missions in mid and high intensity conflict, and can focus them instead on antiterrorism and Third World contingencies, we will enhance our ability to deter the latter.

In most situations involving low intensity conflict, the US response will include security assistance. By strengthening our allies and friends, security assistance programs serve as an economy-of-force measure which allows the United States better to husband its deployed military forces and to avoid direct involvement in hostilities. In that sense, a cogent security assistance program could narrow opportunities for the Soviet Union or its surrogates and lessen the prospects for direct US–USSR confrontation. Unfortunately, the priority recently accorded to the Middle East has left few funds for dealing with the rest of the Third World. For example, the apportionment of security assistance funds to the American republics has, in the past several years, been about three percent of the worldwide total. The administration's FY 86 budget seeks to raise this amount to five percent, barely sufficient for our closest neighbors given the wholesale penetration by the Soviet Union into Peru, the bold Cuban-Soviet endeavor in Nicaragua, and the revelations of Cuban-Soviet complicity in Grenada.

The mention of Grenada raises the critical importance of accurate intelligence for low intensity conflict. If we are to gauge where to allocate our security assistance and how to support other US actions, we need timely and accurate intelligence. Such intelligence—evaluations of the reliable, timely information available to our several intelligence organizations—provides access and influence for US ambassadors and military officers. Overseas, knowledge literally is power. In addition to permitting sound US management, intelligence can be used for strategic or tactical support of an ally. Our superior means of collection will often be the sole recourse of a foreign government seeking to acquire an advantage in intelligence over an adversary, especially if the latter employs the clandestine methods taught by the Soviets or Cubans.

Unfortunately, the best as well as the majority of US intelligence units are manned and equipped to collect against Soviet targets, and are often inept in dealing with cultural and linguistic peculiarities of Third World targets. Designed to operate as part of a larger force in mid intensity wars, these units are often awkwardly robust and expensive to support, politically as well as logistically. Moreover, intelligence units with missions in the Third World are often issued older, less capable, more manpower-intensive equipment, which creates problems for host countries and US commanders who wish to minimize their visibility and maximize the security of the intelligence collectors. Insufficient DOD research and development funding has been directed at this problem, with the result that military intelligence which could be a decisive response to low intensity conflict remains only marginally efficient. Some recent research efforts with robotic collection and electronic transmission of intelligence, however, show great promise.

Communications are *sine qua non* for collecting and disseminating intelligence and otherwise dealing with low intensity conflicts. For democratic governments under attack, access to modern communications technology can be a force multiplier. For the United States, it is essential if the plethora of US government agencies in oversea country teams are to be assisted by intelligence and helped to act in concert with authorities in Washington and with each other. The drawback is that our better military communications equipment is often reserved for the "major contingencies" of mid and high intensity conflict, and readiness for these is cited in denying requests to support low intensity contingencies. The solution to this problem lies in making broader use of commercial communications, suitably protected.

Units capable of providing civil affairs support or conducting psychological operations have all but disappeared from the active forces. The Army, which possesses most of these, now has 98 percent of its civil affairs and 61 percent of its PSYOPS personnel in its reserve components. Active or reserve, these forces are conceptually and technologically obsolescent, bypassed by the age of television. Nonetheless, the skills called for in such units are useful in prosecuting low intensity conflict and could contribute to containment.

Whenever a Third World government faces an internal or external threat, it faces a choice between extensive mobilization of manpower or enhancement of the tactical mobility of existing forces. One of the first items for which it is likely to ask is helicopters, and helicopters are likely to be among the first items a US ambassador is likely to offer. But like security assistance, US military helicopters are expensive. US military trucks are no bargain, either. Fixed wing intratheater airlift might provide an equally important boost to mobility, but here the options are even fewer and more expensive—the services have no contemporary transport smaller than the C–130 Hercules, which for many countries requires too much runway and is too big, too expensive, and too complicated to fly and maintain. Similarly, we seem to have forgotten that in most Third World countries the population clusters on coasts and rivers, where a "brown water" navy built around small boats and landing craft would be useful. Again, the "brown water" capability of the US navy is at minimal strength and is outdated. Here, too, commercial alternatives, made in the United States or by other allies abroad, would answer the need.

There is a clear recognition in the Third World of the value of military engineer units, with the equipment and discipline to undertake construction tasks in remote areas where security may be questionable, or in a natural disaster zone where operations by commercial contractors are unlikely. And in any less-developed country, military engineers can dig wells, build water distribution and flood control systems, and construct the roads and bridges essential to economic progress. There is a concomitant demand for US expertise in organizing and training such units. Yet in our own force structure, 68 percent of Army engineers are in the reserve components.

There is a comparable demand for US military medics. Like our military intelligence, communications, and engineering, our military medicine is respected, even venerated, for its sophistication. Any Third World country which has a bloody

emergency thrust upon it is likely to find that its medical establishment is unequal to the challenge of providing first-aid treatment to the injured and evacuating them to hospitals fast enough
to save their lives. Most countries have never considered seriously the concept of a medical service corps trained and
equipped for the field. Here US ideas and techniques can exert
powerful leverage on manpower. It is expensive to recruit,
train, and season a soldier; his needless loss is an expensive stu-
pidity and a moral violation of the soldier-state compact. But
again, when we look for resources with which to help allies, we
need to remember that over half of our medics are in the
reserves.

If Third World notions of military medicine are outdated,
the approaches to logistic support found there are antediluvian.
Shortsightedness, limited managerial skills, corruption, and
simple lack of organizational know-how often produce such
dysfunctional practices as troops foraging on the peasantry or
commanding officers being issued operating cash based on
unverified muster rolls. Standard field rations, bandages,
batteries, boots, uniforms, load-bearing equipment, and rain
gear, which often could be manufactured within a given country
from indigenously produced materials, usually are not or cannot
be purchased locally with US security assistance funds. There
are, therefore, few alternatives to buying expensive US products
or continuing with traditional makeshift means. Here again, relatively simple production and quality-assurance technology, or
such inexpensive upgrades as minicomputers for material or personnel management, usually await a US assist. Using security
assistance for locally produced items would also create jobs in
troubled economies.

US combat power, fire support and maneuver, would probably be the last force function to be exercised in any low intensity conflict. There are exceptions, of course; recent events
show the usefulness of carrier-borne F–14 fighters, for example.
But the other measures cited above, if used in a timely and

judicious manner, should preclude the introduction of US shooters. Nonetheless, an American ability quickly to employ fire or maneuver should help to deter adventurism by the Soviets or a surrogate. US combat forces have, however, like the other force functions, been poorly designed for low intensity conflict. We need more light land and air forces, more "brown water" naval forces—all more strategically mobile and better fitted to support other nations in defending themselves.

Capabilities for Mid and High Intensity Conflict

One of the burdens imposed by a strategy of containment—or its contemporary equivalent, the broad spectrum deterrence described by Secretary Weinberger—is geographic. To use the Senate Armed Services Committee staff formulation, five of the six major missions of the Department of Defense involve either maintaining military forces overseas or moving forces abroad in an emergency. We are likely to deter only to the extent that we have the ability to generate force to meet threatening situations. Maritime forces can fill the bill in many of these situations, but there are others where we will have to put forces on foreign soil to do the job. Generally speaking, we need to think about five means for projecting force, which relate to force generation somewhat as shown in figure 4.

Forward deployed forces can be the most prepared to contain, but they are also the most costly in terms of resources or political capital. Pre-positioning supplies and equipment abroad conserves airlift and sealift and takes advantage of our relatively plentiful passenger aircraft. But it is expensive, because the predeployed material has to be sheltered and maintained carefully, and because we usually will buy another set of equipment to support training and ensure that units are equipped and ready for missions in areas where their pre-positioned gear may be inaccessible. Pre-positioning in ships at sea offers strategic flexibility but adds to strains on ports. Airlift can project force quickly, but is now and will remain for the foreseeable future a scarce resource, and airlifted forces will remain, therefore,

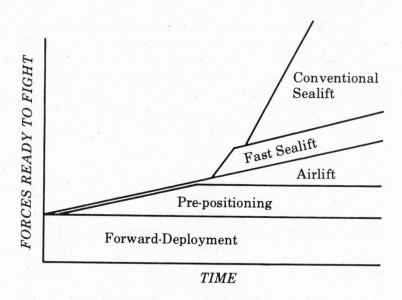

Figure 4

Projection of Forces

constrained in size and capability. Sealift, though somewhat slower than airlift, is essential if the force is large and the operation extensive in time and territory. Fast sealift refers to 30-knot SL–7 freighters, ships which may be uneconomical to operate commercially but which would be obviously advantageous supporting an expeditionary force; these are, however, few in number. Amphibious assault shipping is also relatively scarce, and slower. It is important to recognize, however, that enhanced transportation capabilities aid not only what the SASC staff refers to as "power projection superiority" but also the major regional missions in defense of NATO Europe, East Asia, and Southwest Asia.

For these latter missions (which entail deterrence of, and hence readiness for, mid and high intensity conflict), we rely on our strategic forces and our general purpose forces. It is instructive to review the relative budgetary emphasis these have enjoyed over the years since World War II. Picking the peak budgets of World War II, Korea, and Vietnam, and adding the Ford, Carter, and Reagan budgets, certain trends are evident:[7]

Percent of Defense Budget

Program	Fiscal Year					
	45	52	69	75	80	84
Strategic Forces	14	20	11	8	8	10
General Purpose Forces	52	46	38	32	37	39
C^3I	3	4	8	7	6	8
Air and Sea Lift	2	2	2	1	1	2
Reserve Components	na	2	3	6	6	5

The make-weight in defense budgets has been the general purpose forces program, which has had its ups and downs but has received consistently some two to four times the share for strategic forces. The growth programs have been communications, intelligence, and the reserves. It is interesting that although the capabilities of allies (especially the British) have decreased while US capabilities and interests (in Asia especially) have increased, budget shares for airlift and sealift have remained fairly constant over the years. But, of course, it is now possible to buy more lift per budget share than was the case ten or more years ago, given the cost-effectiveness of modern aircraft and ships. Some parallels exist for general purpose forces.

The same gains in efficiency can be seen in general purpose forces. The Army is more manpower-efficient today than at any time since 1945; fewer soldiers are in the active force for each combat division, yet the current division has something like ten times the firepower of its World War II counterpart and, given its much improved mobility, communications, and intelligence, is able to control forty to fifty times as much terrain. The

Navy has, in the past two decades, upgraded the fleet's diesel-electric submarines to nuclear-powered boats. A modern *Los Angeles* class nuclear attack submarine can search through 10,000 square miles of ocean in a 24-hour period, nearly ten times what its predecessor craft could cover, detecting enemy forces six times further away, attacking with homing torpedoes from three times as far or with antiship missiles from over the horizon at ranges up to sixty nautical miles. The Tomahawk cruise missile extends that strike range to 250 nautical miles, a far cry from the eight-mile reach of the old subs. During August 1944, as allied forces broke out of the Normandy beachhead, 30,000 crew members in 3,000 heavy bombers of the US 8th Air Force flew more than 18,000 sorties. Today, the same tonnage of bombs could be delivered, much more precisely, by 800 single-seat F–16 fighter-bombers.

We may be on the verge of an even more dramatic surge in force productivity. The combination of communications, intelligence, and long-range precise weapons may make devastating attacks possible on arrays of armor such as Soviet forces would present if attacking in Europe or elsewhere. SACEUR's Follow-on Forces Attack concept anticipates such technologies, and the ongoing NATO Conceptual Military Framework, approved by the national military staffs and the Military Committee in May 1985, provides a mechanism for coordinating the efforts of the alliance in this direction. In prospect are combinations of non-nuclear weapons more powerful against tactical targets like tanks and armored personnel carriers than even modern enhanced radiation nuclear weapons. And it appears possible to field such weapons in the near future without major budgetary implications.

But do these new weapons—for example, the Lance missile with conventional warhead, the Multiple Launch Rocket System, remotely deliverable mines, the TR–1 reconnaissance aircraft, the (German) MW–I submunition dispenser, the (UK) JP 233 runway cratering munition—obviate the need for tactical nuclear weapons or permit a "no first use" policy? General

Rogers has said that the new conventional weapons will reduce, but not eliminate, NATO's reliance on nuclear weapons:

> The price of an attack on Western Europe must remain the possibility of triggering an incalculable chain of nuclear escalation. This incalculability, this uncertainty, has been and will remain a vital component of NATO's deterrence.[8]

The same might be said for other theaters where a US confrontation with the USSR might take place.

Indeed, if containment is to operate on the Soviet mentality, and if we wish to contain in the future what X referred to as "Russian expansive tendencies," "incalculability" should be a major component of our deterrent posture across the continuum of possible conflict and the gamut of possible weapon choices. I, for one, would not define away by declaratory policy any unsureness in Moscow about our willingness or our ability to act militarily as our interests, and those of our allies, may dictate. One bit of advice from X, regrettably, remains current:

> The United States must continue to regard the Soviet Union as a rival, not a partner, in the political arena. It must continue to expect that Soviet policies will reflect no abstract love of peace and stability, no real faith in the possibility of a permanent happy coexistence of the Socialist and capitalist worlds, but rather a cautious, persistent pressure toward the disruption and weakening of all rival influence and rival power.[9]

Notes

1. George F. Kennan (writing as 'X'), "The Sources of Soviet Conduct," *Foreign Affairs* 25 (July 1947), pp. 575–76.

2. Ibid., p. 582.

3. Cf. Paul Hollander, "The Two Faces of George Kennan, From Containment to 'Understanding,' " *Policy Review,* No. 33 (Summer 1985), pp. 32ff.

4. Kennan, "Reflections (Soviet-American Relations)," *New Yorker* 61 (25 February 1985), p. 62.

5. B.M. Blechman and W.J. Lynn, eds., *Toward a More Effective Defense* (Cambridge, Mass.: Ballinger, 1985), p. 17.

6. US Senate, Committee on Armed Services, *Defense Organization: The Need for Change,* staff report, 99th Congress, 1st Session, S. Prt. 99–86, p. 2.

7. John M. Collins, *U.S.-Soviet Military Balance, 1980–1981* (Washington: Pergamon Brassey's, 1985), pp. 295ff.

8. General Bernard W. Rogers, "Follow-on Forces Attack (FOFA): Myths and Realities," *NATO Review* 32 (December 1984), p. 9.

9. Kennan, "The Sources of Soviet Conduct," pp. 580–81.

10

Flexible Military Containment: Forward-Deployed Expeditionary Forces

John E. Endicott

W RITING AS 'X' in *Foreign Affairs*, George Kennan called
in July 1947 for "a long-term, patient but firm and vigilant containment of Russian expansive tendencies."[1] As the fortieth anniversary of his article nears, it is appropriate to pause and reflect on the impact a changing international and domestic environment will have on containment.

Power Shifts Since 1945

Containment of Soviet adventurism came as the second of two major American foreign policies after World War II. The first centered on efforts to provide economic redevelopment assistance to allies and former enemies and to restore, as much as

John E. Endicott, Colonel, US Air Force, is the Acting Director of the Institute for National Strategic Studies at the National Defense University.

possible, a world economic system that had suffered from the effects of prewar protectionism. The Marshall Plan signaled a new path for victorious powers, and Soviet refusal to participate marked the beginning of the bipolar world that characterized the international order for approximately thirty years.

Early bipolarity, however, was more feigned than real, given US industrial, technical, and nuclear superiority. As late as 1968, Stanley Hoffmann wrote that the Pax Americana was secured by numerous assets, "capabilities for limited war to match those of the USSR but also ... a greater willingness to use them...." "Imperial primacy" existed, according to Hoffmann, only as an optical illusion that arose from the basic differences between Soviet and American power. One state was a continental land mass and the other an island continent. Primacy was, in the first place, temporary and, in the second, maintained only by a wise use of US defensive power from established bases throughout the world.[2]

Shortly after Hoffmann made these observations, Soviet power was blatantly used in Czechoslovakia under the guise of the Brezhnev Doctrine. Since then, Russian troops have seen action on the Sino-Soviet border and in Afghanistan. Soviet surrogates have been active in Cambodia, Vietnam, Angola, Ethiopia, South Yemen, Chile, Somalia, and Nicaragua; only in Chile has a communist movement been replaced after achieving power. As the above list indicates, Soviet power has tested America's will in many places, but the American response has been selective, according to the country's national interests. We have been following a policy of flexible containment, and doing so successfully.

The outward thrust of Soviet power over the past forty years, realized so far only in Afghanistan, has been accompanied by fractionization in the Soviet bloc and a general trend toward multipolarity in the international system. Sino-Soviet differences, lack of solidarity in the Warsaw Pact, the development of a more neutral nonaligned movement, and the general bankruptcy of Marxist economic development theory have all weakened a once cohesive bloc. Similar trends toward multipolarity can also be observed in the Western alliance, but such diversity is not nearly as threatening to its overall viability.

This gradual weakening of the bipolar international structure reflects relative changes in economic and military power among the states of both alliance systems. Our own failure to appreciate the development of significant constraints on US power was reflected in President John F. Kennedy's famous inaugural speech in 1961, in which he said,

> Let the word go forth from this time and place to friend and foe alike, the torch has passed to a new generation of Americans, tempered by war, disciplined by a hard and bitter peace, proud of our ancient heritage and unwilling to witness or permit the slow undoing of those human rights to which this nation has always been committed, and to which we are committed today, at home and around the world.

The new president went on to say that the United States would "pay any price, bear any burden, meet any hardship, support any friend, oppose any foe, to assure the survival and success of liberty."[3] He was, ironically, opening the umbrella of American protection at the very time when our ability to provide that protection was beginning to wane.

The assumptions of 1947, questionable in 1961, are not valid today. Nations formerly dependent on American economic aid are now stronger, in some instances, than the United States. Germany and Japan especially, but many other states as well, have developed first-rate production systems and now compete successfully with the United States in many markets. It is time to recognize their progress as a measure of our success, but it is also time to recognize developing trends in the international system that might necessitate fundamental change in the structure of American political, economic, and military arrangements with the rest of the world.

Although the United States may have lost its unchallenged primacy, that status was never a goal of containment. And the Soviets need take little satisfaction from the development of a "correlation of forces" more favorable to their interests. The growth of Chinese independence, the return of Egypt, Somalia, and Chile to the Western camp, the general criticism of Soviet activities in Afghanistan and Poland by the community of nations, and the failure of the Marxist development model have undermined confidence in the inevitability of their triumph.

Given such realities on both sides of the bipolar relationship, US policymakers must recognize that continued containment of Soviet outward pressures will only be possible within the context of a more flexible and innovative application of American resources. Force multipliers of the twenty-first century, be they high-tech weapon systems or nations heretofore outside our alliances, must be sought out and integrated into a flexible strategy of containment that utilizes American power as a critical, but not the sole, ingredient.

A credible nuclear deterrent will remain central to successful containment in an era of omnidirectional constraints. The ability to inflict unacceptable levels of damage on the Soviet heartland remains essential to providing stability at the highest levels of the conflict spectrum. But while dependent on this nuclear base, flexible containment will focus on the ability of the United States to project conventional power in defense of its vital national interests.

Conditions after 1985

We live in a fast-changing world. Making long-range projections from a single reference point has led in the past to such dangerous shortsightedness as the pre–World War II Japanese light tank (sufficient for operations against lightly armed opponents but overwhelmingly outclassed by its chief adversary) and the use of horse cavalry long past the introduction of the machine gun.[4] US defense planners will have to come to terms with major new imperatives if they hope to extend containment into the twenty-first century.

In some respects, however, the world of tomorrow will *not* change. The Russians will continue to pursue the policy of indefinite expansion which has been their hallmark since even before 1917. In seeking to enlarge its empire, the USSR will continue to use force aggressively—conventional force, terrorism, proxy forces, and subversion. In all events, the threatening menace of nuclear weapons will remain just over the horizon.

As we approach the twenty-first century, several factors will have increasing impact on our ability to assure future containment of the Soviet Union. First are interlocking economic dependencies. States within the Western alliance are less and less able individually to build and maintain the industrial production base necessary for national defense. EEC nations experienced these constraints early in the aerospace industry and created various consortia (e.g., for Toronado production) to pool expertise and share expenses. In other areas (including shipping, machine tools, and electronics, to mention only a few) off-shore production is commonplace, and even basic industries, such as steel, are increasingly moving to the developing world. Access to key raw materials and energy sources is more and more problematic.

Second, demographic pressures will gradually reduce the size of the cohort of young men available for military service. If this occurs among friends as well as adversaries, a balanced reduction could occur. It is more likely, however, that certain nations—India and Vietnam, for example—will not experience reductions at the same rate as the USSR, the United States, Japan, or other members of the Western alliance. The PRC's cohort should shrink markedly as its population control programs take hold. Generally speaking, population trends will be placing downward pressure on the size of standing armies of the most significant actors on the international stage.

Third, moderate rates of economic expansion and the overall debt ratios of states like Japan and the United States, as well as Western European states, will maintain pressures to hold down military expenditure rates. The military will remain the lowest priority among China's four modernizations as that country follows the highly successful model of postwar Japanese redevelopment. Only a marked change in the threat environment would alter this picture of relatively meager military growth.

Fourth, however, great expectations can be held for scientific and technical advances. Significant breakthroughs in the cost of spacelift can be expected as transatmospheric flight is perfected and new materials make their full impact. Of special interest to the Pacific basin states will be the development of a hypersonic airliner providing rapid transportation between the nations of that vast area. The costs of weapon systems developed from these scientific advances will continue to rise and, particularly if SDI progresses, will increasingly cause a reconsideration of existing force structures. Moreover, not all changes resulting from the race toward the high-tech future will be hardware or force-level oriented, since pressures for innovation (and creative research and development regimes) may cause significant changes in societal structure in some of the more vertically organized societies.

Fifth, part of the scientific and technical developments, the information revolution will lead to significant breakthroughs in artificial intelligence, with great repercussions in command and control. This will be especially so if SDI deployment leads to time-sensitive strategic defenses for use against depressed trajectory SLBMs or as responses to attacks on portions of the system itself.

Finally, we must also be alert to the continuing growth of public skepticism within the Western alliance as to the meaningfulness of sacrifices for national independence and sovereignty, as well as the general lack of awareness in many countries of the primary importance of the balance of power in the international system. The growth of materialism as an end in itself and a reluctance to place national values above economic imperatives is a reality that, paradoxically, arises from the very success of nuclear deterrence. In addition, movements led by members of the scientific and religious communities call for the abolition of the very system that has assured the pax atomica.

If the above developments are likely to occur over the next few decades, what is their probable impact on the military and national security communities in the Alliance and, thus, on containment?

Increasing interdependencies must surely affect the question of logistics, especially prehostility stockpiles of key weapons. Increased emphasis on pre-positioning equipment overseas would seem essential to ensure minimum amounts of critical munitions and replacement parts. Greater stress on the interoperability of allied nations' weaponry and on protecting regional lines of communications would also be important. Offshore areas producing critical weapon elements would seem to deserve a greater US interest in their survivability than might otherwise be the case. Ultimately, questions of regional stability may increase American willingness to come to hitherto unpopular accommodations with powers that could provide stability, even at the cost of some of their neighbors' freedom of action; India and Vietnam are the most obvious cases. Given demographic pressures on Western states, smaller standing armies, greater reliance on reserves, and an innovative use of force multipliers (be they either weapon systems or hitherto untapped allies) would be likely.

Continued technological advance will likely return the defense to the role it lost when aircraft were mated with nuclear weapons and internal combustion engines with armor. Antitank, antiaircraft, antishipping, and anti-ICBM missiles will permit ground forces—lightly configured—to play a much greater role than during the past forty years. Unavoidably, the cost for these new weapons will place far more upward pressure on budgets than they can accommodate. As a result, manpower will generally be reduced to provide necessary funds (perhaps making the demographic trend discussed earlier appear to be less of a problem). The primary reduction will occur in active-duty ground forces, but naval and air elements could also be affected.

In essence, then, mobilization, reserve forces, prepositioned equipment and supplies, and weapon systems common to or interoperable among allies will be of increasing importance.

The need, especially for the United States, to successfully end a conflict before losing domestic political support should be appreciated—although the increased availability of nuclear weapons makes war termination short of the nuclear threshold increasingly problematical.

Forward-Deployed US Expeditionary Forces in Europe

> Perhaps ... the total-force policy and the commitment to maintain a long war-sustaining capability are an anachronism of a past era when a large mass Army was the order of the day. In any event, in an era of volunteerism, the willingness of the American people to support the armed forces and participate therein should determine the level of strategic commitment.[5]

The statement above reflects part of the complex problem facing policy planners in the United States today. On the one hand, our long-term commitment to the defense of Western Europe is increasingly difficult to man and almost impossible to reinforce, while on the other, we have added new commitments to the defense of Middle Eastern oil resources and the stability of Southwest Asia. Simultaneously, strategic necessity demands an adequate US and allied conventional response if we are to avoid using nuclear weapons in either theater.

Given these factors, the restraints noted above for the 1990s and beyond will be all the more important. The two years originally seen by Franklin D. Roosevelt as the period US forces would stay in Europe after World War II have passed twenty-fold. It is appropriate to consider alternatives that will continue to uphold our commitment to the independence of Western Europe but offer the US and allied governments more flexible methods for ensuring containment in regional conflicts elsewhere.

A forward-deployed US expeditionary force to be made part, if possible, of combined allied regional expeditionary forces would be such an option. A force of this kind would recognize the absolute necessity, in tomorrow's operating environment, of having the ability to reach contested areas with a force capable of stabilizing urban areas, oil fields, and air facility networks in order to allow the Western alliance freedom of choice and initiative in contests with state terrorists or Soviet adventurists. The ability to introduce significant US or allied forces into a deteriorating environment can induce stability and, more importantly, forestall capricious action by the Soviet bloc.

The heart of this concept is the recognition that US forces in Europe are in garrison status. Ideally suited for the demanding role of helping to defend Western Europe if a full-scale assault is launched by the Warsaw Pact, US forces committed to Europe sit, wait, train, exercise, and deter as do all garrison forces. As retired General Georges Fricaud-Chagnaud of the French army noted in his defense of the *Force d'Action Rapide,* "limited financial and human resources do not permit tying down forces awaiting to perform improbable missions."[6] The problem for US planners is the high cost in manpower and materiel of the fortress in Europe during a period of "further reduced manpower in the 1980s and 1990s,"[7] a cost that somehow must be moderated in light of widening responsibilities. To defend against the possibility of attack in areas other than Europe, some accommodation must be made, but in ways that are not destabilizing for Europe itself. That accommodation lies with the recognition by NATO allies that US involvement in the Middle East would be in the common interest, in line with the general thrust of the Harmel Resolution of 1967.[8]

Just what does this sort of "dual mission" envisage? Currently, American Army divisions in Europe are either "heavy" in terms of their armor component or "reinforced." As such, they require a great amount of surface and air lift in order to be employed outside Europe. Preparing for the dual mission would involve identifying an extractable core from each division, around which a somewhat smaller and lighter division could be formed. The 82d Airborne Division, which is slightly smaller than the normal US division (approximately 11,000 men), could serve as the model.[9] Each designated division would carry a basic ammunition load and a five-day supply of fuel and rations. Another model that demonstrates the concept is the French *Force d'Action Rapide,* an existing light force with great firepower using the concepts of mobility, high technology, and austere logistics support.

It was estimated that the movement of the 82d Airborne from its American base to the Middle East during the 1973 crisis would have taken one week.[10] Using today's lift capabilities, relocating light divisions from bases in Europe to crisis areas in the Middle East could take half as long, or even less. Heavy armor would be left in Europe, but expeditionary force divisions would carry with them the newest in high-tech force multipliers. Antitank missiles, drones, support and antitank helicopters, surface-to-air and surface-to-surface missiles, and the most modern artillery-delivered cluster bomb units would become the center of the awesome firepower such units would have to carry. Possession of shocking and staying power, without heavy armor, would be the hallmark of such forces. They could be tied to selected units in the United States which would be subject to immediate mobilization, requiring that the United States accustom the world to frequent, but limited or specific, mobilizations.

Non-US NATO forces would be invited to participate out of area, but their primary assignment would be to provide the required backfill for the American forces extracted from Europe. Heavy armor with American crews would remain in place to provide the stopping power required to match Soviet armor. Extensive training in combined operations between these elements left behind would be necessary to assure optimal integration of forces likely to speak two different languages. However, if regimental assignment techniques were completely incorporated into US Army personnel practices, long-term assignments with parent regiments could minimize disruptions.

The ultimate objective would be to structure a force that, because of its forward deployment and readiness, could react with the speed and ferocity needed to forestall cavalier resort to battlefield nuclear weapons. Through a judicious selection of logistic support bases, an interlocking network of pre-positioned depots could provide the necessary near-term supplies for such expeditionary units after their basic loads have been expended. Such locations currently exist to support the RDF concept. Indeed, this proposal would provide readily available forces to the Rapid Deployment Force for areas and missions clearly of interest to our NATO allies.

As an alternative to denuding NATO of American forces and undermining the entire fabric of the Western alliance, this concept would provide American and allied planners with increased responsiveness and ability to contain Soviet power. As Kennan wrote, the Soviet Union's "political action is a fluid stream which moves constantly, wherever it is permitted to move, toward a given goal. Its main concern is to make sure it has filled every nook and cranny available to it in the basin of world power."[11] US forward-deployed expeditionary forces would ensure that all the "nooks and crannies" judged in our national interest would be given the benefit of rapid and effective US presence.

The concept would also benefit the US Army internally. Grown accustomed to garrison duty in Europe, American forces have distanced themselves from the concept of the expeditionary force so useful during previous periods of our history. Thought patterns that stress new and varied missions would be beneficial from an institutional standpoint. Adopting the expeditionary force concept would also go far in showing members of the reform caucus in the US Congress that the Army is capable of innovation directed toward increasing American foreign policy options. Finally, the willingness of European allies to backfill the US divisions would demonstrate to American critics that the NATO nations are full partners in Western defense.

In a word, adoption of the expeditionary force concept would permit the United States and its allies to follow a policy of "flexible containment" in the face of growing political, economic, and security difficulties. It would enable the Western allies to place their forces where they are needed most. The dual mission concept constitutes neither a withdrawal from Europe nor an end to our commitment to NATO. It would, however, end a period of silent subsidy for our European allies that has effectively reduced our ability to respond adequately and rapidly throughout the world.

Forward-Deployed US Expeditionary Forces in Asia

The concept of flexible utilization of available military forces is not new to our Asian-based contingent. US Marine forces on Okinawa have long been looked upon as the Pacific *force mobile,* as have US Army units based in Hawaii. Naval forces have been stationed at various locations throughout the Pacific basin, but have maintained the flexibility warranted by that region's size.

Only one area has consistently received dedicated US military elements since 1950; that, of course, has been South Korea. The likelihood of conflict is much higher on the Korean peninsula than in Western Europe. The potential adversary, North

Korea, is entering a period of transition with the succession of Kim Il Sung by his son, Kin Jong Il. The level of volatility, which (as the Rangoon bombing incident of 1983 shows) is normally very high, will be even higher as the Asian Games, the 1988 Olympics, and the likelihood of new leaders for both countries approach.

Given such a charged environment, it would make little sense to adopt a declaratory policy incorporating dual missions for US ground troops in Korea. It would also be unwise to upset the delicate balance which seems to be permitting minute forward progress in normalizing relations between the two Koreas. However, it is only a matter of time until South Korean ground forces will be able to contain and repulse any attack from the North.

By the 1990s, then, US troops in Korea could be assigned an expeditionary force status along the lines discussed for US troops in Europe. This designation would only affect one Army division, but having such a force available in addition to regional Marine and Army units would considerably enhance US Pacific resources. Bringing this one division back to the continental United States would provide little, if any, cost advantage unless it were completely deactivated. If forces must be reduced, their continued stationing abroad places us in a better position than keeping them at home. The emphasis in a reduced military would be better placed on US-based reserve units, with skeleton active-duty structures, subject to rapid mobilization.[12]

Creation of combined, allied expeditionary forces in Asia should also be encouraged where objectives are shared among nations. However, political constraints are significant in this region, and it is likely that the range of combined opportunities would be somewhat smaller than in Europe.

By 1990, the Japanese force improvements envisaged under the *Showa 59 Chugyo* will have been achieved, with the result that Japan will enjoy significant defensive power. The SSM1 surface-to-surface missile, with a 100-kilometer range, will be integrated into a reorganized Ground Self-Defense Force, F–15s will make up a significant portion of the Air Self-Defense Force, and a significant antisubmarine capability will have been achieved by the Maritime Self-Defense Force. It takes only a little imagination to picture a Japan with enough defensive power to effectively deter or defeat most credible conventional attacks.

With such a secure base, the United States will be able more effectively to counter the Soviet Pacific buildup, principally centered on increased naval and air strength, the introduction of the SS–20s, and access to the Danang and Cam Rhan Bay facilities in Vietnam. The Soviet Union's ability to project conventional power toward Japan will be effectively thwarted by an integration of Japanese air power, the SSM1, dynamic antisubmarine warfare, and creative use of Japan's strong suit, high technology. Japan will possess the ability to deter capricious aggression while relying on the United States to deter nuclear threats.

The Search for the Fulcrum

Despite the developing constraints noted above, then, there is reason to look at the coming decade and beyond with optimism. By making relatively minor, but long-overdue, alterations in missions of US forces overseas, the United States can significantly enhance its ability to extend containment into the twenty-first century. By giving garrison units contingency assignments as expeditionary forces, the utility of forward-deployed US forces can be maximized.

The costs for such reform will come largely in the form of logistical support and non-US personnel needed for emergency backfill. Political costs should be minimal, since the plan would use hitherto stationary garrison troops. The US commitment to the defense of Western Europe and South Korea would be reaffirmed, as would the nuclear umbrella. Most importantly, a degree of flexibility would be reintroduced into the tools available to the policy planner.

Notes

1. As reprinted in *American Defense Policy,* 4th Edition, John Endicott and Roy Stafford, eds. (Johns Hopkins University Press, 1977), p. 63.

2. Stanley Hoffmann, *Gulliver's Troubles* (New York: McGraw Hill, 1968), pp. 17–51, as reprinted in *American Defense Policy,* 3rd Edition, Richard Head and Ervin Rokke, eds. (Johns Hopkins University Press, 1973), pp. 6–19.

3. President John F. Kennedy, *Vital Speeches of the Day,* 1 February 1961, p. 226.

4. Edward L. Katzenback, Jr., "The Horse Cavalry in the Twentieth Century," in Endicott and Stafford, eds., *American Defense Policy,* 4th Edition, pp. 367–70.

5. Kenneth J. Coffey, "Defending Europe Against a Conventional Attack: The Increasing Gap Between the Army's Capabilities and NATO Commitments and What To Do About It," in Bennie J. Wilson III, ed., *The Guard and Reserve in the Total Force* (Washington: National Defense University Press), p. 216.

6. General Georges Fricaud-Chagnaud, "Origins, Capabilities and Significance of the Force d'Action Rapide," unpublished paper, 30 October 1984.

7. Arthur L. Moxon, "U.S. Reserve Forces: The Achilles' Heel of the All-Volunteer Force?" in Wilson, ed., *The Guard and Reserve in the Total Force,* p. 105.

8. The Harmel Resolution of 1967 encourages Allies which wish to do so to cooperate on expeditions outside the treaty area, and use NATO facilities in the process.

9. Coffey, "Defending Europe Against a Conventional Attack," p. 312.

10. Fricaud-Chagnaud, "Origins, Capabilities and Significance of the Force d'Action Rapide."

11. George Kennan, "The Basis for the Containment Policy," in *American Defense Policy,* p. 63.

12. One must admit in any such scheme to utilize most of our forces overseas that there is a problem of manpower retention. With increasing percentages of active-duty forces overseas, the US military may or may not face pressures from dependents unwilling to spend a significant part of their professional lives overseas.

11

The Impact of the Strategic Balance on Containment

George H. Quester

HAVING COMPLETED FOUR DECADES of the nuclear age, we are also approaching four decades since the doctrine of containment was enunciated for American foreign policy. It is altogether natural for analysts to see important connections between the two, hypothesizing that the ratios of US to Soviet nuclear arsenals somehow explain the successes or failures of American efforts to keep Soviet political domination from spreading. The case is made here that the relationship of containment to the nuclear balance is very complicated, and that recent shifts to "parity" or "Soviet superiority" hardly suffice to explain the apparent opening of holes in our barriers of containment. Even the very origin of the policy of containment, in years when the United States alone had nuclear weapons and had just used them at Hiroshima and Nagasaki, demands some quite complicated explanations.

George H. Quester is Chairman of the Department of Government and Politics at the University of Maryland and a member of the International Institute for Strategic Studies and the Council on Foreign Relations.

Ambition, or a Limit to Ambition?

The most elementary question about containment goes to its very essence. Was this a doctrine expanding America's role in the world, or modestly limiting it?

Compared to earlier historical periods of American "isolation," periods when the United States was benefiting from a global balance of power arranged by others, the commitment implied by containment to holding the line against Soviet expansionism looks very ambitious. Indeed, if one thinks of the traditional American aversion to war and international commitments, the decisions required by containment were certainly even a greater departure for the Republic than Wilson's involvement in World War I. However, compared to the unconditional surrender just imposed on Germany and Japan, containment amounted to a major restraint and reduction of ambitions.[1] The United States had not been content merely to "contain" Nazism or Japanese militarism, to demand that German armies simply retreat once again across the Rhine, or that Japanese armies be withdrawn back to their home islands. Rather, the American logic in World War II was that there was no point to winning that war unless a politically democratic form of government could be established in Germany and Japan, as well as in Italy. In the Japanese case, this ambition was admirably served by the sudden US monopoly of nuclear weapons; the message of Hiroshima and Nagasaki was that Japanese cities would be destroyed one by one unless Japan surrendered and submitted to the establishment of free elections. Americans had been willing and prepared to fight on into 1947 or 1949 to impose this kind of surrender on Tokyo, so the atomic bomb came as a pleasant surprise for most Americans, facilitating the surrender in a shorter time and at lower cost. If Americans were willing to go to such lengths to impose political democracy in Japan and Western Germany (in retrospect, with great success—despite all the cliches about how the "American model" cannot be transplanted abroad), should we not have expected much more ambition about imposing free elections on Warsaw and Bucharest, or perhaps even on Moscow?

In short, which of the following two is the proper question: "Why did we do as much as containment?" or "Why did we settle for as little as containment?" And directly relevant to the theme of this paper, what role did the state of the nuclear balance play in whatever change occurred?

Kennan's Own Perspective

Our puzzle on how "containment" is to be differentiated from alternative foreign policies is closely linked to the continuing question of what George F. Kennan himself meant by the word, and whether his meaning was somehow immediately misinterpreted by the American government and people.

Various interpreters of Kennan's thinking[2] (and indeed Kennan's own retrospective interpretation of what he meant[3]) suggest that containment was not intended to be a radical alteration of American foreign policy, that the doctrine did not require manning a perimeter around the globe to hold in Soviet power. In this view, containment was not very different from the balance of power diplomacy which had been second nature to Britain in the nineteenth century, a policy which watched for threats from abroad and sought to check them by building up other rival power centers.

Just as Britain would build up France when Spain was too powerful, and Spain when France was too powerful, so the United States would want to build up Western Europe now that the Soviet Union had become too powerful. Just as Britain would never have allowed France or Spain to swallow too much of the Continent's sources of economic and military power (lest the result pose a threat to England itself), so the United States would work to keep Western Europe from coming under Moscow's control. Containment, by this interpretation, was simply a ringing of an alarm bell within a traditional alarm system, an identification of a new direction of threat. Moscow, in particular, now needed to be "contained," or kept from becoming too powerful, just as other threats had to be checked or contained in the past.

But a considerably different view of the uniqueness of Kennan's message might have seen it as instead proposing a new and necessary alternative to the old balance of power.[4] Since the older major states (Germany, Japan, Britain, and France) had become so weakened by World War II, it was now necessary for the United States actively to man the frontiers against the menace to American interests. Since more than American interests were threatened—indeed, communism threatened all political democracy around the globe (as did the earlier spread of fascism)—many supporters and critics of Kennan's containment message saw it as a call for a uniquely active, continuous, and multifaceted American involvement in world affairs. The balance of power formulation promised some rest period, when inherent checks and balances were operating, and thus seemed a moderate commitment of American energies. But this new formulation of containment offered little opportunity for rest and demanded more continuous commitment of resources.

The recent history of international politics had involved two states, Nazi Germany and Imperial Japan, which apparently would never give up hopes of conquest and could not be checked short of war. A power-politics view of Kennan's thinking would characterize them as unusual and special threats to other nations' vital interests that had required total defeat rather than a mere cutting down in size. Kennan's analysis of the Soviet Union was that no such total defeat would be needed to keep Moscow from attacking the outside world, that the USSR was less threatening in practical terms than the Axis powers had been.

Yet was the only reason for pursuing the unconditional surrender of Germany and Japan the likelihood of further aggression from these powers? After Germany had been driven back to the Rhine again, and after the Japanese had lost even Okinawa, was it not plausible that Hitler or the Japanese Army would have been content to be contained for a while? As suggested earlier, was it the obnoxious internal nature of the Nazi and Japanese regimes, rather than the prospect of fresh aggression in 1946 or 1947, that had made the Allies ready to go further? Or was it instead a fear in Washington that Hitler or the Japanese might soon come into possession of nuclear weapons which led to the demand for unconditional surrender and a total territorial occupation? But if this was the reason to go beyond the dictates of the balance of power—even to destroy the balance by destroying Germany and Japan as military entities—what, then, of the fact that Stalin would get atomic bombs sooner or later, and that the West had to look forward to this precisely as Kennan was composing his analysis?

Pre-1949: "Why Did We Settle for Containment?"

Anyone trying to explain the ups and downs of containment by the state of the nuclear balance thus encounters one problem right at the outset. If we consider the containment doctrine as an embodiment of restraint, it can hardly be explained by nuclear factors, for the United States was as safe against nuclear retaliation in 1947 as in 1945. A few years later, by 1949 to be exact, the nuclear monopoly would be definitively ended; but the limits of the containment doctrine at its conception have to be traced to some form of discouragement other than "mutual assured destruction." If Hitler had possessed nuclear weapons, would not the United States have had to give up its goal of unconditional surrender for something more like containment? Conversely, since Stalin did not have nuclear weapons in 1946, why was containment embraced rather than something more ambitious? Why, in other words, did Kennan seem to endorse a different treatment for the USSR than for Germany and Japan?

Kennan's analysis at the time was tied importantly to his sense of the unwillingness of Americans to pay the prices and make the sacrifices for any venture in international politics. His analysis does not seem to entertain the possibility that the new nuclear arsenal could make a war with the Soviet Union as inexpensive for the United States as had been the last week of World War II against Japan. Utterly repulsed by the damage conventional bombings had done to cities like Hamburg and Dresden, Kennan considered nuclear weapons so destructive as to be useless for political or even military purposes, justifiable only to deter the use of similar weapons against the United States.[5] His analysis thus was that the US nuclear monopoly did not offer any special opportunities; i.e., he accepted restraints on US behavior at the time when the Soviets had no nuclear weapons that the rest of us might have accepted, with resignation, only after the Soviets acquired them. (Yet we all understand today that nuclear proliferation makes a tremendous difference. Was there ever a greater difference than that between the US-Japanese confrontation of 1945 and the US-Soviet confrontation by 1950? And why does Kennan's interpretation make so little of this difference?)

If the containment doctrine had been publicized by George Kennan in the immediate aftermath of the Soviet nuclear test, in other words, we would all today be analyzing it as a sensible and inevitable resignation to the limits imposed on US foreign policy by a totalitarian dictator's ability to destroy American cities. In military terms, containment makes perfect sense when a dictator already has nuclear weapons. He might not dare to use them when he is simply trying to grab another piece of territory; but he would have no incentive not to use such weapons if we were trying to depose him and free his people. But containment was not a response to Soviet nuclear weapons potential, or even to their imminence, at least as far as we can tell from the documents and the memories of the doctrine's drafters.

One might perhaps attempt to reconcile the nuclear issue with the inception of containment, to dispel the apparent paradox, by assuming some degree of temporal discounting in Kennan's views. Perhaps he was assuming that the Soviets would have the bomb very quickly, say by 1948, or perhaps he assumed more generally that any aggressive American policy (forgoing some kind of galvanizing Soviet conventional sneak attack) would take longer than Soviet nuclear technology to fall into place. If Kennan, subliminally or more consciously, was thus already resigned to Soviet possession of the nuclear ultimate-veto weapon, then his endorsement of containment might be regarded as illustrating the determining impact of the nuclear factor right from the start.

Yet there would be problems with this interpretation. The typical forecast by American experts was that it might be 1955 before the Soviets acquired nuclear weapons. The commitment and urgency of the original American effort to develop atomic bombs was based on 1940 forecasts that Hitler's dictatorship might be seeking such weapons. Should not similar forecasts about Stalin's dictatorship have called for attaching some greater significance to an interim that might also last another two or three years? Just as the American commitment to "unconditional surrender" and the total occupation of Germany was premised in part on worries about German nuclear capability (a capability then unrealized, or else America might have had to abandon the goal of surrender and occupation for the alternative of a "containment"), so the as-yet-unrealized Soviet nuclear capability might have amounted to an argument to move beyond containment rather than be satisfied with it.

Comparing Stalin with the Axis

Kennan would afterward contend that minor ambiguities in the wording of his 'X' article were to cause major misunderstandings and mistakes in policy.[6] He states that words like "counterforce" led to too much emphasis on military confrontation rather than non-military checks against the Soviets.

Yet in making these arguments Kennan seems to ignore the differences between conventional and nuclear military power. Once the Soviets had detonated their first atomic bombs, the drafters of NSC–68 feared the possibility that the Soviet bomb

might now check the threats and influence of the US bomb.[7]
Following (they believed) the logic of Kennan's NSC–20 as it
applied to the end of the US nuclear monopoly, they called for
substantial offsetting increases in conventional military
preparations.

But what, then, of the logical obverse of NSC–68, an analysis of how the United States could handle Soviet threats when
Moscow still had no nuclear weapons? Should the logic not
have been that more could be made of the US nuclear stockpile?
In his criticisms of NSC–68's derivations from his own premises, Kennan criticized all of the arms buildup, nuclear and
conventional, that was to occur as part and parcel of the implementation of containment. Yet this ignores the nuclear jolt that
NSC–68 was responding to.

Consistent with the retrospective interpretation that Kennan
was advocating not an expansion of American commitments but
their moderation, we must note his belief that Stalin could not
be as total or immediate a threat as Hitler had been.[8] Moscow,
with its Marxist-Leninist ideology and world view, was seen by
Kennan as much more cautious and patient. Firm resistance
might suffice here, where it had not sufficed for the Japanese
and Germans.

The differences between Hitler and Stalin were real
enough, and very much along the lines that Kennan outlined,
but one still wonders whether they were the sole explanation for
the American shift from "unconditional surrender" to "containment." Assuming that without the atomic bomb the United
States would have been expending nearly a hundred thousand
American lives storming the beaches of Japan in the months
when Kennan was instead analyzing the postwar Soviet Union,
was imperial Japan really so qualitatively different from Stalin's
Russia that Tokyo needed to be occupied while Moscow only
needed to be fenced in at some distance? Such reasoning suggests that the early history of containment was much more directly affected by nuclear weapons than Kennan tends to admit.

But for the bomb, we very plausibly would still have been fighting against Japan in 1946 and 1947, with the Soviets overrunning all of Manchuria and Korea, and with Moscow and Washington jointly worrying about the casualties to be incurred in an invasion of the Japanese home islands. Under such circumstances, would Kennan have gotten the same attention for his analysis of Soviet behavior?

The differences between Japan's situation and Russia's, each facing an American nuclear monopoly, still require more analysis than Kennan was willing to provide, for Kennan's 'X' article was in part an explanation of why the United States would not do as much against the USSR as against Japan. What could the USSR have threatened to do in retaliation if President Truman had ordered US nuclear weapons into action in response to the violations of the Yalta pledges? As Soviet cities were being destroyed and the death toll mounted from twenty to forty or fifty million, conjoined with some American demand for a Soviet surrender, no US cities could have been similarly destroyed. But the cities of Western Europe could indeed have been occupied by the Soviet army in revenge.[9] The rapidity of the US demobilization after the German surrender, along with the demobilizations of British and French forces, ensured that there would be nothing except Russian exhaustion to halt such an advance. The Soviets had also demobilized their forces after the Summer of 1945, but not nearly so completely.

By comparison, the Japanese already were in occupation of many Chinese cities (and had already done their worst to Nanking). The means of retaliation available to Japan were not sufficient to amount to a counterweight to the threat demonstrated at Hiroshima and Nagasaki, but the means available to the Soviets, given the easier geographical access to all of Western Europe and the advanced deployment of Soviet forces after the defeat of the Germans, were.

This difference in retaliatory options, which may explain the differing vulnerabilities of Japan and the USSR to the US nuclear monopoly, may also explain Kennan's failure to accord any significance to that monopoly. Yet the difference in these options is only in part explained by geography. In a far more important part, it is explained by American attitudes, attitudes which Kennan was taking as given rather than as something malleable.

Why, indeed, did the United States not maintain at least enough of a conventional defense of Western Europe so that some use could have been made of the nuclear monopoly? In part, Americans were tired of war, eager to get their sons home regardless of what this did to the combat effectiveness of the military units from which they were being released. They were unwilling to pay the costs of the necessary conventional auxiliary to a use of nuclear power.[10] But in larger part, Americans were incapable of launching a war against a state like the USSR, no matter how many pledges it had broken about respecting systems of free elections in Eastern Europe, unless Moscow first attacked the United States, just as Japan had attacked at Pearl Harbor. If Hitler had not declared war on the United States on 11 December 1941, it might even have been difficult for President Roosevelt to get the United States committed to taking part in the European war.

Such an American attitude, of never beginning wars but then fighting them through to unconditional surrender, is hardly explained by any astute commitment to the considerations of power politics. Neither is it explained by ideological considerations of the importance of supporting democracy against totalitarianism.

"War fatigue" thus has to be put into context. Almost no Americans would have guessed at the beginning of August 1945 that World War II was to end within the month. However fatigued they may have been with the costs of that war, very few would have considered any kind of negotiated peace whereby Japan would escape occupation and democratization. Americans were to disarm after August 1945 in the face of the Russians, but they would not have disarmed in the face of the Japanese if Japan had continued to resist.

Perhaps what was missing, in ways Kennan sought to correct, was a full awareness that Stalin's regime could be just as dictatorial as Tojo's had been. Yet the wartime naivete which had convinced some Americans that Stalin's Russia was really a government by the consent of the governed was rapidly fading. What was more crucially missing was any sense of an enemy's having brought a war on himself, an enemy's having started the war in question. Kennan indeed advised that Russia was unlikely to start such a war. And he recognized that the United States could not start such a war, even if one might have been appropriate from the standpoint of the balance of power or concerns about the spread of political democracy.

Changes in the Nuclear Balance

Everything changes, it is being argued here, with the Soviet tests of nuclear weapons detected in 1949. From that point, the question, "Why did we settle for as *little* as containment?" has a simple answer, rather than a complicated one. Stalin and his successors now have the means for destroying major cities of the United States in a last-gasp nuclear retaliatory attack, so we can never eliminate the Soviet menace in the way we eliminated the Nazi and the Japanese menaces. But at the same time, the question, "How can we do as *much* as containment?" becomes much more complicated.

Skeptics might intervene here to question the significance of 1949. Wasn't the United States still very much "superior" to the Soviets in nuclear weaponry, even after the first Soviet atomic bomb was detonated? If the lack of ambition in containment requires an explanation before 1949, would not some of the same puzzle remain as long as the US Air Force and nuclear weapons stockpiles continued to be far larger than those of the Soviet Union?

It is not uncommon for surveys of the evolution of the Soviet-American nuclear balance to settle into a phraseology of "superiorities," listing steps in the progression as follows:

American monopoly	1945–1949
American "superiority"	1949–1968
"parity" or "essential equivalence"	1969–1979
Soviet "superiority"	1980–?

Yet there are all too many misleading inferences that tend to be drawn from such a list, and even the historical pacing of this sequence can be questioned.

A first misleading inference is the implied next step of the logical chain, which an elementary sense of symmetry reveals as "Soviet monopoly." On reflection, it seems unlikely that the pendulum would ever swing out so far. Moscow and Leningrad will never be as secure against an American retaliatory attack as Washington and New York were in 1947 against Soviet retaliation (or in 1945 against a Japanese nuclear strike). Neither the worst-case scenarios put forward by the Committee on the Present Danger before 1980 nor the cases examined by the Scowcroft Commission in 1983, often labeled "the window of vulnerability," come even close to offering Moscow the kind of safety from retaliation that the United States had in 1945 or 1948.[11]

Any pendulum model of the evolution of the Soviet-American nuclear confrontation also misleads us in a second way, in how we reconstruct history. What were American analysts looking forward to in the 1950s, the period we now remember as one of "US superiority"? In fact, this "superiority" had already been functionally discounted into a mutual deterrence parity in the writings of Brodie and Kissinger and others, including the authors of NSC–68. Perhaps Americans are always inclined to be pessimistic, indulging in a prudential worst-case analysis, and thus were unable to sense whatever advantages the nuclear balance was offering.

Yet the pessimism at that time was hardly limited to a writing-off of US advantage, for the dominant worry after the middle of the 1950s was of something far worse. An effective Soviet *monopoly* loomed if the USSR succeeded in passing the United States in the development of intercontinental ballistic missiles (the "missile gap"). Because bombers were so vulnerable on their bases, and because the USSR could be so secretive, the scenario of a Soviet first strike catching all US bombers before any retaliation could be inflicted did not seem so unreal or impossible in those years.

As presented in the writings of professional analysts like Generals Taylor, Gavin, and Medaris,[12] Moscow by the early 1960s might well have had what Washington had possessed in the mid-1940s: the ability to use nuclear weapons itself and escape all nuclear retaliation. What would have happened to "containment" then? Would the Soviets have been content with "containing" the United States, or would they have elected to strike while they held such a new monopoly, imposing the same kind of change of government on the United States that the United States had imposed on Japan? Kennan, for his part, feared that they might.

As we try to plot possible links between the US-Soviet nuclear balance and the failures of containment, we thus might rather outline the progression of the more important *anticipated* balance as follows:

	seen in:	*looking forward to:*
US monopoly	1947	1955
US "superiority"	1949	1960s
Soviet monopoly (bomber gap, missile gap)	1957	1959
US monopoly? (missile gap in reverse)	1961	1970
US "superiority"	1963	1970s
parity	1968	1970s
Soviet "superiority"?	1974	1980s

The third, most relevant point obscured by conventional retrospectives on the nuclear balance is that there is only one tremendously important transition here, and it is not the shift from one side's nuclear superiority to another's. Rather, it is the shift from US monopoly to anything else, the point when New York and Washington and other US cities could no longer be assured against Soviet retaliation. Once the Soviet possession of even Hiroshima-sized bombs had been established—however many fewer bombs the Soviets had and however primitive their means of delivery—the US Air Force could not have been certain of protecting all US cities against attack, even in the most "splendid" of preemptive first strikes. If a resignation to containment did not make nuclear sense before 1949, it did so immediately thereafter.

When one looks at the analysis of nuclear weapons offered in the late 1940s and the 1950s, it is indeed remarkable how little weight is attached to "US superiority" as compared with "US monopoly." Any US superiority where the Soviets have nuclear weapons with which to strike at American cities is again and again rounded down to very little advantage for the West, with the immediate prospect, therefore, of conventional wars and failures of containment.

Bernard Brodie suggested this outcome as early as 1946, in his chapters of *The Absolute Weapon:*

> The bomb cannot but prove in the net a powerful inhibition to aggression. It would make relatively little difference if one power had more bombs and were better prepared to resist than its opponent. It would in any case undergo incalculable destruction of life and property.[13]

The authors of NSC–68 worked from a similarly pessimistic premise when asked to respond to the 1949 discovery that the Soviets had tested an atomic bomb:

> In the event of a general war with the U.S.S.R., it must be anticipated that atomic weapons will be used by each side in the manner it deems best suited to accomplish its

objectives. In view of our vulnerability to Soviet atomic attack, it has been argued that we might wish to hold our atomic weapons only for retaliation against prior use by the U.S.S.R. To be able to do so and still have hope of achieving our objectives, the non-atomic military capabilities of ourselves and our allies would have to be fully developed and the political weaknesses of the Soviet Union fully exploited.[14]

The North Korean attack on South Korea in June of 1950, repulsed only by the introduction of substantial US and allied conventional ground forces, illustrated this hypothetical scenario only too clearly. The United States could not use nuclear weapons to get the North Koreans out of Seoul (as it had used such weapons, in part, to get the Japanese out of Seoul), for the North Koreans were now shielded by a patron who had nuclear weapons of his own.

A number of authors in the mid-1950s developed the argument of limited war more fully, contending that nuclear forces (even if quite different in total size) basically cancelled each other out because each side would fear for the safety of its cities. William Kaufmann outlined such a conclusion clearly enough in *Military Policy and National Security:*

> If the Communists should challenge our sincerity, and they would have good reasons for daring to do so, we would either have to put up or shut up. If we put up, we would plunge into all the immeasurable horrors of an atomic war. If we shut up, we would suffer a serious loss of prestige and damage our capacity to establish deterrents against further Communist expansion. Indeed, given existing conditions, there is no escaping the conclusion that the doctrine of massive retaliation would be likely to confront us continually with having to choose between one or the other of these two most distasteful alternatives.[15]

Henry Kissinger's first book, *Nuclear Weapons and Foreign Policy*, developed at length the case that strategic nuclear forces had already cancelled each other out, though he went on to argue that nuclear weapons could somehow be used profitably, within the restraints of a limited war, to defend Western Europe.

> The growth of the Soviet nuclear stockpile has transformed massive retaliation from the least costly into the most costly strategy. With the end of our traditional invulnerability.... [a]ll-out war has turned into a strategy which inevitably involves trading a life for a life; it has become the war of attrition par excellence.[16]

As noted, the United States may earlier have been kept from using its nuclear monopoly for anything more than containment by the counter of the Soviet conventional military advantage. Washington's ability to drop atomic bombs on Minsk was balanced against the Soviet Army's ability to occupy Frankfurt. But what, then, when the Soviets also had atomic bombs? What would hold back the Soviet conventional attack if the two nuclear forces deterred each other's use?

Before 1949, any war between the two World War II victors would have seen atomic bombs as the exclusive weapon of the United States, but a great preponderance of conventional military force for the Soviets. As Soviet nuclear forces joined such a conventional imbalance, one again has to ask how the United States could be so ambitious as to aspire to containment. Just as Mao's communist armies overwhelmed those of Chiang to take over China, would not Stalin's communist hordes be able to sweep over Western Europe sooner or later? If the United States had not felt able to aspire to liberate Poland from Stalin, as it had liberated Belgium from Hitler, could it now even hope to defend Belgium against Stalin?

The relationship of containment to this comparison of conventional forces is not the subject of this paper. The US monopoly of nuclear forces had some prospect of cancelling out the impact of the conventional imbalance. After 1949, however, it is altogether plausible that the conventional imbalance would alone explain any failure of deterrence.

Post-1949: "How Can We Do as Much as Containment?"

Yet, before we write off the impact on containment of comparisons of the nuclear stockpiles (that is, once the Soviets had any stockpile at all), we have to address some lingering possibilities of significance for the transitions from US superiority to parity and from parity to Soviet superiority. Just as with the impact of conventional forces, some of the questions here are posed by the paradox of the years before 1949, precisely the years when containment was drafted as a doctrine.

If we were limiting ourselves by the containment doctrine, was this because Soviet conventional forces made up for the US nuclear monopoly? Or was it because American timidity, and Soviet resolve, eliminated any impact of this monopoly? If the United States has always tended to be overly frightened by other nations' arsenals and insufficiently confident of its own, then the comparative evolution of the stockpiles might regain some importance subjectively, despite its objective irrelevance. From this perspective, those worried about Western resolve in facing up to communist dictatorships could extrapolate such a conclusion from the mere fact that the United States had not gotten more out of its nuclear monopoly. Once the monopoly was converted into a nuclear duopoly, would the Soviets not feel free to move westward, challenging the containment barrier, for some of the very same reasons that the West had felt unable to move eastward as a liberating force? The more the Soviet nuclear arsenal grows, by this interpretation, the more the Soviets will push forward against the barriers of containment. Rather than watching two permanent alliance shields settling in with the nuclear duopoly, we will see the Western shield become ineffective.[17]

Yet this kind of argument for a significant tie between the nuclear arms confrontation and the viability of containment remains difficult to prove. As we survey the years after 1949, the linkage between growing Soviet nuclear power and the undoing of containment will not be so clear and easy to demonstrate.

A very simple and symmetrical picture of mutual deterrence would allow no military invasions of a nuclear power's homeland. And barring some isolated instances of terrorist outrages, the United States has indeed remained immune. By the same logic of nuclear deterrence, an adversary assault should not come against allied territories which the nuclear protector values highly. No conventional military aggressions would be directed against areas for which the protector has plausibly committed himself to nuclear escalation, either by verbal declaration or by deploying "tactical" nuclear weapons into such territories. Again, there have been no invasions of Western Europe.

Similarly, the lines of containment would be more challengeable where the patron could not plausibly attach much value to the territory, where theater nuclear weapons were not deployed, and where nuclear escalation would not be credible. Places like Angola, Zaire, and Grenada, or Afghanistan and Vietnam, are thus very much open to be contested. A portion of the Western failures of containment since 1960 may thus have to be explained not by the Soviet-American nuclear balance, and not even by the comparison of conventional military strength, but by the emergence of fundamental doubts among many Americans about the appropriateness of resisting communist forces in places like Southeast Asia, Africa, or even Central America. At the same time, in a parallel development (which may also have little to do with nuclear or conventional weaponry, but might interestingly support aspects of Kennan's containment thesis), the political future of Eastern Europe is also now more open to contest than it would have seemed at the end of the 1940s. Perhaps the West here is no longer so much inclined to "limit itself" to containment.

Explaining Containment Failures

Let us now walk through the specific sequence of "failures of containment" since 1949, attempting to discern the pattern of any impact that nuclear force levels may have had.

Fidel Castro's takeover of Cuba in 1959 must be viewed as such a failure of containment, since Cuba was the first country to fall under communist rule after the 1954 partition of Indochina. These were indeed years when the United States dreaded an imminent "missile gap," a coming period when Moscow might somehow be able to have an effective nuclear monopoly in its favor, roughly comparable to what the United States had possessed before 1949. But the linkage to Havana is hardly so direct. Castro did not proclaim himself a Marxist until he had consolidated power, and he had based his guerrilla campaign on a program of ousting the Batista dictatorship and restoring a liberal system of political democracy, garnering a great deal of private American material support in the process.[18]

Castro thus had given out far less advance warning of a failure of containment than Mao had in China, when only a few venturesome analysts inside the State Department had speculated that the Chinese Communists were "agrarian reformers" who might in the end be largely independent of Moscow. If such uncertainties can account for even part of the slowness of the extension of containment logic to Asia, far greater surprises were probable on the basis of how the confrontation between Castro and Batista had gone. Americans were not the only ones surprised when Castro's regime turned out to be a communist dictatorship modeling itself on and aligning itself with Moscow. Many of Castro's supporters within Cuba were just as rudely surprised. In any event, America's passivity before Castro's accession to power seems to have had little to do with how the United States was counting Soviet nuclear forces in comparison with its own.

The unsuccessful Bay of Pigs invasion, launched by the Kennedy administration in an attempt to depose Castro and restore the barrier line of containment, occurred after the Kennedy team had discovered that there was no missile gap. Indeed, since Khrushchev had been bluffing about the production rates of Soviet ICBMs, there was now possibly a "missile gap in reverse," and an all-out war might not see many nuclear warheads reaching North America (although Soviet deployments of the shorter-range SS–4 and SS–5 missiles would certainly have ensured very great nuclear destruction of Western Europe).[19] The total failure of the Bay of Pigs invasion was a more conscious failure of containment than Castro's rise to power, in that everyone was now aware of Castro's political leanings. It failed predominantly because of the weakness of the anti-Castro forces the United States was backing and the flaws in their conventional military situation.

Much more plausibly tied to the nuclear weapons issue, then, was the Cuban missile crisis of October 1962.[20] For reasons which remain obscure, Khrushchev tried to sneak Soviet medium-range nuclear missiles into bases in Cuba after having assured Kennedy that no such deployments were being contemplated. The ensuing crisis saw the United States threatening both conventional and nuclear war to force the Soviets to withdraw these weapons.

There are many interesting problems and paradoxes about how to interpret the Cuban missile crisis. First, it was not strictly a round in the contests of containment, since the issue was not the political future of Cuba but rather its use for deployments of nuclear weapons. Khrushchev, afterwards rationalizing his venturesome deployment and ignominious retreat, argued that he had extracted from Kennedy an assurance that Cuba would not again be invaded.[21] This would amount to "containment" of American power, an interpretation by which the Soviet missile deployment was merely intended (like the deployments of American medium-range nuclear weapons to West Germany or South Korea) to add credibility to extended nuclear deterrence.

By the time of the Cuban missile crisis, the line dividing the communist and noncommunist worlds had been drawn through Cuba, and nothing happened then or later to shift this particular segment of the Iron Curtain. The missile deployment may have established that Moscow values Cuba as much as the

United States values South Korea; and the relative strengths of the two sides' nuclear forces in the crisis bears less on the shifting back and forth of the demarcation line than on the powers' willingness to risk nuclear war in defense of that line.

A failure of Western containment is only at issue here if the Soviet missile deployment is seen as intended to facilitate the spread of communist regimes beyond Cuba. Perhaps Khrushchev was also trying to humiliate Kennedy and the United States, so as to impress Latin Americans and others with the increase in Soviet comparative power and hence to open up new corners of the world to Soviet influence and intimidation. It is also plausible that the Soviet dictator was instead fearful that "the missile gap in reverse" had too much restored US nuclear power, that he was trying to convert his SS–4 missiles into the functional equivalent of ICBMs by moving them forward to where they could hit targets in the United States instead of in Western Europe. Before the first successful tests of US ICBMs and submarine based SLBMs, the Eisenhower administration had similarly moved some intermediate-range nuclear missiles to bases in England, Italy, and Turkey as a "quick fix" to plug a possible missile gap. In this view of Khrushchev's 1962 deployment, the background of strategic power had hardly slipped so badly from the standpoint of the United States.

The next major failure of containment would come with the culmination of the wars which had raged in Indochina since 1945: the 1975 fall of South Vietnam, Cambodia, and Laos to communist rule. It is very difficult to explain the American defeat here, any more than the French defeat earlier in Dienbienphu, as the result of growth in Soviet nuclear power. The very nature of the terrain and tactics chosen suggests that the Marxists were at all points avoiding the nuclear issue, utilizing the "nickle and dime" "salami tactics" of guerrilla warfare to preclude the West from drawing some line which might bring nuclear escalatory threats into play. Although one sees an occasional Western speculation about applications of nuclear weaponry to reverse the outcome of the wars in Indochina, such speculations fail less because of an awareness that the other side might have retaliated than because there is little reason to feel that nuclear weapons had any utility in the conflict.

The places that have figured the most prominently in threats of nuclear escalation since the 1950s—West Germany, Korea since 1952, and Quemoy and Matsu—have not seen failures of containment. The places where containment has failed have been much further removed from nuclear threats, either because they were not worth as much to the two sides or because they did not lend themselves even to ordinary conventional battle.

At the outer extreme, one wonders what would have happened in Vietnam if the Soviet Union had never acquired nuclear weapons, somehow being unable to master the technology. Would the United States have been able to contain the advance of Marxist rule into South Vietnam if it held a nuclear monopoly, any more than it was able to stop Mao from taking over all of China? Would it have been willing enough and committed enough to make the necessary sacrifices?

The real breakdown of containment in Vietnam might be traced more to something that had already begun showing itself in the fall of China: a doubt among many Americans about whether we were supporting the better kind of person in Diem (or in Chiang Kai-shek) as opposed to Ho Chi Minh (or Mao), whether the United States really had something to offer the underdeveloped world. When the comparison is made between Eastern and Western Europe, where the line of containment was originally defined, the moral bases of American self-confidence are reinforced. Where the comparison is made in the guerrilla-prone Third World countries, these bases are eroded. It is here that Americans begin speculating that "economic democracy," a fairer division of land and resources and income, might be more important than "political democracy," free elections, and the press and individual freedoms that go with them.

Whatever sympathies many Americans might have had for Mao were reduced in the public affiliation that the Communist Chinese declared with Moscow, and in the blatant North Korean aggression, surely sanctioned by Moscow, followed by Chinese entry into the Korean War. Yet the political and economic disappointments of the decolonization process around the globe in the next two decades produced a deeper shaking and weakening of what had once been an American consensus about the goals of foreign policy, and with it a real weakening of containment.

It is thus no accident that the places where nuclear weapons are brandished the least have been the places where containment has been most under communist attack. In some part, this has simply been the result of a sound strategy of the communist central command, intent on avoiding nuclear punishment in any Western escalatory retaliation. In large part, it is because the places to which we are the least willing to commit our nuclear retaliatory capacities—whether we be in a state of superiority or parity or inferiority (or perhaps even when we had a monopoly)—are the places where we are in general the most confused about American purposes in the world.

In the immediate wake of the collapse in Vietnam, the next two memorable failures of containment came in Mozambique and Angola. The US Congress seemed determined to forbid any active participation by US forces, even clandestine forces, in resisting the imposition of Marxist regimes in these former Portuguese colonies. Was this determination a result of senators and representatives counting Soviet missile warheads? Or was it because of the count of young American soldiers who had been killed and wounded in Vietnam, and the feeling that we had been backing "the wrong side" for too long in Portuguese efforts to hold on to these colonies, just as we had in Vietnam?

Another break in the barrier of containment in the same period occurred in Ethiopia, where, after the fall of Emperor Haile Selassie, a junta of army officers (most of whom had been trained in the United States) declared a Marxist regime and joined in a mutual embrace with the Soviet bloc, in the end bringing into operation the same Soviet military aid and Cuban troops that had turned the tide in Angola. Again the missile rattling was virtually nil. Again the American commitment was minimal, with many Americans seeing the old regime as bad for the Africans involved, and viewing the "socialism" and "economic democracy" of the new regime as preferable to anything that could be extracted from the American model.

Someone seeking a more complete list of failures of containment would of course have earlier listed Egypt, Syria, and Somalia, along with Algeria and Libya, each of which was once written off as "in the Soviet camp." For a time such worries were interestingly rebutted and complicated by a pattern in which the Soviets, in control for a time, were later expelled. Thus, while the first signs of a pro-Moscow leaning in a regime like Nasser's would once have brought alarmed visions of a failure of containment, by the middle of the 1960s the general analysis became more optimistically cynical about whether Soviet-style regimes could really be imposed in Africa. "African countries can't be bought, they can only be rented," was the waggish summary, perhaps intended to be a deprecating comment about the ideological fidelity of African leaders, but actually amounting to a compliment on the ability of the region to fend for itself and avoid becoming a pawn of either of the superpowers.

Egypt thus was once viewed as a failure of containment, a judgment largely forgotten today. At one time, the same worries were held for Algeria. Somalia was written off as a Soviet military base and satellite, until Moscow suddenly switched its allegiances in the seemingly intractable conflict between Ethiopia and Somalia about the future of the Ogaden region. It is possible, of course, that today's Ethiopia (if not Angola and Mozambique) violates the facile generalization that African countries will never become duplicates of Bulgaria or Cuba—that perhaps these countries really are failures of containment. Yet the basic proposition remains: that containment did not fail because Americans or Russians (or Ethiopians or Angolans) were regularly comparing the totals of Soviet and US nuclear missile warheads. It failed because the regions involved were as far removed as one can get, on this globe, from any direct shadow of nuclear warfare.

The next failure of containment, then, occurs in Central America, with the fall of the pro-American Somozas in Nicaragua and the victorious opposition soon slipping into a one-party Marxist regime. Again, anyone trying to explain the path of events in Nicaragua, and up the domino chain in El Salvador or elsewhere in Central America and the Caribbean, would hardly bet very much on the comparison of strategic power as compared with local applications of conventional and guerrilla forces. If the United States had shifted many of its missiles from land based silos to additional SLBM submarines in the 1970s as a way of heading off any vulnerability of such missiles to Soviet ICBMs, or if the United States had replaced MIRVed missiles with some sort of early version of "Midgetman," can anyone really argue that these actions by themselves would have preserved the chances of political democracy in Nicaragua or El Salvador or Ethiopia?

The events in Grenada, with a US military intervention restoring some chances for a free-election system, similarly illustrate how containment in either direction may not depend on the missile balance. The arrival of a Marxist regime on the island could have been seen as a containment failure from the standpoint of the West, and some might argue that it was a result of increases in Soviet strategic power. Yet the American intervention shows how little the augmentation of Soviet missile power can affect events when the territory involved is not plausibly crucial to Moscow, when no means have been found to deploy nuclear weapons to that territory, and when (as a result) nuclear escalation is not plausible. Castro and his Soviet partners failed to contain Western influence in Grenada. In their private discussions, it is hardly plausible that they are lightly shrugging off the precedent of its loss.

One more example of Soviet expansionism, challenging the containment principle, would of course be Afghanistan. Yet Afghanistan might instead be seen as a failure of another Kennan formula, developed as an alternative when he became dissatisfied with how the barriers of containment had taken shape across Europe: that of "disengagement."[22] Along with Austria and Yugoslavia, and the pair of Sweden and Finland, Afghanistan might have been a neutral buffer zone between the Soviet bloc and the Western alliance, helping reduce tensions and avoid direct face-offs between the military forces of Washington and Moscow.

Yet as Kennan recognized, such a "disengagement" buffer is a success only when it has some strength and viability of its own, when it does not instead become a power vacuum. At various times the West has feared that Yugoslavia might become such a vacuum instead of a buffer. A neutralized, disarmed, unified Germany, as proposed by Kennan, might similarly become such a power vacuum, tempting each side to race in to preempt the other's political and military moves. Afghanistan apparently became such a vacuum at the end of the 1970s, at least in Moscow's view; and what had been tolerated and left alone, as a noncommunist neighbor of the USSR, was tolerated no longer.

Yet the important point is that the United States had never staked out any alliance commitments to Afghanistan, or hitched its nuclear potential to shielding this state. Such an extension of nuclear deterrence had been proffered at various times to Iran and Pakistan, but not to Afghanistan. And the Soviets have intervened militarily in Afghanistan, not in Iran, despite all the tumult and convolutions that have occurred in Tehran since the fall of the Shah. Once again, would a Martian visitor, having been briefed on the changes in the Soviet-American nuclear confrontation and the challenges to containment on the ground, conclude that there was much of a link between the two?

A Final Irony

With the single slight exception of Grenada, we have listed our breaks in containment entirely by a measure pessimistic for the West. Yet the accounting of whether containment is working, or is failing, may be somewhat more two-sided than this. Offensives have moved across the 1948 demarcation line in both directions, involving different tactics and different sectors of the line, and always related only in very complicated ways to the balance of nuclear arms.

We noted earlier that such Western defeats as Vietnam may have stemmed from American self-doubt about whether we had any good cause to defend in the poorer LDCs, and self-doubt will now hamper us also in the contests erupting in Central America. Yet there are other corners of the world for which Americans will have less self-doubt, where any boiling up of political turmoil actually amounts to a tonic for their commitment to resisting and opposing Moscow.

The clearest cases emerge in what Kennan's formula had resigned us to leaving under Soviet control: the countries of Eastern Europe. Many Americans may now shrug off the harshness of a Marxist regime in Vietnam by stressing economic factors: "the people may not be able to read free newspapers, but at least they are not starving anymore." When the discussion shifts instead to Poland and the restlessness exemplified by Solidarity, however, the common-sense summation comes out quite differently, something more like "the people lost their freedom, and haven't gained anything on the economic side either."

The agitation Americans have felt about violations of the Helsinki accords on human rights, and about repression of the Solidarity movement or dissidents within the Soviet Union itself, suggest that we on our side are hardly content with containment. The Soviet leadership must thus feel itself as much on the defensive as on the offensive, in Eastern Europe and even at home, in fear of Western influences transmitted by blue jeans and movies and in a hundred other ways, in fear of signal events like the election of a Polish Pope or the awarding of a Nobel Peace Prize to a dissident. Moscow has to worry that containment will not work any better in its sphere than it has worked to shield American interests in Central America, and that the details of Soviet and American missile totals will not make a very great difference.

It is important to note that Western successes in getting around containment might cut quite close to the bone of Soviet interests, closer than has been true to date in Soviet attacks on US interests. Could the Soviet Union really tolerate the loss of Poland, East Germany, or Hungary to any kind of internal agitation without responding with as massive a military intervention as in East Berlin in 1953, Hungary in 1956, or Czechoslovakia in 1968, even brandishing its nuclear weapons in the process? Some American government spokesmen are fond of noting how close El Salvador is to the United States geographically, "closer to Texas than Texas is to Washington"; but Poland is even closer to the USSR geographically, and much more important economically, socially, and politically.

Kennan's containment doctrine was criticized in 1947 by Republican opponents of the Truman administration, and by some others, as too unambitious, as resigning Americans to continuing communist control over all of Eastern Europe against the wishes of the peoples of these countries. Even in the USSR there was no reason to believe that most Russians would have voted communist if they had a choice of any other political alternatives; many of them had welcomed Hitler's armies even when they came as invaders in 1941.

Defenders of containment could rebut such criticism by referring to places where Kennan outlines a prediction, not just a hope, that a Marxist regime will be disestablished by containment, by being kept from realizing and fulfilling its "historical-scientific" mission to spread revolution and communist political arrangements.[23] We are now contemplating some four decades of further evolution of the Soviet role in the world since Kennan's analysis, more than doubling the USSR's age. Has the disillusionment in Moscow that Kennan foresaw actually occurred? Has any of such disillusionment caused the grip of the Communist Party on the Soviet bloc to slip?

There are indeed widespread signs of malaise and self-doubt in the Soviet system, even if it is not clear that containment has been causing them. From the perspective of many an alarmed Western analyst, Soviet power today is not really contained: the barriers seem to be crumbling as Soviet naval squadrons reach into all the oceans and Soviet influence grows in Africa and Central America. Yet the Soviet Union is hardly viewed around the Third World as the model of an improved life for the future, and it is decidedly not viewed as such in Eastern Europe. And the leadership and rank-and-file back inside the USSR are becoming painfully aware of this.

Perhaps Solidarity, together with dissidence within the Soviet Union, is indeed what George Kennan forecast and hoped for as the ultimate results of a negation of Soviet expansionism, his answer on whether we would always have to be content with nothing more than fencing in Marxist totalitarianism. Yet the problem remains as it has been ever since 1949: with Soviet nuclear weapons in existence, capable of destroying New York and Washington, how far can we let the challenge to the Soviet empire go before too much endangering our own interests?

We have thus arrived at the second paradox in Kennan's failure to attach much significance to the prospect of that initial instance of nuclear proliferation, Moscow's acquisition of nuclear weapons. It is not clear how sanguine Kennan or anyone else looking ahead to Soviet atomic bombs could have been about containment's success in debunking the canons of Marxist ideological cant, stripping the Communist Party of its confidence in its world role, denuding the Soviet population of whatever faith it had in the Party, and provoking internal ferment analogous to the toppling of the Shah in Iran. How would the world react today to riots in the streets of Moscow, comparable to what Solidarity had going in Warsaw? Is it not again an unfortunate but inexorable consequence of the existence of nuclear missiles that we would have to be more worried than cheered by such developments? Just as an army advancing to liberate

Moscow might remove the last restraints keeping a Soviet leadership from devastating the world, so might a process of internal revolution or turmoil portending the toppling (and future trial) of the Communist Party leadership.

Kennan may thus have been too ambitious in suggesting the possibility of a de-communization of the Soviet Union. In the nuclear duopoly that was barely two years away, such a political change within the Soviet world could be just as dangerous as a liberation of the Russian people by outside military forces. We may thus have been reading too much into Kennan by arguing that his "settling for containment" reflected an advance perception that Soviet nuclear forces would soon come into being; for his "hopeful" suggestions of another way out of the confrontation must then be faulted for not taking nuclear weapons nearly enough into account.

The world as yet sees no signs of a Solidarity movement in Moscow. We might think that we would very much welcome such a development, a decisive break through Soviet efforts to "contain" Western liberal influences. Yet, when we contemplate the state of the world's nuclear arsenals and the problems of avoiding nuclear war, we have to have some second thoughts.

Notes

1. The US commitment to "unconditional surrender" is discussed in Anne Armstrong, *Unconditional Surrender* (New Brunswick, New Jersey: Rutgers University Press, 1961).

2. For a sympathetic analysis of Kennan on these points, see John Gaddis, *Strategies of Containment* (New York: Oxford University Press, 1982), pp. 25–54.

3. George F. Kennan, *Memoirs: 1925–1950* (Vol. I) (Boston: Little, Brown, 1967), pp. 354–67.

4. For perhaps the most widely read of the interpretations viewing the 'X' article as advocating more of a commitment than the traditional balance of power, see Walter Lippmann, *The Cold War: A Study in U.S. Foreign Policy* (New York: Harper, 1947). See also Charles Gati, "What Containment Meant," *Foreign Policy*, No. 7 (Summer 1972), pp. 22–40.

5. George F. Kennan, *Memoirs* I, pp. 296, 311, 437; *Memoirs: 1950–1963* (Vol. II) (New York: Pantheon, 1972), pp. 244–46.

6. Kennan, *Memoirs* I, pp. 358–59.

7. The text of NSC–68 can be found in *Naval War College Review* 27 (May-June 1975), pp. 51–108.

8. Kennan (writing as 'X'), "The Sources of Soviet Conduct," *Foreign Affairs* 25 (July 1947), pp. 574–76.

9. On this Soviet counter-leverage, see the analysis in NSC–68, *Naval War College Review*, p. 81.

10. The rapidity of the US demobilization is recounted in Samuel P. Huntington, *The Common Defense* (New York: Columbia University Press, 1961), pp. 33–38.

11. On the "window of vulnerability," see the Scowcroft Report, *Report of the President's Commission on Strategic Forces* (Washington: 6 April 1983).

12. Maxwell Taylor, *The Uncertain Trumpet* (New York: Harper and Row, 1960); John G. Medaris, *War and Peace in the Space Age* (New York: Harper, 1958); and James Gavin, *Countdown for Decision* (New York: Putnam, 1960).

13. Bernard Brodie, ed., *The Absolute Weapon* (New York: Harcourt Brace, 1946), p. 75.

14. NSC–68, in *Naval War College Review*, pp. 83.

15. William W. Kaufmann, ed., *Military Policy and National Security* (Princeton: Princeton University Press, 1956), pp. 24–25.

16. Henry A. Kissinger, *Nuclear Weapons and Foreign Policy* (New York: Harper Bros., 1957), pp. 154–55.

17. An argument of this sort is presented by Paul Nitze, *Is SALT II a Fair Deal for the United States?* (Washington: Committee on the Present Danger, 1979).

18. On Castro's rise to power, and the first years of his regime, see Ernst Halperin, *Fidel Castro's Road to Power* (Cambridge, Mass.: MIT Center for International Studies, 1970).

19. The assessment of the strategic nuclear confrontation in the first years of the Kennedy administration is discussed in Desmond Ball, *Politics and Force Levels* (Berkeley: University of California Press, 1980).

20. On the Cuban missile crisis, see Elie Abel, *The Missile Crisis* (New York: Lippincott, 1966); Albert and Roberta Wohlstetter, *Containing the Risks in Cuba,* Adelphi Paper No. 19 (London: International Institute for Strategic Studies, 1965); and Arnold L. Horelick and Myron Rush, *Strategic Power and Soviet Foreign Policy* (Chicago: University of Chicago Press, 1965).

21. Nikita Khrushchev, *Khrushchev Remembers* (Boston: Little Brown, 1970), pp. 500–05.

22. For an overview of various proposals for disengagement, including those of George Kennan's BBC Reith Lectures, see Eugene Hinterhoff, *Disengagement* (London: Stevens and Sons, 1959).

23. Kennan, "The Sources of Soviet Conduct," pp. 580–82.

Containment

Concept and Policy

Text and display lines in Times Roman and Italic
Book and cover design by Thomas Gill
Cover mechanical and illustrations by Laszlo L. Bodrogi

Special thanks to the Carnegie Endownment for
International Peace for its support of Terry L. Deibel,
Resident Associate there, during the editing of
the papers published in these volumes.

NDU Press Editor, Thomas Gill
Editorial Clerk, Carolyn Valentine

SYMPOSIUM COORDINATORS

Colonel Giles Harlow, USAF
Director, External Programs

Dr. Harold W. Holtzclaw
Director, Symposia

Lieutenant Colonel Robert Walker, USAF
Director, Operations

Dr. Terry Deibel
Program Advisor, National War College

Lieutenant Colonel M. D. Krause, USA
National War College Coordinator

Ambassador J. Bruce Amstutz
Industrial College of the Armed Forces Coordinator

Master Sergeant G. C. Huff
Symposia Noncommissioned Officer